Phenomenology and the "Theological Turn"

The meaning of transcendence in immanence

Phenomenology and the "Theological Turn"

THE FRENCH DEBATE

DOMINIQUE JANICAUD, JEAN-FRANÇOIS COURTINE,
JEAN-LOUIS CHRÉTIEN, MICHEL HENRY, JEAN-LUC
MARION, *and* PAUL RICŒUR

Fordham University Press
New York

The Theological Turn of French Phenomenology was originally published in French as *Le tournant théologique de la phénoménologie française* by Éditions de l'Éclat. Copyright © 1991—Éditions de l'Éclat, Paris.

Phenomenology and Theology was originally published in French as *Phénoménologie et théologie* by Fleurus-Mame. Copyright © 1992—Criterion, Paris.

Perspectives in Continental Philosophy, No. 15
ISSN 1089–3938

Library of Congress Cataloging-in-Publication Data

Tournant théologique de la phénoménologie française. English.
    Phenomenology and the "theological turn" : the French debate /
Dominique Janicaud . . . [et al.].—1st ed.
        p.   cm.—(Perspectives in continental philosophy ; no. 15)
    Contents: pt. 1. The theological turn of French phenomenology—pt. 2.
Phenomenology and theology.
    Includes bibliographical references.
    ISBN 0-8232-2052-4—ISBN 0-8232-2053-2 (pbk.)
    1. Phenomenology.   2. Theology.   3. Philosophy and religion.
4. Philosophy, French—20th century.   I. Janicaud, Dominique,
1937–   II. Ph'enom'enologie et th'eologie. English.   III. Title.
IV. Series.
B829.5 .T6313   2000
142'.7'0944—dc21   00-04267

Printed in the United States of America
06 07 08 09 10   6 5 4 3 2
First edition

CONTENTS

Part I

The Theological Turn of French Phenomenology

By DOMINIQUE JANICAUD
Translation by BERNARD G. PRUSAK

Translator's Introduction

HAS THERE BEEN a "turn toward the theological" in recent French phenomenology? Does it make sense to talk of a "theological phenomenology"? In his 1991 essay translated here, Dominique Janicaud affirms that there has indeed been such a turn, and argues against it that "phenomenology and theology make two." He emphasizes, however, that his essay is not "a synoptic and systematic study of the relations between phenomenology and theology," but instead a critique of and a polemic against what he takes to be perversions of the phenomenological method for explicit or implicit theological ends. Janicaud takes a stand on which way French philosophy ought to go, and it is not the way of Emmanuel Lévinas, Jean-Luc Marion, Jean-Louis Chrétien, and Michel Henry.

The purpose of the present introduction is to provide the reader with a context for understanding Janicaud's essay and to show the way into the controversy its argument has aroused. Janicaud opens his essay by giving its background: "The present essay originated as a report [*constat*] made at the behest of the International Institute of Philosophy."[1] A "*constat*" is also, however, a legal term for the statement of the facts read by a court clerk at the opening of a proceeding. A "*constat*" reports the constants of a case: etymologically, how it stands with that case. What Janicaud does in what follows is to put Lévinas, Marion, Chrétien, and Henry on trial. Marion, Chrétien, and Henry represent the "second generation" of French phenomenologists, also known as the "new phenomenologists." Janicaud's charge, simply put, is that the "new phenomenology" they practice is no longer phenome-

---

[1] See Dominique Janicaud, "Rendre à nouveau raison?" in *La philosophie en Europe* (Paris: Gallimard, 1993), ed. Raymond Klibanksy and David Pears, pp. 156–93. In the sequel to *The Theological Turn*, *La phénoménologie éclatée* (Paris: Éditions de l'éclat, 1998), p. 7, n. 2, Janicaud records that he wrote this report three years before its publication, that is, in 1990.

nological. Put dramatically, Janicaud inverts the scenario of Plato's *Apology*: he indicts Lévinas et al. for corrupting the future of French philosophy by introducing into phenomenology a god—the biblical God—who does not belong there.

Janicaud is not the first in the history of French philosophy to warn against mixing phenomenology and theology. Long before him, Jean Hering, a former student of Husserl's at Göttingen, called attention to the "dangers of the phenomenological movement" in *Phénoménologie et philosophie religieuse,* his 1925 thesis presented to the Protestant theology faculty at Strasbourg.[2] "It is not difficult to foresee," writes Hering, "that the hour when [phenomenology] will become *à la mode* . . . will see the springing forth of a whole pseudophenomenological literature."[3] Hering is particularly critical of Scheler's popular writings (though not of his philosophical works), which in his estimation imprudently use the tools and the terms of the phenomenological method for theological-political ends.[4] In such use Hering discerns "dangers" not only for the autonomy of phenomenology as a philosophical discipline, but for the phenomenology of religion as well. The problem, as he sees it, is not the use of the phenomenological method to clarify what he calls "religious phenomena"—his book actually concludes with a positive assessment of what phenomenology can bring to the study of "religious philosophy" (the study of God, the world, and man "from the angle of natural or positive religion")[5]—but rather the abuse of this method in "the *premature* and *unreflective* application of certain eternal truths to facts *hic et nunc.*" As an example he gives the use of the εἶδος of a Christian church "in order to prove the excellence of this or that empirical church."[6]

Hering and Janicaud alike ask what is, and what is not, phenomenological. They also likewise specify several "general principles of phenomenology," Hering first and foremost the "principle of all principles" articulated by Husserl in §24 of *Ideas I,* Janicaud

---

[2] Jean Hering, *Phénoménologie et philosophie religieuse. Étude sur la théorie de la connaissance religieuse* (Strasbourg: Imprimerie Alsacienne, 1925).

[3] Ibid., p. 73.

[4] Ibid., pp. 74–75.

[5] Ibid., p. 7.

[6] Ibid., p. 74.

the importance of the reduction and eidetic intuition. But the "dangers" to phenomenology discerned by Janicaud extend well beyond the confounding of the empirical and the ideal. His warning is not new, but the problem, as he sees it, is. According to Janicaud, recent French phenomenology has subordinated the description of phenomena to the quest for the "essence of phenomenality," and has surrendered a positive phenomenological project to make way for the advent of the "originary." In his 1998 encyclical letter *Fides et Ratio*, Pope John Paul II (who, as Karol Wojtyla, made a name for himself with his writings on Scheler) calls for philosophers "to move from phenomenon to foundation," through the immanent to the transcendent.[7] This is just what Janicaud claims the "new phenomenologists" have done. In violation of both the letter and the spirit of the phenomenological method, they have committed "[s]trict treason of the reduction that handed over the transcendental I to its nudity."

Reviewing *The Theological Turn* for the journal *La quinzaine littéraire*, Michel Haar concluded: "[This book] opens a great debate. Now it is up to the accused to respond!"[8] The responses, however, were slow and fitful in coming,[9] and a debate has only recently begun. At Villanova University in September 1997, for example, Marion and Jacques Derrida debated on the question of "the gift."[10] Arguing that the pure gift cannot be described as such without destroying it (by inscribing it within an economy of exchange), Derrida essentially reiterated Janicaud's critique. According to Derrida, Marion is no longer doing phenomenology since what he is trying to think, the pure givenness of the gift, cannot be known: intuition is lacking, in violation of Husserl's "principle of all principles." Marion countered that "we can describe the gift" as such, and that, "as long as description is possible

---

[7] John Paul II, *Fides et Ratio: On the Relationship between Faith and Reason*, §83. The full text is posted at http://www.vatican.va.

[8] Michel Haar, "Philosopher à l'âge de la science," *La quinzaine littéraire* 592 (1991): 22.

[9] So Marion's "Saturated Phenomenon" (included in this volume), which once alludes to *The Theological Turn*, but only to deny its relevance.

[10] September 27, 1997, moderated by Richard Kearney, at the conference "Religion and Postmodernism."

. . . , we remain in the field of phenomenology." But this did not satisfy Derrida: Marion's "extraordinary extension of *Gegebenheit*," he replied, only makes sense against a theological background. Exasperated, Marion finally exclaimed that the question of whether or not he is doing phenomenology is unimportant. For, like Heidegger, he remarked, he is more interested in the things that interest phenomenology. . . .

Marion's response is obviously inadequate—he retracts his concession even while proffering it—but his exasperation is quite understandable: the question of what is, and what is not, properly phenomenological risks eclipsing what phenomenology is fundamentally about, namely, "the things themselves." An interest in advancing the debate likewise animates Janicaud's 1998 sequel to *The Theological Turn*, *La phénoménologie éclatée*; but the argument of this book (whose title translates several ways[11]) finally falls back upon that of *The Theological Turn*.[12] It falls to the readers of this

---

[11] To call phenomenology "*éclatée*" may be to say that phenomenology has been blown to bits, shattered. It may also be to say, however, that phenomenology has opened beyond itself and onto the world—manifested its potential, come into its own. Yet further, the title may be taken to indicate Janicaud's intention to show how phenomenology's parts go together in the functioning of the whole—the purpose of a "*dessin éclaté*," a drawing that breaks a thing down in order to show how it is articulated. Janicaud's text supports all three of these readings.

[12] While seeking to move beyond polemics, Janicaud nonetheless reaffirms the need for a debate on phenomenology's "methodological exigencies"—the elements "any phenomenology worthy of this name" must exhibit (*La phénoménologie éclatée*, p. 8). "[This debate] has, at least, been broached," he writes (pp. 8–9); but in his estimation it has too often been diverted by peripheral objections, in particular to the propriety of his naming the turn "theological" rather than "religious" or "metaphysical" (pp. 9–10). ("At bottom," Janicaud observes, "no one has been able to contest, and with reason, that there has been a turn in French phenomenology" [p. 11]. The question is rather how to qualify what, in *The Theological Turn*, he identifies as the two distinguishing characteristics of recent French phenomenology: its "rupture with immanent phenomenality" and its "opening [*ouverture*] to the invisible.") According to Janicaud, these objections have effectively given comfort to precisely what he meant to challenge: "a too confident conception of the 'possibility' of phenomenology" (p. 9)—a conception that, he argues, risks exploding phenomenology by overextending it.

Against this conception, as allegedly exemplified in the work of Marion (whose work is discussed at the center of both *The Theological Turn* and *La phénoménologie éclatée*), Janicaud puts forth a minimalist and pluralist conception of phenomenology (pp. 21–24, 94–119). In his view, there is no such thing as "*the* phenomenology" (p. 9)—progressing, say, from Husserl to Heidegger to

translation, then, to work out the questions for themselves. This introduction will try to clarify two of the most important, while indicating further questions in notes along the way.

Janicaud's critique relies primarily on Husserl's 1911 essay "Philosophy as Rigorous Science" and his 1913 book *Ideas I*. Against Marion, he cites, for example, §58 of *Ideas I*, where Husserl extends the reduction to the transcendence of God. In this instance, however, Janicaud simply cites Husserl without offering an interpretation, as if it were self-evident what this reduction finally means regarding the question of God in phenomenology and as if it disposed of the question once and for all. Here as elsewhere, Janicaud is vulnerable to the charge that he ignores Husserl's development and turns Husserl's method into a doctrine.[13] He also invites the following questions: First, in what sense is his essay a "critique"? Second, what is the status of theology (and of God) after the reduction?

To begin with the first question, "it is tempting," Janicaud writes toward the end of *The Theological Turn*, "to establish an ultimate court of appeal to pronounce on the question *quid juris* in things phenomenological." But this is, he has just reflected in his text, a temptation that must be resisted. For the legitimacy of this or that phenomenological inquiry cannot be decided in advance, in terms of an overarching critical system, but must be considered on a case-by-case basis. "In this sense," Janicaud writes, "phenomenology does not cease to 'cut its teeth' anew." Janicaud intends his critique, then, to be not comprehensive and once-and-for-all (like Kant's first *Critique*), but "precise and delicate," discriminating. "Thus, for [Marion's theme of] givenness," he remarks, "the distinction must be made between the *Selbstgegebenheit* of a determined essence, the givenness of a temporal dimension or of time itself as a dimension, and finally givenness 'in itself' (which is without doubt no more than a limit-concept on which nothing can be constructed . . .)."

Marion—but a "pluralism of methods and approaches" (p. 23) that remain phenomenological insofar as they respect what, in *The Theological Turn*, he calls phenomenology's "two sui generis methodological instruments, the reduction and eidetic description." The whole debate, however, is to know in what this respect consists; and on this point the jury is still out.

[13] Remarkably, Hering also warned against *this* danger; see *Phénoménologie et philosophie religieuse*, pp. 35–37, 43.

The Kantian tone of Janicaud's work is nonetheless striking. He is not advocating a return to Kant (to "the thing in itself" rather than "the things themselves"); but the framework of his critique cannot but recall the first *Critique*. According to Janicaud, the defining characteristic of the "new phenomenologists" is that, following the later Heidegger, they have abandoned Husserl's concern for "scientificity" and "constancy to the rational ideal": in other words, they have abandoned Husserl's intention to develop phenomenology in the sure path of a science. But it was precisely this intention, Janicaud maintains, that saved Husserl from falling back into the darkness and contradictions of "the *metaphysica specialis* of the tradition"—delimited, it seems to go without saying, in Kant's transcendental dialectic. Further, this intention "safeguarded [Husserl's] capacity to pose the problem of the sense of the lifeworld" against naturalism and psychologism (or the more traditional scourges of materialism, skepticism, and subjective idealism), which would otherwise make freedom and traditional faith both unthinkable and impossible. Accordingly, "the polemical part of this little book," Janicaud writes toward its beginning, "is not at all directed against the theological as such. On the contrary, maintaining the constraints of scientificity" serves to make space for theology and other speculative disciplines, space within which they may legitimately elaborate themselves through hermeneutics or "another mode of 'thought' finer still."

The upshot is that it could well be asked whether Janicaud's critique is sufficiently "precise and delicate," or not rather more systematically Kantian than he wants it to be. Against Marion, Janicaud and Derrida alike argue that pure, unconditioned givenness—beyond the horizons of subjectivity (Husserl) and of being (Heidegger)—cannot be rendered phenomenologically evident. As they see it, such givenness is finally a mere concept without intuitions, a concept that it might be possible to think, but that is impossible to experience and to know. But, for Marion, this just means that they have not understood Husserl's phenomenological "breakthrough" in the *Logical Investigations*. For Marion, the Kantian distinction between what can be known and what can only be thought (signified, but not fulfilled) is not the end of the analysis, but its beginning. According to his interpretation, "The phenomenological breakthrough consists neither in the broadening of intuition [as on Heidegger's interpretation], nor in the autonomy of signification [as on Derrida's], but solely in the unconditioned primacy of the givenness [*donation*] of the phenomenon . . ."[14]—that is, in the realization that both signification and the categorial intuition of being *give* themselves, and that it is this "givenness" that calls first and foremost to be thought.[15] Whereas Derrida reads Husserl as a prisoner of the metaphysics of presence, bound by the idea of a theory of knowledge,[16] Marion reads Husserl as showing the way out of the metaphysics of presence and thus beyond deconstruction.[17] Marion takes from Husserl the insight—pregnant but undeveloped— "that, in its basis [*dans son fonds*], every phenomenon surges forth as a gift [*don*], and therefore that all phenomenality comes to pass [*advient*] as a donation."[18] Proper to the gift as Marion understands

---

[14] Jean-Luc Marion, *Réduction et donation. Recherches sur Husserl, Heidegger et la phénoménologie* (Paris: Presses Universitaires de France, 1989), p. 53; English trans., *Reduction and Givenness: Investigations of Husserl, Heidegger, and Phenomenology* (Evanston, Ill.: Northwestern University Press, 1998), trans. Thomas A. Carlson, p. 32 (trans. modified).

[15] See ibid., p. 47 (on the givenness of signification) and p. 58 (on the givenness of being); trans., pp. 28 and 36.

[16] See Jacques Derrida, *La voix et le phénomène* (Paris: Presses Universitaires de France, 1967), pp. 16, 3; English trans., *Speech and Phenomena* (Evanston, Ill.: Northwestern University Press, 1973), trans. David B. Allison, pp. 16, 5.

[17] In his article "Réponses à quelques questions," *Revue de métaphysique et de morale* 1 (1991): 65–76, written in response to the editors of the journal, Marion cites several other phenomenologists, including Derrida, who have studied the question of givenness "in strict philosophy" (p. 69). Commenting on Derrida in a footnote (n. 1), Marion asks whether "the gift does not precede being [*être*] and time" and implies that it is anterior not only to the ontological difference, but to *différance* (p. 70).

[18] Ibid., p. 72. In his interpretation of Husserl's "principle of all principles," Marion stresses, first, that "intuition defines itself as originally giving [die *originär gebende Anschauung*], and not at all as intuition on the basis of being [*être*] or objectivity." On this reading, givenness, not being, becomes basic, and *da* the key to *Da-sein*. Marion stresses, second, that the apodicticity of intuition "comes only from pure givenness": so he reads Husserl's dictum "that everything that offers itself to us in 'intuition' is simply to be taken in as what it itself gives [*als was es sich gibt*], but also only in the limits in which it gives itself [*aber auch nur in den Schranken, in denen es sich da gibt*]." Marion concludes: "It thus belongs to givenness not only to define originally intuition (intuition must be brought back to givenness, so make itself giving [*donatrice*], not givenness make itself intuitive); and not only to fix the measure in which a phenomenon can be received (there are phenomena to the strict measure of givenness, and not the inverse); but

it is that, while it can be fully experienced and known as such (for example, the gift of love, or of freedom, or of being), it can never be made fully present or exhausted. "Given/giving," Marion writes, "the gift opens the horizon where being [être] can appear."[19]

The theological interest of Marion's work would be hard to deny, and he does not deny it himself. "[A]n insightful reader," he writes, "could not fail to divine that the question of revelation rather essentially governs [Reduction and Givenness]."[20] What Marion does deny is that this work is essentially theological. It is, on his presentation, strictly, radically phenomenological insofar as, in accordance with the "principle of all principles," it seeks to suspend all "conditions of visibility" in order to receive the phenomena purely as they give themselves.[21] Phenomenology thus purified becomes what Marion calls "the method of revelation"—not the content of Revelation (as if phenomenology could do away with revealed theology), but the way of opening to the possibility of an event without cause.[22]

---

above all to unite the two terms of the reduction," intuition and phenomenon, in itself (p. 71).

For the "principle of all principles," see §24 of Ideen zu einer reinen Phänomenologie und phänomenologischen Philosophie: Erstes Buch, Husserliana Band 3 (The Hague: Martinus Nijhoff, 1950), ed. Walter Biemel, p. 52; English trans., Ideas Pertaining to a Pure Phenomenology and to a Phenomenological Philosophy: First Book (The Hague: Martinus Nijhoff, 1983), trans. F. Kersten, p. 44. Marion's critique of Husserl (as of Heidegger) is that he did not apply the reduction in its radicality. It could be asked, however, whether this critique does justice to Husserl. In Reduction and Givenness, Marion ignores Husserl's analyses of passive synthesis and time consciousness—even though time is, for Husserl, as for Heidegger, the ground level of constitution. For Marion on time, and on the temporality of the gift (in this instance, the Eucharist), see his Dieu sans l'être (1982; Paris: Presses Universitaires de France, 1991), pp. 239–58; English trans., God without Being (Chicago: University of Chicago Press, 1991), trans. Thomas A. Carlson, pp. 169–82.

[19] Marion, "Réponses à quelques questions," p. 72. Givenness may not, then, be onto-theological in Heidegger's sense; but its relation with classical metaphysics is complicated to say the least. In Dieu sans l'être, p. 241, God without Being, p. 171, Marion summarizes the task of the overcoming (dépassement) of metaphysics as that of acceding to "the nonmetaphysical essence of metaphysics."

[20] Marion, "Réponses à quelques questions," p. 73.

[21] Ibid., p. 74. Marion enumerates three such "conditions" to be overcome: the principle of sufficient reason, the law of noncontradiction, and the stricture of subjective intelligibility.

[22] Ibid. See here John Milbank, "Only Theology Overcomes Metaphysics,"

At this point it makes sense to ask the second question: What is the status of theology (and of God) after the reduction? Janicaud insists that the "hermeneutic indetermination" in which his critique leaves theology is not an expression of scorn, but in fact respects the autonomy of theology. To support this thesis, he cites Heidegger's 1927 essay "Phenomenology and Theology," in which Heidegger argues (or, more accurately, dictates) that theology is a positive science whose object is not God,[23] but the *positum* of faith itself.[24] "[T]he positive science of [Christian] faith does not need philosophy," Heidegger writes, "for the grounding and primary disclosure of its positivity, Christianness. This grounds itself in its own way."[25] But, according to him, theology does need philosophy (understood at this time as fundamental ontology) *"as a corrective of the ontic and so pre-Christian content of basic theological concepts"* (Heidegger's italics).[26] Theology needs ontol-

---

in *The Word Made Strange* (Oxford: Blackwell, 1997), pp. 36–52. Milbank nicely observes that Marion seeks to correlate "the twentieth-century theology of divine word and gift" with phenomenology radically understood, "as if . . . to be both [Karl] Barth and Heidegger at once" (pp. 36–37). As his title indicates, Milbank does not think that this correlation can work. As for why not, he argues to begin with that, in Marion's phenomenology as in Husserl's, the *ego* retains its priority, "an initial 'I' constituted first as the ground of intentional representation" (p. 39). But this criticism is, at least, highly questionable, if not simply empty. First, in what sense is the I "first" if "constituted"? Also, what does it mean to call the I "the ground of intentional representation"? For again, in what sense is the I a "ground" if "constituted"? In the end, Milbank's criticism ignores the whole problematic of the constitution of the *ego* and seems to reduce phenomenology to a kind of psychology. He concludes that theology "must entirely evacuate philosophy, which is metaphysics . . ., leaving it nothing to either do or see, which is not—manifestly, I judge—malicious" (p. 50). But this is not yet to say what it is.

[23] Heidegger, *Phänomenologie und Theologie* (Frankfurt am Main: Vittorio Klostermann, 1970), p. 25. See also *Wegmarken* (where this essay was republished), 2nd ed. (Frankfurt am Main: Vittorio Klostermann, 1967), p. 59; English trans., *Pathmarks* (Cambridge: Cambridge University Press, 1998), ed. William McNeill, trans. James G. Hart and John C. Maraldo, p. 48.

[24] Ibid., p. 21. See *Wegmarken*, p. 55, *Pathmarks*, pp. 45–46.

[25] Ibid., p. 27. See *Wegmarken*, p. 61, *Pathmarks*, p. 50 (trans. modified).

[26] Ibid., p. 30. See *Wegmarken*, p. 64, *Pathmarks*, p. 52 (trans. modified). For an analysis of Heidegger's understanding of philosophizing at this time, see Daniel O. Dahlstrom, "Heidegger's Method: Philosophical Concepts as Formal Indications," *Review of Metaphysics* 47 (1994): 775–95. Dahlstrom suggests, at the end of this paper, that "Heidegger's method is only understandable in terms of his theism, that is to say, his understanding of the ontic science, Christian theology" (p. 795). Heidegger argues in "Phenomenology and Theology" that theol-

ogy in order to secure its scientific character—in order to develop in the right way. Phenomenology does not give theology its content (for example, the concept of sin), but phenomenology can be used by theology to understand the significance of this content (insofar as it applies to the particular being of *Dasein* and not, say, to mere atoms in the void).[27]

Heidegger's understanding of the relation between phenomenology and theology is nevertheless questionable. The theologian John Macquarrie, for example, has asked whether Heidegger's understanding of theology is not too restrictive, too dogmatically committed to "the new theology of Bultmann, [the early] Tillich, and above all Karl Barth, a theology which explicitly rejected natural theology and was resolved . . . to confine itself to a hermeneutic of faith."[28] Marion has also questioned Heidegger's circumscription of theology. According to Marion, "the question of 'God' "—within scare quotes, since its content is made to depend upon what fundamental ontology can approve—is made relative to *Dasein* and thus effectively secularized and undercut.[29] Crucially, however, Marion does not challenge the right of phenomenology in general to clarify theology, but only the right of Heidegger's phenomenology to do so. By rethinking phenome-

---

ogy has "sense [*Sinn*] and legitimacy [*Recht*] only as [an] ingredient of faith," and not as a disinterested theoretical discipline (p. 20). See *Wegmarken*, p. 54, *Pathmarks*, p. 45. On the basis of extensive citations, Dahlstrom argues that Heidegger likewise understands philosophy "as a way of being in the world that at the same time aims at determining this being" (p. 789).

[27] See *Phänomenologie und Theologie*, p. 31, *Wegmarken*, p. 65, *Pathmarks*, p. 52.

[28] John Macquarrie, *Heidegger and Christianity* (New York: Continuum, 1994), p. 55. Heidegger dedicated *Phänomenologie und Theologie* to Bultmann. For the relation of Bultmann's theological work to Heidegger's fundamental ontology, see Macquarrie's *An Existentialist Theology* (London: SCM, 1955).

[29] Marion, *Dieu sans l'être*, p. 104, *God without Being*, p. 69. According to §9 of *Sein und Zeit* (Tübingen: Max Niemeyer, 1993), p. 42, English trans., *Being and Time* (New York: Harper & Row, 1962), trans. John Macquarrie and Edward Robinson, p. 67, it is *Dasein*, and no longer God, whose essence it is to be: "*The 'essence' of Dasein lies in its existence.*" Heidegger seems to mean this paradigmatically "speculative sentence" to cut against Thomistic theology in particular and speculative theology in general. It could be argued, however, that, ironically, Heidegger's approach opened the way for Marion's restoration of the most speculative of theologians, Dionysius the Areopagite. See Marion, *L'idole et la distance* (Paris: Grasset, 1977), pp. 178–243.

nology "out of the logic of the gift,"[30] Marion seeks at once to preserve the "new theology" and to give it a philosophical footing—not to "ground" it in a philosophical system alien to it, but to liberate it from uncritical dependence on any such system.[31]

Another relevant consideration is what kind of God is excluded by the reduction. In his 1997 book *Étant donné*, Marion argues that "the 'God' bracketed" by Husserl in §58 of *Ideas I* "defines itself only as the foundation [*Grund*] of the facticity of the world" and "thus leaves intact" the "*theo*-logical names" of revealed theology, which "defines God by immanence as well as transcendence."[32] In his 1997 book *Personne et sujet selon Husserl*, Emmanuel Housset argues further that, in Husserl's later thought (especially his unpublished manuscripts), God is no longer merely a "limit-concept" expressing the teleology of reason, but plays a constitutive role in opening the subject to its vocation.[33] In *La*

---

[30] Marion, "Réponses à quelques questions," p. 72.

[31] In "Heidegger's Method," Dahlstrom cites the Protestant theologian Gerhardt Kuhlmann's 1929 attack "against what he regard[ed] as his contemporaries' naive appropriation of an atheistic existentialist analysis that reduces the phenomena of faith and revelation to the 'projection' [*Entwurf*] of *Dasein*" (pp. 775–76). See Gerhardt Kuhlmann, "Zum theologischen Problem der Existenz (Fragen an R. Bultmann)," *Zeitschrift für Theologie und Kirche* 10, no. 1 (1929): 28–57. As Dahlstrom documents in a forthcoming paper, "Scheler's Critique of Heidegger's Fundamental Ontology," Scheler too was suspicious of "the worldview inform[ing] Heidegger's existential analysis." In §62 of *Sein und Zeit*, p. 310, *Being and Time*, p. 358, Heidegger acknowledges that "a definite ontic conception of authentic existence, a factical ideal of *Dasein*," underlies his fundamental ontology. He writes, further, that this fact must not be denied, but "grasped in its *positive necessity*" (Heidegger's italics). But, as Dahlstrom puts it, Heidegger "remains exasperatingly mum" about what that "factical ideal" is: he never says. According to Dahlstrom, Scheler, however, had no doubts: he saw this worldview as "theological, specifically Protestant, even more specifically 'the Barth-Gogartian theology, a kind of Neo-Calvinism' " (so Scheler in the 9th volume of his *Gesammelte Werke, Späte Schriften* [Bern: Francke, 1976], ed. Manfred Frings, pp. 295, 260; Dahlstrom's translation). "What Scheler understands by the latter," Dahlstrom writes, "is a Protestant conception of 'the absolute symbolic transcendence of God' together with the utter thrownness of human beings into the world" (Scheler, *Späte Schriften*, p. 296)—a conception which, by absolutizing being, ultimately leads to the devaluation of human being.

[32] Marion, *Étant donné. Essai d'une phénoménologie de la donation* (Paris: Presses Universitaires de France, 1997), pp. 106, n. 1, 336.

[33] Emmanuel Housset, *Personne et sujet selon Husserl* (Paris: Presses Universitaires de France, 1997), pp. 265, 266, 268, 274, 275, 278, 279, 280–90.

phénoménologie éclatée, however, Janicaud simply denies this thesis, without even so much as referring to Housset.[34]

As the reader might have conjectured, the conclusion to be drawn is that the debate must go on. The value of *The Theological Turn* for this debate is twofold: to awaken an awareness that there is something eminently questionable afoot, however this something may finally be assessed; and to recall that, in phenomenology, questions can be decided only by going back to experience. In *Étant donné*, Marion asks, "Why try to disqualify [givenness] in assigning it a theological origin (supposing, of course, that theology implies in itself a disqualification)?" He answers his own question: "Because challenging it on phenomenological grounds alone would prove too delicate, indeed impossible."[35] But if Janicaud has not answered all outstanding questions, neither have Marion and his fellow "new phenomenologists." What, after all, *is* the origin of the idea of the pure gift? In his introduction to *Phenomenology and Theology*, Jean-François Courtine asks, in speaking of what he calls "the religious phenomenon . . . apprehended in its greatest generality," "[T]o what experience do [we] refer here?" He answers: "once again to the experience (plural, multiform, no doubt essentially heterogeneous, theological and atheological) of the divine, of the passing of the god," whether such an experience has actually taken place, or is envisaged only in its "possibility." But the question needs to be asked again, for what is Courtine talking about? He seems to say too much. Is not an experience that admits of such variation equivocal? How, if it is "essentially heterogeneous," can it go to show anything at all? Once more, then, what experience attests to this possibility? Or must this possibility finally be taken on faith? Janicaud's essay provokes such questions from its beginning to its end.

For help with my translation, I wish to thank first and foremost Nicolas de Warren, who generously read and corrected the entire manuscript; Dominique Janicaud, who kindly and patiently saved

---

[34] Janicaud, *La phénoménologie éclatée*, p. 12 ("God remains a limit-concept for phenomenology") and p. 39 ("Husserl's unpublished manuscripts . . . cannot be utilized to claim that there was already in [him] a 'theological turn' "). Housset, for his part, does not even refer to Janicaud.

[35] Marion, *Étant donné*, p. 105.

me from several howlers; Jorge Pedraza, who did the same; and Amapola Tô, who got me over several stumbling blocks.

For help with my introduction, I wish to thank once more Nicolas de Warren for our many discussions; and my teacher, Daniel O. Dahlstrom, for his encouragement and direction.

Finally, I wish to thank John D. Caputo for engaging me to do this project and supporting me throughout it.

BERNARD G. PRUSAK
Boston, 1 April 1999

1

Contours of the Turn

EVERY CONCEPTION, however modest, is born from some seminal idea. The present essay originated as a report [*constat*] made at the behest of the International Institute of Philosophy.[1] Having agreed to do a kind of review of French philosophy from around 1975 to 1990, and thus to write a *post scriptum* to Vincent Descombes's rich retrospective, *Modern French Philosophy*,[2] I found myself facing a quite complex landscape of thought, one much more subtle than the parade of clichés too often imposed by harried journalists. The history of philosophical thought has never been constituted of a series of slides all moving in the same direction; the history of contemporary philosophical thought, in particular French philosophical thought, is still less easily schematized than that of previous epochs. The combat of ideologies, conflict of interpretations, and play of "influences" have but intensified themselves in this intersection of the world of ideas which Paris has remained.

I spoke of a report. Without revisiting analyses that an interested reader will be able to find elsewhere,[3] it appeared to me that French phenomenological studies—pursued with seriousness and tenacity (in particular, by Paul Ricœur and Michel Henry), distinguished by a singular originality (exemplified by Emmanuel Lévinas), and withdrawn from the fashions and slogans of the 1960s and 1970s—harbored a fecundity whose fruits and coherence revealed themselves in the light of more recent developments. This fecundity is obviously not entirely to be captured under the rubric

---

[1] In cooperation with UNESCO.

[2] Vincent Descombes, *Le même et l'autre. Quarante ans de philosophie française* (Paris: Éditions de Minuit, 1979); English trans., *Modern French Philosophy* (Cambridge: Cambridge University Press, 1980), trans. L. Scott-Fox and J. M. Harding.

[3] Dominique Janicaud, "Rendre à nouveau raison? Dix ans de philosophie française (1979–1989)," in *La philosophie en Europe* (Paris: Gallimard, 1993), ed. Raymond Klibansky and David Pears, pp. 156–93.

of a theological "turn," no more than it would be justified to insist on the idea of a passage from an atheist phenomenology (exemplified by Jean-Paul Sartre, Maurice Merleau-Ponty, or even Mikel Dufrenne) to a "spiritualist" phenomenology (with the masters previously named and several inheritors whose names will emerge little by little in this study). But at the start, it is only a question on my part of setting things in historical perspective.

It will be objected that any "report," even at this level, is already interpretive. I do not deny it, but hold that this "setting in perspective" can be done at a preliminary level, in some minimal way, not yet implying any value judgment—neither praising nor condemning—or any methodological critique. At this preliminary level, it is only a question of testing the coherence of an interpretive intuition concerning French phenomenology over the last thirty or so years. Is there a trait that distinguishes it decisively from the time of the first reception of Husserl and Heidegger? And is this trait the rupture with immanent phenomenality? The opening [*ouverture*] to the invisible, to the Other [*Autre*], to a pure givenness [*donation*],[4] or to an "archi-revelation"? The response to these two connected questions is totally affirmative. The task of this first chapter will be to provide evidence and other considerations supporting this judgment—evidence and considerations that will prove almost too prolific and, let us hope, rather convincing. Then, with more detailed analyses, will come critique and perhaps even polemic, aiming at a sole goal: methodological clarification.

In order to understand the theoretical conditions of possibility for the theological turn, we must ourselves make a brief turn back, not only for historical assurance, but to bring into light the specificity and the limits of the first French phenomenological "breakthrough."

THE HUSSERLIAN SHOCK

With a half-century of perspective, the original reception of Husserl in France appears to us today to have been an oversimplifica-

---

[4] *Translator's note*: The French "*donation*" is used by Jean-Luc Marion, not

tion. But could it have been otherwise? What was not inevitable was the conjunction of exceptional talents and intense interest in a new methodology.

In this regard, the most significant text is brief, but dazzling. It is signed "Sartre" and entitled "Intentionality: A Fundamental Idea of Husserl's Phenomenology." What must we retain from these several pages, dating from January 1939, which were to play the role of manifesto for the new "phenomenological ontology" in the 1940s and 1950s?[5] What is first of all striking is the anti-idealist polemic. Against André Lalande, Léon Brunschvicg, and Émile Meyerson, who analyzed and celebrated the mind's power of assimilation and unification, Sartre lays claim to "something solid," without however wanting to return to either a gross sensualism, an objectivism, or a more subtle type of realism à la Henri Bergson (distinguishing between the reality of our perception and the virtual ensemble of images).[6] Intentionality, then, is this new and almost miraculous solution: the duality idealism/realism is overcome (as well as the duality subjective/objective) by a prior correlation, this "irreducible fact that no physical image can render"—the bursting forth [éclatement] of consciousness in the world, and from the very beginning consciousness "of something other than itself." There is no pure consciousness; the celebrated formula, "All consciousness is consciousness of something," proclaims that the pseudopurity of the cogito is always abstracted from a prior, intentional correlation.

What is striking today, on rereading this text, is the contrast between the importance of the methodological stakes and Sartre's

---

uncontroversially, to translate the German "Gegebenheit." (The controversy centers on the alleged theological overtones of "donation.") The standard English translation for "Gegebenheit" is "givenness," which has also become the standard English translation for "donation."

[5] Jean-Paul Sartre, Situations. I (Paris: Gallimard 1947), pp. 31–35; English trans., "Intentionality: A Fundamental Idea of Husserl's Phenomenology," trans. Joseph P. Fell, Journal of the British Society for Phenomenology 1–2 (1970): 4–5. We find testimony to the immense impact of this text in an article, dating from 1945, by Jean Beaufret: "The intelligence of the subject treated was equaled only by the happiness of the expression." See Beaufret, De l'existentialisme à Heidegger (Paris: Vrin, 1986), p. 41.

[6] See chap. 1 of Matière et mémoire; English trans., Matter and Memory (New York: Zone Books, 1988), trans. Nancy Margaret Paul and W. Scott Palmer, to which Sartre alludes in Situations. I, p. 32; trans., p. 4.

cavalier manner. The manifesto is done up in the most glittering and sensational colors: "Husserl has reinstalled the horror and the charm in things." We find ourselves delivered from the "interior life" and even from . . . Marcel Proust! But there is no wrestling with texts, and still less perplexity. This forecefulness is not innocent: Sartre thus masks real difficulties, of which the most serious is how the method of eidetic description is going to enable us to encounter and to restore the concrete—in particular, in the affective domain—without falling into essentialism. The affective life is characterized by a dynamism that does not lend itself easily to the grasp of the *eidos*, and this dynamism itself is not wholly monolithic. What will become of singular, somehow secondary, intensities? Must we sacrifice as too interior the "intermittences of the heart" so finely evoked by the suddenly shameful Proust? It would seem to be incumbent, at least, to signal how the problem of constitution inevitably crosses that of the lifeworld. Admittedly, Sartre is a little less expeditious in the introduction to *Being and Nothingness*: he cannot mask the truth that, if the existent [*existant*] is reduced "to the series of appearances that manifest it,"[7] the being [*être*] of the intentional phenomenon is not "thing-like" ["*chosique*"]. It is therefore necessary to preserve its specific transcendence, without falling back into idealism. But does not the Husserlian enterprise of constitution restore a kind of transcendental idealism? Sartre has to concede this point, sending Husserl back to the Kantianism he was unable to overcome.[8] Recourse to the Heideggerian concept of preontological understanding, however, allows Sartre to suspend the Husserlian aporia in order to disengage what interests him in the first place: the description of the immediate structures of the for-self [*Pour-soi*], sui generis, nonthetic modalities of (self-) consciousness.

Already in *The Transcendence of the Ego*, dating from 1936, Sartre had wanted at once to detach the Husserlian *cogito* ("all lightness, all translucence"[9]) from the Cartesian *cogito* and to critique what

---

[7] Sartre, *L'être et le néant* (Paris: Gallimard, 1943), p. 11; English trans., *Being and Nothingness* (New York: Washington Square Press, 1953), trans. Hazel E. Barnes, p. 3.

[8] Ibid., p. 289; trans., p. 329.

[9] Sartre, *La transcendance de l'ego. Esquisse d'une déscription phénoménologique* (Paris: Vrin, 1966), p. 25; English trans., *The Transcendence of the Ego: An Existentialist Theory of Consciousness* (New York: Hill and Wang, 1960), trans. Forrest Williams and Robert Kirkpatrick, p. 42.

he presented as Husserl's return to the classical thesis of the transcendental I. In returning to an intentionality burst forth beyond itself [*éclatée*], to a prior correlation between our transcendence and the world, Sartre did not fear to venture daring if not contradictory formulas, like that which made the *ego* a "being [*être*] of the world."[10] Likewise he did not hesitate to reintroduce the me [*moi*] after having systematically criticized it. He was above all obliged, all the while laying claim to the Husserlian *epochē*, to suppose a "bad" evolution on the part of the Master, turning back from the intuitive radicality of the *Logical Investigations* to the neoidealism of the *Ideas* (an evolution that is supposed to be already perceptible within the *Logical Investigations*). Unfurling (nonegological) transcendental consciousness as "impersonal spontaneity," Sartre made himself the champion of a radical phenomenology already in league with historical materialism, but not without multiplying the ambiguities toward Husserl (whom Sartre freely used as an imposing reference while leaving aside the reasons for his "evolution"). Decidedly, Husserl's "evolution" was an accommodating alibi that was used and abused.

Obviously Sartre is not the only party in question here. The difficulties he suspends or minimizes were retrieved by Merleau-Ponty and examined with more patience and scruples, though without being totally resolved. Merleau-Ponty steadfastly maintains that the phenomenological return to the things themselves is "absolutely distinct from the idealist return to consciousness"[11] and strives, not without trouble, to anchor the investigations of the *Phenomenology of Perception* in Husserl's last works on "genetic phenomenology."[12] Under the pretext that eidetic phenomenology must resituate "essences in existence" and open itself to the complexity of being-in-the-world [*être-au-monde*] as to that of intersubjectivity, the end somehow justifies the means. Phenomenology is spirited away by Merleau-Ponty's existential project; the density of descriptions manages to excuse the thinness of method-

---

[10] Ibid., p. 13; trans., p. 31. Trans. modified: Williams and Kirkpatrick render "du monde" as "in the world."

[11] Maurice Merleau-Ponty, *Phénoménologie de la perception* (Paris: Gallimard, 1945), pp. iii ; English trans., *Phenomenology of Perception* (London: Routledge, 1962), trans. Colin Smith, p. ix.

[12] Ibid., p. i; trans., p. vii.

ological justifications. Intentional analysis is put itself to the service of the "perceptive genius" and the prereflexive *cogito*.

Of course, no more than Sartre, Merleau-Ponty cannot totally mask the true situation: that the Husserlian legacy has been more used for its goods than respected as a whole. Thus the following concession is important:

> For a long time, and even in some recent texts, the reduction has been presented as the return to a transcendental consciousness before which the world is spread out in an absolute transparence, animated through and through by a series of apperceptions which it is the philosopher's charge to reconstitute on the basis of their result.[13]

This is to admit, in fact, that Husserl never liberated himself from an idealist metaphysics and that the recourse to intentionality does not at all guarantee, under the pretext of focusing on the existential, an exit out of the horizon and presuppositions of a philosophy where the *cogitatio* continues to play a central role. To break this lock, Merleau-Ponty and Sartre would have had to engage, more seriously and fundamentally, with Heidegger (and not use him as a lure to augment the value of the later Husserl). Consequently, they would also have had to cease this strange game of sacralizing the reference to Husserl. In effect, in the young Sartre and the early Merleau-Ponty, this reference to Husserl plays the role of collateral for the absolute, foundational novelty of the phenomenological method. This operation only succeeded because, at the same time, criticisms of Husserl were minimized either by rhetorical concessions, or on account of the Master's real or supposed evolution. It is not certain, though, that this tactic was entirely deliberated and mastered. As in every operation of transfer, the authority is at once welcomed and rejected (an ambiguous status from which Nietzsche, Freud, Marx, and Heidegger have also benefited).

In spite of everything, it would be bad form to deny two eminently positive traits to this original reception of Husserl. Faithful or unfaithful to the first inspiration, intelligent and provocative works were produced: Sartre's *Psychology of Imagination* and

---

[13] Ibid., p. v; trans., p. xi (trans. modified).

Merleau-Ponty's *Phenomenology of Perception* stimulated phenomenological research and refertilized French philosophy. What's more, the rupture with the classical philosophy of representation and neo-Kantianism did indeed register an earthquake provoked by Husserl himself, one that Heidegger had at once exploited and displaced.

INTERTWINING AND APLOMB

During the decade following the liberation of France, the workplace of French phenomenological investigations stayed open, but unsteady. Sartre abandoned it to turn resolutely toward politics and an ethics of engagement. In his debate with the Marxists, he plainly conceded that his phenomenological ontology remained abstract in relation to social and dialectical reality; the passiveness of Husserlian transcendental idealism finally seemed too heavy to him. Neither the *Notebooks for an Ethics* nor *Saint Genet* reveals the least further interest in properly phenomenological questions—too "pure," too detached from concrete situations and sociopolitical struggles.

At this time, phenomenology was attacked by Marxists in terms and according to presuppositions that appear to us partisan and dogmatic today, but produced their effects on the moment. Tran Duc Thao denounced the ambiguous neutrality of matter as phenomenology treats it: brute *hylè* or cultural object, matter for phenomenology is no longer either dialectical, or worked by man. To be sure, the reduction leads to a givenness of sense that is a human and dynamic truth, but this givenness does not keep us, in Husserl, from falling back into a kind of "total skepticism."[14] Only Marxism could save phenomenology from abstraction.

These arguments tended more to quarantine phenomenology than truly to integrate it into Marxist investigations. And they did

---

[14] Cited by Jean-François Lyotard, *La phénoménologie* (Paris: Presses Universitaires de France, 1954), p. 112; English trans., *Phenomenology* (Albany, N.Y.: State University of New York Press, 1991), trans. Brian Beakley, p. 125. A Marxist critique of Husserlian phenomenology was presented with finesse (but in terms its author today judges outdated) by Jean T. Desanti in his *Introduction à la phénoménologie* (1963; 2nd ed., Paris: Gallimard, 1976).

not at all dissuade Merleau-Ponty, Lévinas, Ricœur, and several others from pursuing exploratory readings of the Husserlian continent. An especially notable contribution to this research and reflection was the publication, in 1950, of Ricœur's translation of Husserl's *Ideen I*.[15] In his introduction, the translator does not mask his perplexity, and it is significant that this is concentrated on the sense of Husserl's transcendental idealism: Is it only a question here of a subjective idealism? Husserl appears to liberate himself from both relativism and Kantianism, however, by both his philosophy of intuition and his reduction of all still "worldly" a priori. Eugene Fink opens an interpretive perspective that Ricœur treats with sympathy, but does not categorically adopt: beyond psychological intentionality and the noetic-noematic correlation, Husserl frees up a third sense of intentionality, the "productive" and "creative" revelation at the origin of the world.[16]

Already at this point, Ricœur formulates the question he retrieves and clarifies in his recent book, *Oneself as Another*: At what stage of the reduction does subjectivity identify itself as intersubjectivity? And in a short sentence, full of underlying meaning, and impossible to pass over indifferently, he lets this slip out: "Is the most radical subject God?"[17] The theological turn is obviously contained *in ovo* in this genre of interrogation, but Ricœur restrained himself from taking the next step. His methodological scruples led him to multiply the hermeneutical precautions prior to any passage from phenomenology to theology.

To salute this rigor does not excuse us from appropriating and deepening the analysis of the difficulties handed down by Husserl. These are extensive, and we shall here encounter them in the course of pursuing our guiding question, metaphysical par excellence: the paradoxical revelation of Transcendence in a source at the heart of phenomenality. We must try to understand, at the same time, why these difficulties were able to be gathered together and "resolved" in two different and on the whole diver-

---

[15] Edmund Husserl, *Idées directrices pour une phénoménologie* (Paris: Gallimard, 1950), trans. Paul Ricœur.

[16] See Ricœur's introduction, pp. xxv–xxx; English trans., *A Key to Edmund Husserl's Ideas I* (Milwaukee: Marquette University Press, 1996), ed. Pol Vandevelde, trans. Bond Harris and Jacqueline Bouchard Spurlock, pp. 47–50.

[17] Ibid., p. xxx; trans., p. 50.

gent directions, which we will designate elliptically by two key words whose explication will follow: *intertwining* and *aplomb*. At stake is how to understand the sense of the reduction, the approach to intersubjectivity, the status to give to the lifeworld, and above all the relationship between phenomenology and metaphysics.

At the heart of Merleau-Ponty's research, arrested in manuscripts collected under the title of *The Visible and the Invisible*, intertwining is introduced to try to name what neither the classical philosophy of representation, nor even Husserl's phenomenology, ever succeeds in apprehending. Certainly the Husserlian notion of horizon prefigures such an approach, but—Merleau-Ponty specifies—"we must take the word strictly."[18] Horizon cannot be reduced to a translucent space of visibility or generality, like a surface, a plane, or even spatiality. Instead, writes Merleau-Ponty, "The body and the distances participate in the same corporeality or visibility in general, which reigns between them and it, and even beyond the horizon, beneath its skin, to the very depths of being [*être*]."[19] Horizon understood as intertwining overflows every delimitation operated by my vision in the visible, even embraces everything visible in a latency that is the *flesh* of things.[20] That is, the visible is never pure, but always palpitating with invisibility, and even the vision I have of it is not anything that could be definitively circumscribed, but is inscribed in corporeality. Intertwining thus gestures toward a double overflowing: of the visible by the flesh of the world, and of my vision by corporeality. These four terms form a chiasm, but one whose point of intersection is never separable from the mysterious emergence of visibility, "now errant, now gathered together."[21]

Renaud Barbaras has clearly shown how the ontology sketched out in *The Visible and the Invisible* overcomes the dualism in which the *Phenomenology of Perception* remained enclosed: between a still classical conception of reflexivity and its prereflexive or natural

---

[18] Merleau-Ponty, *Le visible et l'invisible* (Paris: Gallimard, 1964), ed. Claude Lefort, p. 195; English trans., *The Visible and the Invisible* (Evanston, Ill.: Northwestern University Press, 1968), trans. Alphonso Lingis, p. 148.

[19] Ibid.; trans., p. 149 (trans. modified).

[20] Ibid., p. 175; trans., p. 133.

[21] Ibid., p. 181; trans., pp. 137–38.

"complement."[22] The separation between culture and nature traversed, unquestioned, Merleau-Ponty's first great work. But in setting out in quest of flesh as the "element" of being [*être*] (itself rethought as intertwining, and not as pure givenness), phenomenology looks to take by surprise a dimension prior to the division between reflexive and prereflexive, also antecedent to the plane where the *ego* poses its face to the *alter ego*.[23] My corporeality is immediately intersubjective; that is why the structure of intersubjectivity is inseparable from the texture of the world. All thinking from above [*de surplomb*] misses this complex and living emergence. In the same way, the aplomb of the Other [*Autre*] breaks the threads of intersubjectivity.

It will have been divined that aplomb designates, under our plume, a philosophical attitude every way different and even antithetical, the attitude that loftily affirms itself in Lévinas's *Totality and Infinity*. Aplomb can mean merely audacity, but this psychological sense is not the principal one intended here. In its philosophical sense, where Lévinas is concerned, aplomb is the categorical affirmation of the primacy of the idea of infinity, immediately dispossessing the *sameness* [*mêmeté*] of the I, or of being [*être*]. *Totality and Infinity* is not only contemporary with the last investigations of Merleau-Ponty, but is concerned with resolving the same problem in and responding to the same deficiency of Husserlian phenomenology: intentionality does not succeed in "reducing" reflexivity; neither emergence in the world, nor access to the other [*autrui*], receives sufficient attention. No matter how transcendental in aspiration, the idealism of Husserl's project of universal constitution remains no less radical. Lévinas makes his call for an overcoming of the purely intentional sense of the notion of horizon in terms quite close to those of Merleau-Ponty:

> Intentional analysis is the search for the concrete. The notion held under the direct gaze of the thought that defines it nevertheless reveals itself implanted, unbeknownst to this naïve thought, in horizons unsuspected by this thought. These horizons endow it with meaning—such is the essential teaching of Husserl. What does it

[22] Renaud Barbaras, *De l'être du phénomène. Sur l'ontologie de Merleau-Ponty* (Grenoble: Jérome Millon, 1991), chap. 1.

[23] Ibid., p. 279.

matter if in Husserlian phenomenology taken to the letter these unsuspected horizons are in their turn interpreted as thoughts intending objects![24]

In contrast to Merleau-Ponty, does Lévinas have the merit of frankness in the liberties he takes with Husserl? The goal, let us underline, is the same, at least at first: overflowing the intentional horizon. And in fact the tactics are very much alike, since they consist—wherever we might locate the letter—in being more faithful to the spirit of phenomenology than Husserl himself. This strategem was first ventured by Heidegger; it finds its expression in the theme of the "phenomenology of the unapparent," and recurs, mimed and reinvented, through Jacques Derrida and Michel Henry.

For the moment, we have to try to understand Lévinas and Merleau-Ponty's radical divergence—a divergence that can only look like a mystery—given their similar overcoming of intentionality and their opening [ouverture] of phenomenology to the invisible. Does it suffice to observe that the first challenges ontology to the profit of metaphysics while the second does the reverse? This pigeonholing must not make us forget the very real stakes here for reorienting thought. Between the unconditional affirmation of Transcendence and the patient interrogation of the visible, the incompatibility cries out; we must choose. But are we going to do so with the head or with the heart—arbitrarily or not? The task, insofar as it remains philosophical and phenomenological, is to follow the sole guide that does not buy itself off with fine words: interrogation of method. It then appears clearly that Merleau-Ponty's way has a most heuristic fragility: it is a moving quest, searching for the very words to approximate the richness of an experience each and everyone can undergo. His is a minimalist method, shunning hasty reductions and the idealist temptation, but not at all attention to the other [autre]. The intelligence is sprightly and quick, but as in Proust eventually doubles back and

---

[24] Emmanuel Lévinas, Totalité et infinité. Essai sur l'extériorité (Paris: Kluwer/Le livre de poche, 1990), p. 14; English trans., Totality and Infinity: An Essay on Exteriority (Pittsburgh: Dusquesne University Press, 1969), trans. Alphonso Lingis, p. 28 (trans. modified). Cf. Merleau-Ponty, Le visible et l'invisible, p. 195; trans, pp. 148–49.

deepens the sensible.[25] Merleau-Ponty's way presupposes nothing other than an untiring desire for elucidation of that which most hides itself away in experience. Phenomenological, it remains so passionately, in that it seeks to think phenomenality intimately, the better to inhabit it. Intertwining excludes nothing, but opens our regard to the depth of the world.

On the contrary, the directly dispossessing aplomb of alterity supposes a nonphenomenological, metaphysical desire; it comes from "a land not of our birth."[26] It supposes a metaphysico-theological montage, prior to philosophical writing. The dice are loaded and choices made; faith rises majestically in the background. The reader, confronted by the blade of the absolute, finds him- or herself in the position of a catechumen who has no other choice than to penetrate the holy words and lofty dogmas: "Desire is desire for the absolutely Other [Autre]. . . . For Desire, this alterity, nonadequate to the idea, has a meaning [sens]. It is understood as the alterity of the Other [Autrui] and as that of the Most High."[27] All is acquired and imposed from the outset, and this all is no little thing: nothing less than the God of the biblical tradition. Strict treason of the reduction that handed over the transcendental I to its nudity, here theology is restored with its parade of capital letters. But this theology, which dispenses with giving itself the least title, installs itself at the most intimate dwelling of consciousness, as if that were as natural as could be. Must philosophy let itself be thus intimidated? Is this not but incantation, initiation?

We would do well to recognize the talent and singular originality of Lévinas without, however, granting him the least concession when it comes to methodological and phenomenological coherence. Thus, to cite for the moment only this example, Desire is lickety-split capitalized, emphatic in the extreme. But in virtue of what experience? Evidently something metaphysical. This circularity is perhaps hermeneutical, but certainly not phenomenological. To be sure, Lévinas acknowledges his transgression of phenomenology's "play of lights,"[28] but his biased utilization of what he presents as phenomenology (to pedagogic

---

[25] Merleau-Ponty, *Le visible et l'invisible*, p. 195; trans., p. 149.
[26] Lévinas, *Totalité et infinité*, p. 22; trans., pp. 33–34.
[27] Ibid., p. 23; trans., p. 34.
[28] Ibid., p. 13; trans., p. 27.

ends? to apologetic ends?) and his inscription of the aplomb of the Other [*Autre*] at the heart of experience makes things infinitely more complex than would be an explicit passage (or conversion) from "phenomenology" to "metaphysics." Vis-à-vis what he names "formal logic," Lévinas likewise walks quite softly—striving to overwhelm it, all the while proclaiming himself faithful to the spirit of intellectual rationalism. With his or her clunky critical clogs, every philosopher has the right to intervene and point a finger at Desire: capitalized, does it not become generic? And likewise the Other [*Autre*]? And after all, even if we agree to consider a "dimension of height," must it immediately yield the "Most High"? Thus could we multiply to our heart's content other equally insolent questions, to which we divine too well that the only response could be a reference to the initial presuppositions: "Take it or leave it."

The present essay will develop the good reasons we have for not following this theological swerve, at least insofar as it means to impose itself by a *captatio benevolentiae* of phenomenology. But this reconnaissance we are conducting on the recently cleared lands of French phenomenology must also enable us to understand how ulterior theological thoughts make use of not only Lévinas's frank breakthroughs, but at the same time the subtle illuminations of the second Heidegger. Does the theological turn peter out, then, in barely perceptible tracks? We must not forget that theology can make itself negative and thus exacerbate our ontological anxiety.

THE "PHENOMENOLOGY OF THE UNAPPARENT" AND THE QUESTION OF GIVENNESS

The expression "phenomenology of the unapparent" appears very late in Heidegger, in 1973, and in a precise context, the Zähringen seminars, whose proceedings were first published, in French, in 1976.[29] Paradoxically, this enigmatic formula causes

---

[29] Martin Heidegger, *Questions IV* (Paris: Gallimard, 1976), trans. J. Beaufret, F. Fédier, J. Lauxerois, and C. Roels. The German translation, *Vier Seminare* (Frankfurt am Main: Vittorio Klostermann, 1977), was done by Curt Ochwadt; Heidegger reviewed the translation of the seminars, whose "minutes" were

difficulties less on the side of the "unapparent" than in its maintaining of the reference to phenomenology. Certainly, the unapparent is ambiguous: it can be that which hides itself away, that which does not appear clearly to the eyes, but also that which cannot be reduced to a single appearance (as opposed to real being [*être réel*]). It is evident that Heidegger excludes this second sense, which falls back on the flatly Platonic conception he precisely wants to shake off. The Zähringen discussions were intended as a response to Jean Beaufret's principal question: "To what extent can we say that there is not, in Husserl, any question of being [*être*]?"[30] The response is clear: despite the breakthrough of the sixth *Logical Investigation*, Husserl still understands being [*être*] as an objective given [*donné*], whereas Heidegger tries to think its "truth" as the "unconcealing" [*désabritement*] of presence. From there, everything is no longer related to intentionality, but consciousness is more originally situated in the "ek-static" of *Dasein*.[31] This gathering of the emergence of presence is unapparent to both metaphysics and common sense; Heidegger confides its care to a more original mode of thinking that he names here "tautological thought."

These indications only confirm the orientation of Heidegger's "turn," seeking—at times audaciously, at times more patiently—the conditions of a release from exclusively metaphysical modes of thought. The aporia of this project, already enough in themselves, have no need to be encumbered by this additional burden: giving a new lease on life to phenomenology, albeit metamorphosized. Does Heidegger really need this reference? Does he always present his "last" thinking as phenomenological? The response to these two questions can only be negative, though it would be legitimate to question the "need" Heidegger still has to maintain a tie, however tenuous, with the phenomenological inspiration. The fact is that, in the Zähringen seminars, as in "My Way to Phenomenology,"[32] the relation to the Husserlian legacy lies at

---

taken in French. *Translator's note:* See also volume 15 of Heidegger's *Gesamtausgabe, Seminare* (Frankfurt am Main: Vittorio Klostermann, 1986), ed. Curd Ochwadt, pp. 372–400.

[30] Ibid., p. 309; *Seminare*, p. 372.

[31] Ibid., p. 322; *Seminare*, p. 383.

[32] Trans. Heidegger, "Mein Weg in die Phänomenologie," in *Zur Sache des Denkens* (Tübingen: Max Niemeyer, 1969), pp. 81–90; English trans., "My Way

the center of the debate, and in such a way that Heidegger finds himself quite naturally (and still very lucidly) led to mark out the unity of his thought's itinerary, from his meeting with Husserl to his well-known dissents and divergences. It must be acknowledged that the unity of this path can be so traced only by paying due heed to the misunderstandings that constantly underlay Husserl and Heidegger's collaboration: their Brentano was not the same,[33] and the young Heidegger was fascinated by the sixth *Logical Investigation*, to which Husserl came to accord scarcely any importance. But next to the upheavals to which *Being and Time* was going to subject the method and above all the presuppositions of Husserlian phenomenology, all that was still nothing.

These reflections lead to a double statement of fact [*constat*]: Heidegger is perfectly within his rights to appropriate phenomenology, which belongs to nobody, not even Husserl, in either its letter or its inspiration; but the "tautological thought" he extols finally has nothing to do with the Husserlian enterprise of constitution, which meant—try as try can—to offer a more fundamental, more true, and more complete knowledge [*connaissance*] of the different facets of being [*l'étant*], including the subjective correlates of ontic reality. Jean-François Courtine has shown that the "phenomenology of the unapparent" could retrospectively assume, within *Being and Time*, the first sense of the "uncovering" [*désocculation*] of phenomena: as a grammar of predication, it could still be understood as a hermeneutic deepening of phenomenology. But the "tautological" radicalization of the Heideggerian project exposes it, according to Courtine, not only to equivocality, but perhaps to the *Unglück*—to the disaster or catastrophe—of abandoning the phenomena.[34]

This evocation of Heidegger's enigmatic path might seem to lead us away from the question of the theological turn. But, on

---

to Phenomenology," in *On Time and Being* (New York: Harper & Row, 1972), trans. Joan Stambaugh, pp. 74–82.

[33] Husserl was inspired by Brentano's *Psychology from an Empirical Standpoint*, whereas Heidegger "learned to read philosophy" in *Of the Several Senses of Being in Aristotle*. See Heidegger, *Questions IV*, p. 323.

[34] Jean-François Courtine, *Heidegger et la phénoménologie* (Paris: Vrin, 1990), pp. 381–405.

the contrary, it places us at the crux of the matter where everything is decided: at the point of rupture between a positive phenomenological project and the displacement of its "possibility"
toward the originary [*originaire*]. What troubles some can gratify
others. If the "phenomenology of the unapparent" finally makes
all rule-based presentation of the phenomena vacillate in favor of
a hearkening to a word whorled with silence, here—against all
expectations—is a line extended toward the originary, the nonvis-
ible, the reserved. Ready to renounce a thematic phenomenology, the candidates to the theological heritage will content
themselves with a phenomenology of points and dots. How could
they remain unmoved by the intrepid return to the originary,
whose ambiguities will fascinate, not discourage, the hermeneuts
of a new version of the *intimior intimo meo* (or at least what they
believe to be so)? If the "phenomenology of the unapparent" is
to be interpreted not as a regression, but as full of promise, then
the most audacious soundings stand permitted. These will exploit
the retrieval of both "givenness" and the most originary dimension of temporality to attain and bind together the traces of a new
approach of the Sacred and of the "God most divine." In fact,
can it be denied that Heidegger's "turn" was conditioned by his
quest for the Sacred, through his reinterpretation of Hölderlin?
Without Heidegger's *Kehre*, there would be no theological turn.
Assuredly. But this affirmation is not a legitimation. The faithful
hearkening easily reverts to orthodoxy. A restless mind, fashioning
new questions, will perhaps seem insolent to be so exacting over
semantic slides and methodological displacements. Yet if its questioning is not a rite, it will demonstrate an acuity in line with
the requirements of the "piety" that must crown, according to
Heidegger, thought worthy of the name. . . .

The logic of our subject matter will lead us, in the third chapter,
to a critical study of the brilliant French sequels to the "phenomenology of the unapparent." Thus we will come upon, at first and
up close, Jean-Luc Marion's audacious inquiry into a "pure form
of the call,"[35] the stakes of a third reduction, neither transcenden-

---

[35] Jean-Luc Marion, *Réduction et donation. Recherches sur Husserl, Heidegger et la
phénoménologie* (Paris: Presses Universitaires de France, 1989), p. 296; English
trans., *Reduction and Givenness: Investigations of Husserl, Heidegger, and Phenomenology* (Evanston, Ill.: Northwestern University Press, 1998), trans. Thomas A.
Carlson, p. 197.

tal nor existential. In what way does this reduction—purported to unfurl a givenness the more originary as it is radical—remain phenomenological? What sense can we make of a call so pure that it claims only an "interlocuted" ["*interloqué*"], without flesh or bones? The author himself recognizes the legitimacy of this objection in principle, which he formulates in these terms: "Does such a transgression . . . still issue in an authentically phenomenological situation, or does it not rather renounce the elementary methodological exigencies of a 'rigorous science'?"[36] In reiterating this methodological question, we will not disregard Marion's response given to it, which must be seriously examined in its motivations and presuppositions. For in this way we shall formulate the further question of whether the narrow way announcing "rigorous and new paradoxes" beyond *Reduction and Givenness* can still lay claim to "phenomenology as such."[37]

Different and yet exposed to like questions, the "phenomenology of the promise" proposed by Jean-Louis Chrétien equally merits an attentive reading, at once welcoming and critical. Worthy of sympathy, perhaps even amazement, the writing of *La voix nue*[38] [*The Naked Voice*] remains certainly phenomenological by the fineness of its evocations and descriptions. But we must immediately add "in the larger sense," and not fail to interrogate the advances, permitted by this latitude, toward the gift in itself, love in infinite excess, the glorious body, and "the promise that always already surrounds us."[39]

Our initial wonderment was methodological; our final inquiries must also be so in order to allow us to draw lessons from other phenomenological trajectories, older and more fruitful, whose explicit or implicit relation to the theological possibility appears worthy of question. Thus the fourth chapter will trace the methodological discriminations by which Michel Henry has explicitly and loftily laid claim to the adequation between phenomenality (elucidated as the essence of all manifestation) and the absolute (understood as the revelation of life itself as affectivity). In opposi-

---

[36] Ibid. Trans. modified: Carlson omits "methodological."

[37] Ibid., pp. 305 and 7–10; trans., pp. 205 and 1–3.

[38] Jean-Louis Chrétien, *La voix nue. Phénoménologie de la promesse* (Paris: Éditions de Minuit, 1990).

[39] Ibid., p. 60.

tion to the concept of the phenomenon reigning not only in Husserl, but in the whole of Western philosophy since the Greeks—the visibility of the object or of the *eidos*—Henry relates the structure of phenomenality to its secret interiority, its constitutive invisibility, the night of its autoaffection. Are we right to detect, here, a theological turn? So far as this thinking means to return to the very foundation of immanence, fashions itself "material,"[40] and prioritizes reflection on method,[41] it would be absurd to reproach it with any surreptitious slippage or whatever other inconsistency. But our question, in what it implies, is still not invalidated. In fact, Henry's theological orientation was already perfectly explicit in *The Essence of Manifestation*,[42] where the critique of Husserl's intuitionist rationalism, as well as Heidegger's ontological monism, made description of the phenomenon subordinate to the approach to the essence of phenomenality.[43] Now this essence was understood as affectivity absolutely revealing the absolute.[44] Were we subtly led, then, back toward God? Assuredly—but less toward the God of a positive theology than toward the Deity in Meister Eckhart's sense:[45] mysterious unity between phenomenal manifestation and the very basis of life.

Our challenge will not bear on Henry's spiritual intention— quite respectable and often of an admirable tenor—but on his strange stubbornness to install this research (essentially fragile and secret, if not esoteric) at the center of a disciplinary apparatus whose principles are all formulated in precisely the rational, unifying, Western terms intended to be challenged. Whereas Heidegger prudently uses the term "thought" for an inquiry requiring a mutation of language, Henry proceeds to a kind of expropriation of the phenomenological house and its methodological instru-

---

[40] Michel Henry, *Phénoménologie matérielle* (Paris: Presses Universitaires de France, 1990).

[41] See ibid., pp. 61–136 ("La méthode phénoménologique"), and "Quatre principes de la phénoménologie," *Revue de métaphysique et de morale* 1 (1991): 3–26.

[42] Henry, *L'essence de la manifestation* (Paris: Presses Universitaires de France, 1963); English trans., *The Essence of Manifestation* (The Hague: Martinus Nijhoff, 1973), trans. Girard Etzkorn.

[43] Ibid., p. 38; trans., p. 30.

[44] Ibid., p. 860; trans., p. 683.

[45] Ibid., §§40, 49.

ments. He even goes so far as to proclaim that the future belongs to a "phenomenology" thus reoriented. But what future and for whom, if the fusion (if not confusion) between the affective approach to the absolute and the constitution of a unified methodological corpus is imposed, in a virtuosic—but dogmatic—autoreference, as if it followed automatically? How is it possible to drive toward the "nonknowledge" of the mystical Night in using the conceptual or terminological instruments of good old academic philosophy? It is this incompatibility that motivates our objection and will oblige us—once we have traversed the inevitable moment of critique—to propose other roads for phenomenology to follow. The fact that Paul Ricœur will be, though discreetly, one of our guides in this positive exploration is the sign, among others, that the polemical part of this little book is not at all directed against the theological as such. On the contrary, maintaining phenomenology in methodological limits, clearly defined and assumed, without losing sight of the ideal and the constraints of scientificity, will facilitate the task of hermeneutics (or another mode of "thought" finer still) in taking up those fundamental questions which, overflowing the phenomenal field, give rise to philosophical thought no less.

Phenomenology is not all of philosophy. It has nothing to win in either a parade of its merits, or by an overestimation of its possibilities—unless it is a temporary imperialism in the academic, francophone canton, or the dubious status of a disguised apologetic, of a spiritualist last stand. But is it not a noble and vast enough task for phenomenology to seek the dimension of invisibility that all describable idealities imply? Merleau-Ponty, who posed a question of this type, remained incontestably phenomenological in laying down the following restriction (which will be the shibboleth of this investigation): "not an absolute invisible . . . , but the invisible *of* this world."[46]

---

[46] Merleau-Ponty, *Le visible et l'invisible*, p. 198; trans., p. 151.

2

The Swerve

HUSSERL, we know, did not recognize himself in the project of *Being and Time*. The success of this book showed him, during the painful last years of his life, that the fortunes of phenomenology might well ride on what was, to his eyes, a fundamental misunderstanding. He saw his radical attempt to refound the scientificity of philosophy transformed into both a "destruction" of metaphysical rationality and a descriptive analytic of the elementary structures of existence. And he could not foresee that a new turn of the phenomenological movement would open onto theological perspectives equally foreign to the spirit of phenomenology "as a rigorous science." Sartre and Merleau-Ponty, whatever liberties they had taken in regard to the Husserlian methodological prescriptions, at least remained faithful to this fundamental Husserlian inspiration: the essence of intentionality is to be sought, by the phenomenological reduction, in phenomenal immanence. If there is an intentional transcendence, it is to be grasped as it is given itself in the world. The suspension of the natural attitude ought not to lead to a flight to another world or to the restoration of absolute idealism, but to a deepening of the transcendental regard vis-à-vis experience and for it.

It is not at all a question here of taking anybody to task for the nonrespect of an orthodoxy. On the contrary, it is a fact that the history of thought is woven in ever new wefts, which enrich it in displacing it. Our subject matter is different and also means to be philosophically more interesting than the simple statement—whether uttered in praise or in condemnation—that there exists a phenomenological inspiration covering a much vaster field than works of "strict observance." (We must acknowledge, in fact, that "strict observance" has led only to restatements or at best to pertinent elucidations of the Husserlian project). It is a question here of analyzing the methodological presuppositions permitting a phenomenologist (or by which a phenomenologist might believe him- or herself permitted) to open phenomenological investigations onto absolute Transcendence while putting aside the Husserlian concern for rigor and scientificity.

Emmanuel Lévinas's *Totality and Infinity* is the first major work of French philosophy in which this theological turn is not only discernible, but explicitly taken up within a phenomenological inspiration. In order to treat our subject matter—which, once more, means to be essentially methodological—with maximum precision, let us return to *Totality and Infinity* and try to establish to what extent this book remains phenomenological. If our response does not support the type of ambiguity wanted by Lévinas, but instead develops into a methodological critique, we will have to follow this business all the way to its end and investigate the "seizure" ["*captation*"] of phenomenology realized by such a philosophical operation. But first of all we must recall what status Lévinas himself explicitly gave to the phenomenological in *Totality and Infinity*.

PHENOMENOLOGY: INSPIRATION OR METHOD?

Prudently, at the beginning of his preface to the German edition of *Totality and Infinity*, dating from January 1987, Lévinas speaks only of a "phenomenological inspiration." Besides Husserl and Heidegger, he salutes Martin Buber, Gabriel Marcel, Franz Rosenzweig, and especially Henri Bergson as masters and inspirations. He makes no effort to situate *Totality and Infinity* in the strict current of Husserlian method. If Lévinas does not do this, it is evidently because this claim is unsupportable and goes against the text itself—to which we must return.

"Phenomenology is a philosophical method, but phenomenology—comprehension by bringing to the light—does not constitute the ultimate event of being [*être*] itself."[1] This announcement warrants our attention for several reasons. For the moment, let us restrict ourselves to noting that it converges with other warnings regarding ontology, the concept of totality, philosophies of representation, and even intentionality: "All knowledge [*savoir*], as in-

---

[1] Lévinas, *Totalité et infinité*, p. 13; trans., p. 28 (trans. modified).

tentionality, already supposes the idea of the infinite, the *nonadequation* par excellence."[2] In the extremely dichotomous framework that is put into place (and by whose direction exteriority breaks open totality), phenomenology falls on the side of ontology and philosophies of representation. It equalizes the noema to the noesis and thereby proves itself incapable of opening itself to the event par excellence, the advent of the Other [*Autrui*]. Phenomenology is a "play of lights" and seems to be only that.[3]

Despite its clarity, this putting-into-place does not avoid raising difficulties and questions. What is clear is Lévinas's challenge to phenomenology as a method. And what goes together with this method is its end: eidetic elucidation, the intuition of essences. The difficulties that arise concern in part the very coherence of Lévinas's project, in part the legitimacy of his assimilatations of phenomenology, intentionality, and representation. This last point is without doubt the most evident: Lévinas lets himself off easy when he reduces phenomenology to the eidetic. For this is to make light of what André de Muralt has called the "two dimensions of intentionality": the phenomenological descriptive point of view does not at all exhaust the phenomenological project, which is also, more fundamentally, transcendental.[4] In the same spirit, we do well to recall, with Jan Patocka, the necessary distinction between the reduction and the *epochē*, which makes manifest the appearing [*l'apparaître*] itself and not only this or that essential apparition.[5] The discovery of the transcendental a priori is the principle driving Husserl's enterprise. This discovery is not at all limited to isolating an *eidos*, but reveals the correlation between the world and intentional transcendence. Reducing it to a combination of representations is tantamount to returning to an associationist or reflexive point of view worthy of Condillac or Hamelin, but certainly not of Husserl.

Second objection: it is equally contestable to assimilate phe-

---

[2] Ibid., p. 12; trans., p. 27 (trans. modified).

[3] Ibid., p. 13; trans., p. 27.

[4] André de Muralt, *L'idée de la phénoménologie. L'exemplarité husserlienne* (Paris: Presses Universitaires de France, 1958), p. 338; English trans., *The Idea of Phenomenology: Husserlian Exemplarism* (Evanston, Ill.: Northwestern University Press, 1974), trans. Garry L. Breckon, p. 341.

[5] Jan Patocka, *Qu'est-ce que la phénoménologie?* (Grenoble: Jérome Millon, 1988), p. 257.

nomenology to ontology, to the extent that phenomenology is defined as a method. Admittedly, Sartre practiced a "phenomenological ontology," but the Husserlian conception was different. For Husserl, the suspension of the natural attitude implies leaving behind all ontological realism, and the project of the constitution of a phenomenological science obeys the *telos* of an infinite rationality and therefore an ideal. Ontology is itself bracketed, whether on the level of the entity [*l'étant*] or on the level of the "there is" ["*il y a*"] of being [*l'être*] (to which Husserl did not at all mean to restrict himself).

There is still much more to object to regarding the additional assimilation Lévinas makes in claiming that all philosophy is an objectivism of knowledge [*connaissance*].[6] Is this true of the Good in Plato, of the One in Plotinus, of the Infinite in Descartes? Not only must we respond negatively, but note besides that Lévinas himself makes use of these experiences of transcendence.

Still, there is something more serious to consider: Lévinas's conception of intentionality leads us to question the very coherence of his thought. At the least, his formulations of it are contestable and disconcerting, for we just saw that intentionality in Husserl is not at all reducible to the adequation of thought and object. But what becomes of it in Lévinas? What strikes us as his essential violence (or "exteriority") is the act or surplus of the idea of the infinite. Now, Lévinas specifies, "The infinite does not first exist [*n'est pas d'abord*], and *then* reveal itself. Its infinition produces itself as revelation, as positing its idea in *me*."[7] But if this revelation is subjectivity (over which there is not any disagreement), what sense does it make to claim that it does not involve, precisely, intentionality? A sham intentionality, purely representative, has been fabricated to prepare the way for the advent of the idea of the infinite. This is an artifical operation, one that Descartes and Husserl were able to do without: for these thinkers, in discovering in me the idea of the infinite, I discover also that my subjectivity exceeds the representation I have of it. There is no need, then, to introduce the Other [*Autre*] face to the Same, nor to claim, as Lévinas does, that the idea of the infinite is "the *non-*

---

[6] Lévinas, *Totalité et infinité*, p. 89; trans., p. 89.
[7] Ibid., p. 12; trans., p. 26 (trans. modified).

adequation par excellence."[8] The intentionality in which the play
between the finite and the infinite is to be discovered is neither
adequate nor inadequate; it is the opening itself of the possibilities
phenomenology brings to light.

Lévinas imposes his schema, then, only at the price of considerable distortions of his methodological referents. In order to rees-
tablish the coherence of his project, we must accept "his"
intentionality, "his" conception of phenomenology. But at what
price? Certainly, explicitly, the price is the abandonment of the
phenomenological *method*, a farewell to the Husserlian ambition
of rigor. We must signal, besides, that Lévinas challenges what he
calls "formal logic" many times over. Is this logic altogether in its
manipulation of key concepts like the other and the same . . . and
in its deployment of a method that waters down into "inspiration"?

A somewhat bitter stroke must be added to our picture. Lévinas's "hermeneutical violence" reproduces, while displacing, the
Heideggerian violence with respect to the same "objectives": eidetic phenomenology, representative subjectivity, objectifying
philosophy. Being [*être*] has simply been replaced on the "good"
side by the Other [*Autre*], and metaphysics is celebrated instead of
being deconstructed. It is fair game to turn the weapons of the
Heideggerian ontology against itself—an operation that Lévinas
will not be the only party to venture, and which does not fail
to recall, all proportions aside, the combats around the Hegelian
heritage. But Lévinas's operation is not, for all that, any more
legitimate. Confronted by the tradition it challenges or claims for
itself, it must also answer for its own coherence. For dismissing
the majority of phenomenology's methodological constraints—
along with phenomenology—is too easy.

A Phenomenology Even So?

Just as Lévinas evokes the event of being [*être*] while challenging
ontology, he reintroduces a phenomenology after having challenged the phenomenological method. As he does not himself

---

[8] Ibid.; trans., p. 27.

theorize this two-timing [*double jeu*], but prefers to treat it as a kind of constant fait accompli by which the absolute anteriority of the Other [*Autre*] is loftily affirmed, it falls to the perplexed reader, unwilling either to submit or to quit, to reckon with the passages to the limit—or contradictions—this discourse allows itself.

So it is for the return to phenomenology in a project that challenges it while situating itself "beyond the face." We want to speak of this "phenomenology of Eros,"[9] which is presented as giving a home to exteriority in sensibility; but we wonder how this phenomenology can be spoken or written about, since it is beyond the face, which already transgresses "the idea of the Other [*Autre*] in me."[10] This is a double transgression, and rather dizzying. But none of this prevents Lévinas from seasoning a work that is otherwise too austere with several evocations, at bottom rather naïve, of the caress, modesty, and tenderness. What, however, remains phenomenological in these several pages, unless it is the description and illustration of a thesis that is already acquired? The description does not play any heuristic role; it discreetly posits its images in an edifying space where conceptuality has been blocked, once and for all, on the Other [*Autre*]. But what Other [*Autre*]? To what degree of transcendence, or of conviviality? And how, from the demanding heights of pure exteriority, will we ever descend to the evocations, more or less suggestive, of a phenomenology for a reduced price?

This "phenomenology" comes down to the edifying and airy evocation of a disembodied caress and a display-window eroticism. "The caress consists in seizing upon nothing."[11] Let us not succumb to irony too easily; it is clear that this "nothing" is not static, but searches for a form that eludes it. Without doubt—but is this not the case with every temporalized gesture? What is specific, here, to the caress? What remains of it, deprived of everything empirical? Will we be happier in turning to the erotic relation as such? "The Beloved [*Aimée*], at once graspable but intact in her nudity, beyond object and face, and thus beyond

---

[9] Ibid., pp. 286–98; trans., pp. 256–66.
[10] Ibid., p. 43; trans., p. 50.
[11] Ibid., p. 288; trans., p. 257.

the existent [*l'étant*], abides in virginity."[12] These lines are again "impossible"! But let us keep going in the understanding that it is a question here of subverting the ambient understanding of sexuality by spiritualizing the erotic relation. But in this instance the capitalized "Beloved" immediately transports us into the country of the ideal, and it will become clear, a few lines further along, that it is a question here of the "eternal feminine." Still, let us assent to the Beloved and to virginity. But the impoverishment of experience attains stupefying proportions when we must acknowledge that this virginity holds itself "beyond the object and the face, and thus beyond the existent [*l'étant*]."[13] Either these words have a meaning, or they have none. In the first case, the virginity in question is *absolutely* ungraspable (and not "simultaneously" discovered and hidden)—but how, then, are we even to speak of this a priori where all corporeality slips away? How, moreover, are we ever to approach the Beloved, if the face is itself packed away—this face that we have been taught, however, was "expression," already beyond all image?[14] So we find ourselves driven back to our second hypothesis: these words signify nothing, just as the caress "seizes upon nothing," a caress that is meant for nobody. For that matter, does this proposition even have an author? Evanescence here, there, and everywhere.

If we move now from the "phenomenological" description to the fundamental level it means to reveal, what is really at issue? Lévinas has apprised us that we must not expect an *eidos*, a representation, an image. And so it is. From hypostasis to hypostasis, we are led to the "Principle"! But Lévinas wants to hold onto the fiction (or two-timing) of his phenomenology of Eros—an Eros that gives pleasure in experience in just the same way that the transcendence of exteriority is supposed to arise in immanence. From here, this circle is squared: a pure experience! Regarding the feminine face in its equivocality, we read: "In this sense voluptuosity is a pure experience, an experience which does not pass into any concept, which remains blindly experience."[15] This concept has an awful lot to bear. If only it were demonstrated to

---

[12] Ibid., p. 289; trans., p. 258.
[13] Ibid.
[14] Ibid., p. 43; trans., p. 51.
[15] Ibid., p. 290; trans., p. 260.

us, to begin with, that the notion of pure or absolute experience makes sense and does not collapse into words, words, words. Obviously, Lévinas is once more playing here on the partially inexpressible (or at least in concepts) character of the experience of desire and pleasure. But speak (or write) of this experience as he will, can he really give himself all the liberties he does in confounding the libidinal with the ideal? Or again in claiming that equivocality can set the stage for a "pure experience"? There is nothing less pure than equivocality. More radically than ever, we must pose this question: Is the notion of "absolute experience" admissible? "The absolute experience is not disclosure [*dévoilement*] but revelation"[16]—all of Lévinas's discourse is suspended on this presupposition. Once he has made his reader assent to it, he may lawfully put all of its variants into circulation. For example, after having imposed a notion of pure exteriority, he can write a sentence like this one about signification: "It is, par excellence, the presence of exteriority."[17] Only, how can exteriority be pure, if it is present?

We will be told that the phenomenological reduction has been replaced by "revelation"; in short, we will have to listen, again, to the refrain of the beyond. But this is always to put off the same question: Why keep playing along at phenomenology when the game is fixed? Why claim to overcome intentionality, only to reintroduce an "intention" of sense[18] or an intentionality of transcendence? We pick up, here, the thread of our question, which is methodological. Lévinas's two-timing can be critiqued as purely and simply contradictory, terminating in a battle of words. Formally, such is the case. But it appears to us philosophically more enriching to unmask, in the workings of these contradictions, a more artful strategy, though one not totally mastered. In systematically displacing the Husserlian concepts and the Heideggerian analyses (the same to the other [*autre*], *eidos* to exteriority, intentionality to expression, the unveiling of being [*l'être*] to the epiphany of the existent [*l'étant*] as such), Lévinas not only produces a (provisional) effect of interference in the mind of the die-

---

[16] Ibid., p. 61; trans., pp. 65–66. See also pp. 67 and 152; trans., pp. 70–71 and 141.

[17] Ibid., p. 61; trans., p. 66 (trans. modified).

[18] Ibid., p. 290; trans., p. 260.

hard phenomenologist who is trying to find his or her way, but succeeds in a veritable *captatio benevolentiae* of the phenomenological method—the better to wring its neck. In fact, phenomenology has been taken hostage by a theology that does not want to say its name. Let us clarify this last critique.

THE THEOLOGICAL HOSTAGE-TAKING

In "Violence and Metaphysics," an essay as precise as it is subtle, Jacques Derrida went to the heart of these difficulties: "By making the origin of language, of sense, and of difference the relation to the infinitely other [*autre*], without relation to the same, Lévinas resigns himself to betraying his own intention in his philosophical discourse."[19] To betray his own intention—the expression follows to the trace [*suit à la trace*] the excess of intention over intentionality or for that matter any other discourse. But Lévinas has a philosophical discourse even so, and how abundant, and eloquent! Presently, the philosophical tribe is not so put out by it; from the moment an œuvre is recognized, it forms a sort of closed totality (how ironic, in the case of Lévinas!) we can compare to other "great" achievements of thought. But this is an expeditious solution we want to challenge. In this regard, so-called analytic philosophy has lessons to teach us: prestigious signatures do not protect against refutation. And Vincent Descombes, on this point, has reason to be ironic, in his *Objects of All Sorts*,[20] on the facilities phenomenological discourse too often accords itself.

To be precise, we have wanted to show that, in Lévinas, phenomenology is at once challenged and put to use, in a manner that is not altogether innocent and refers back, fundamentally, to the line of questioning indicated by Derrida. Here nothing less

---

[19] Jacques Derrida, *L'écriture et la différence* (Paris: Éditions de Seuil, 1967), p. 224; English trans., *Writing and Difference* (London: Routledge, 1978), trans. Alan Bass, p. 151. Trans. modified: Bass omits "without relation to the same."

[20] Vincent Descombes, *Grammaire d'objets en tous genres* (Paris: Éditions de Minuit, 1983); English trans., *Objects of All Sorts: A Philosophical Grammar* (Baltimore: Johns Hopkins University Press, 1986), trans. Lorna Scott Fox and Jeremy Harding.

than the status of metaphysics as discourse is at stake. Contradiction, incoherence—these words have already been written by Derrida to describe Lévinas, though with much respect and circumspection. "Like pure violence, pure nonviolence is a contradictory concept. Contradictory beyond what Lévinas calls 'formal logic.' "[21] The irony of the situation is that, in rejecting ontology as warlike and by opposing to it morality as peace, Lévinas does violence to ontological phenomenality. This is given neither as pure unveiling, nor as brutal conflictual rage, nor as the simple appeasement of letting-be.

Something important is at stake here: whether we can manipulate experience, or must, on the contrary, patiently describe it in order to know it. Without any doubt, Husserl chose the second way, with a will for total coherence. His concern for the "thing itself" made him, before the real, constantly revitalize the spirit of investigation. But, with Lévinas, everything is different. The relation to experience is subordinated to the restoration of the metaphysical (and theological) dimension; in this regard—contrary to Derrida's suggestions at the end of "Violence and Metaphysics"—it is no longer a question here of empiricism. Admittedly, Derrida has in mind the essence of empiricism when he thus qualifies Lévinas's radical quest for exteriority; but we must not fall victim to the word and fail to recognize to what point Lévinas's metaphysical/theological project leads him to schematize experience.

Let us return for a moment to the phenomenology of Eros. The reader may have observed that it did not succeed in seducing us. But beyond personal preferences, a question of method has been posed. It is perfectly legitimate to challenge, for example, the Sartrean vision of the relation to the other [*autrui*] as conflict and to reject the importance given in *Being and Nothingness* to masochism and sadism, as well as other situations of conflict. (The extent to which Lévinas reacted against this vision is palpable.) But it is undeniable that Sartre wanted to bring into evidence the *essence* of love, and that he tried to do so phenomenologically, working from contradictions in the lover's consciousness: "In love . . . , the lover wants to be 'the whole world' for the be-

---

[21] Derrida, *L'écriture et la différence*, p. 218; trans., p. 146.

loved."[22] Even if it is not so easy to isolate "the concrete relations with the other [*autrui*]," it is undeniable that the Sartrean project remains phenomenological in opening onto variations and contradictions of the attitudes studied (in particular, altruism and the essence of "being-with" ["*être-avec*"], which Sartre does not ignore, but discusses). The same fidelity holds, all proportions aside, in Merleau-Ponty, where "the body as sexed being [*être sexué*]" is studied in situ and on the basis of pathological cases.[23] In Lévinas, no such thing occurs: adversity, like the adverse thesis, is globally rejected as "warlike"; the obsession with the Other [*Autre*] permits him to put the realities of this relation under uppercase cover. As Michel Haar has noted, ethics—having become "irresistible requisition, instant and anticipatory abolition of all egoism"[24]—is imposed as a traumatism, even as it demands transcendence. An impossible *requisit*, phenomenologically untenable, whose truth could only be secured in an alliance with another order. Such a dogmatism could only be religious. It has its grandeur, but also its limits.

Another word on phenomenology and its method. What is the result of the seizure carried out by Lévinas? An original and inspiring œuvre? Perhaps. But we can also ask if the two-timing of phenomenology does not compromise Lévinas's profound intention by enclosing it in an abstract schema. He wanted to avoid the pitfalls of the eidetic, but did he truly? Has he not produced an eidetic discourse in reverse, whose extreme term is the exteriority of the Other [*Autre*] and which is more empiricist than empirical (which Derrida wanted, without a doubt, to point out)? Apart from the anemia of his existential evocations, Lévinas leaves us with profoundly Hegelian sentences (which again Derrida saw), only emptied of all dialectical force: "Desire is desire for the absolutely Other [*Autre*]."[25] Alterity, having passed into exteriority, makes common cause with an indeterminate absolute where all cats are black and all cows are grey—as you like it.

---

[22] Sartre, *L'être et le néant*, p. 435; trans., p. 479.

[23] Merleau-Ponty, *La phénoménologie de la perception*, pp. 180–202; trans., pp. 154–173.

[24] Michel Haar, "L'obsession de l'autre: L'éthique comme traumatisme," in *Lévinas* (Paris: Cahier de l'Herne, 1991), ed. Catherine Chalier and Miguel Abensour, p. 451.

[25] Lévinas, *Totalité et infinité*, p. 23; trans., p. 34.

Do these critiques oblige us to restore a discourse of the Hegelian type? For do they not oppose to Lévinas's inspired provocations the rules of conceptual or speculative logic? Not at all. Our irony is intended to reintroduce and maintain a methodological uneasiness and critique before the "all or nothing" Lévinas wants to impose. The incantory force with which he infuses altruism is undeniable, but conceals on its dark side—and in the name of a dogmatic conception of transcendence—a kind of violation of critical consciousness. But as it appears useless or naïve to reproach Lévinas for this violence—he emphatically affirms this "traumatism of transcendence,"[26] my being taken hostage by the face of the Other [*Autre*]—we would like, at least, provisionally to conclude these critical remarks by showing that things still hold together. A phenomenology attentive to experience is within its rights to contest the "defection from phenomenality"[27] that would be forced on it.

PHENOMENOLOGICAL DESCRIPTION OR METAPHYSICAL INCANTATION?

Experience being vast, open to the infinite, the objection is legitimate that Lévinas's œuvre reveals, at least, the limits or borders of phenomenality. Thus Marc Richir, drawing attention to the "infinitization" characteristic of phenomena like recurrence, persecution, substitution, and especially prophecy, suggests that Lévinas's infinite is the "other" shore, beyond phenomenality,[28] of a phenomenology of the symbolic order. Under Lévinas's regard, the far side of experience somehow touches us by its absence (however willed and forced this is). His phenomenology is then above all negative, yet ultimately precious—precious for its sense of passivity irreducible to all apophantic discourse and representation.

We do not contest that it is possible to disengage this interest,

---

[26] Lévinas, *Autrement qu'être ou au-delà de l'essence* (Paris: Kluwer/Le livre de Poche, 1990), p. 10; English trans., *Otherwise Than Being or Beyond Essence* (Dordrecht: Kluwer Academic Publishers, 1991), trans. Alphonso Lingis, p. xliii.

[27] Ibid., p. 141; trans., p. 90.

[28] Marc Richir, "Phénomène et infini," in *Lévinas*, p. 256.

or this range, in Lévinas's œuvre. But we affirm that the most intimate movement of his thought consists in transporting it from phenomenology to metaphysics, in line with the radicality of the "expropriation" of the subject by the Other [*Autre*]. To tell the truth, the metaphysical diktat is so patent that it is not even contestable; but we must underline that its abrupt and directly moral formulation is simplifying (which is not the case with all metaphysics, as is proved by rich sequences in Hegel's *Phenomenology of Spirit*). We read, for example, in *Totality and Infinity*:

> To be for the other [*autrui*]—is to be good. . . . Transcendence as such is "moral conscience." Moral conscience accomplishes metaphysics, if metaphysics consists in transcending. . . . The primary phenomenon of signification coincides with exteriority. Exteriority is significance itself. And only the face is exterior in its morality.[29]

Do these lines have any phenomenological meaning that is not entirely predicated on metaphysical definitions (and choices)? If the assimilation of metaphysics and morals is already contestable, what are we to say (phenomenologically) of an exteriority so pure that it glistens like "the nudity of the principle"?[30] And what kind of appearing [*apparaître*] is to be welcomed, discovered, and described, if the face gives nothing to decipher without hesitation, but only a "first phenomenon" whose significance is immediately guaranteed and indeed coincides with itself, before all givenness of sense?[31]

Phenomenology is thus doubly short-circuited: in its transcendental grasp of intentionality as in the neutrality of its descriptions. On the first point, the preeminence of the Other [*Autre*] (a figure as abstract as it is transcendent) removes all sense from the Husserlian rediscovery of intentionality: any noetic-noematic correlation is immediately transgressed by an "ek-stasis" whose hyperbolic if not obsessional character *Otherwise Than Being* reinforces. In this schema, the subject is posed (or exposed) as the hostage of the Other [*Autre*].[32] Paul Ricœur has shown that the already hyper-

---

[29] Lévinas, *Totalité et infinité*, pp. 292–93; trans., pp. 261–62. Trans. modified: Lingis twice omits "moral."

[30] Ibid., p. 293; trans., p. 262.

[31] Ibid., p. 292; trans., p. 261: "The face signifies by itself; its signification precedes the *Sinngebung*."

[32] Lévinas, *Autrement qu'être*, p. 282; trans., p. 184.

bolic character of these analyses becomes even paroxysmal.[33] And he goes on to find "scandalous" the extreme hypothesis of an emphatic openness to the Other [Autre] as offender—an extreme conception of expiation that, according to Ricœur, terminates in a dead end and profoundly mistakes the complementary, dialectical movement between the Same and the Other [Autre], as well as the dissymetry between the gnoseological dimension of sense and the ethical dimension of the injunction.[34]

These remarks must be completed at a more modestly methodological level—where we find our second short circuit. The exigence of neutrality in phenomenological inquiry does not fizzle out, in Husserl, in an oratorical or rhetorical precaution, but expresses a methodological rule of scientific spirit going well beyond simple scruples of conscience. Be it in the epochē itself, imaginative variations, or all the intellectual work of description and specification, the phenomenologist presupposes nothing other than the minimal methodological rules he or she has fixed. The phenomenologist is neutral, in the sense that he or she is open to the thing itself, without any other teleological prejudice than the ideal of rational and scientific truth. It will be countered that Lévinas precisely wants to break with the neutrality of the objectifying regard, which he assimilates (abusively to our eyes) to ontology. And that is exact. It would fall upon Lévinas, then, to renounce the seizure of phenomenology we have already brought to attention and which is reformulated, in a most contestable manner, at the end of Otherwise Than Being: "Our analyses lay claim to the spirit of the Husserlian philosophy, whose letter has been the call to order for our epoch to a permanent phenomenology, rendered to its rank as the method of all philosophy."[35]

This claim obviously must be taken seriously, but that does not mean we must pass over in silence, or underestimate, the methodological difficulties it raises. Lévinas was clearer and more convincing when he spoke frankly of "overflowing" phenomenology.[36] As

---

[33] Ricœur, Soi-même comme un autre (Paris: Éditions de Seuil, 1990), pp. 387–93; English trans., Oneself as Another (Chicago: University of Chicago Press, 1992), trans. Kathleen Blamey, pp. 335–41.

[34] Ibid., pp. 390 and 393; trans., pp. 338 and 340–41.

[35] Lévinas, Autrement qu'être, p. 280; trans., p. 183.

[36] Lévinas, Totalité et infinité, p. 13; trans., p. 27.

to the spirit of the Husserlian "philosophy," no one is its guardian; the discussion risks, then, losing itself in the imponderable. What is contestable, though, is, on the one hand, Lévinas's appeal to the bizarre and not very rigorous notion of a "permanent phenomenology" together with, on the other hand, his addendum that the evocations of *Otherwise Than Being* remain faithful to "intentional analysis."[37] For it is just this analysis that gets written off, or in any case seriously displaced, by the affirmation of the "anarchy" of a subjectivity that is no longer principally consciousness, but opens a perspective onto the greater glory of the infinite.[38] Admittedly, Lévinas takes his cue from intentionality, just as he does not cease to frequent phenomenology for what purportedly results from it. But if there is still a measure of phenomenology in his project, it is constantly conditioned by his "just war" led against the ontological war.[39] It becomes the defense and illustration of a cause whose incontestable nobility finds its proper titles elsewhere.

We must not confound two orders: philosophical genealogy and methodological legitimacy. From the first point of view, Lévinas's personal bond to the phenomenological tradition is incontestable, if only by the Husserlian anchorage of his first works.[40] Under the second heading, the question remains open. Indeed, our sole goal here has been to call to mind that the stature of an author and the train of his references cannot authorize considering this question closed. Could maintaining our astonishment before this metaphysical flight—refusing to consider this Other [*Autre*], who is singularly worldless, as self-evident—be to persevere, perhaps, as a phenomenologist, and to prepare to pose other questions? If it is true that the impatience to attain the beyond can lead us to mistake the resistance of things and beings, then yes indeed.

---

[37] Lévinas, *Autrement qu'être*, p. 280; trans., p. 183.

[38] See ibid., the beginning of chap. 4 ("Principle and Anarchy"), and chap. 5 ("The Glory of the Infinite").

[39] Ibid., p. 283; trans., p. 185.

[40] See Lévinas, *La théorie de l'intuition dans la phénoménologie de Husserl* (Paris: Vrin, 1930); English trans., *The Theory of Intuition in Husserl's Phenomenology* (2nd ed., Evanston, Ill.: Northwestern University Press, 1995), trans. André Orianne; and *En découvrant l'existence avec Husserl et Heidegger* (Paris: Vrin, 1949).

3

Veerings

In carrying out our inquiries on quite recent works, we still do not abandon the most ancient questions and their constraints. These gather round the fold already immanent in Aristotle's thought, divided between a science of being [être], such as it is given in general, and a science of the Highest Being, the noetic illumination of the divine. The theme of onto-theology has so intimately penetrated reflection on the history of metaphysics that it seems quite legitimate to turn this magic wand back on contemporary writings whose "postmetaphysical" character is often more proclaimed than proved. With Lévinas's thought, we faced a complex puzzle and a paradoxical and strategic blurring of the boundaries between the phenomenological and the theological. I say a strategic blurring, for, by installing the transcendence of the Other [Autre] at the heart of a phenomenology that can no longer quite be considered one, Lévinas expressly divests the philosophical regard of the neutrality of which he ought, in principle, to make it his duty to protect. I say a paradoxical blurring, for the trouble stirred up in the phenomenological field does not at all sit well with mystical drunkenness and does not prevent Lévinas, moreover, from vigorously re-posing the question of the philosophical status of the idea of God. "Questions relative to God are not resolved by answers in which the interrogation ceases to resonate or is wholly pacified. . . . One asks if it is possible to speak legitimately of God without striking a blow against the absoluteness that his word seems to signify."[1] How can we contest the philosophical legitimacy of this question?

Whereas a gunslinging rationalism (today less and less prevalent) would enclose itself in a double refusal—of the opening [ouverture] of philosophy onto the "unapparent," and of the elevation of

---

[1] Lévinas, De Dieu qui vient à l'idée (Paris: Vrin, 1986), p. 8; English trans., Of God Who Comes to Mind (Stanford, Calif.: Stanford University Press, 1998), trans. Bettina Bergo, pp. xi–xii.

thought to the question of God—our critical inquiry means, on the contrary, to make room for all phenomenological and philosophical possibilities. Thanks to a methodological discrimination, we mean to permit each project to retrieve its specificity and to respect the type of rigor specific to it. For example, Wassily Kandinsky magnificently enriched abstract art, and it would be aberrant to challenge his pictorial œuvre in the name of "social realism" or any other theory. Nevertheless, the manifesto entitled *Concerning the Spiritual in Art,* however stimulating it may be, exposes itself to contradiction when it claims to actualize the great spiritual rebirth it announces by means of the paths of theosophy.[2] Every allowance being made, we find ourselves in a comparable situation in philosophy: in this special marketplace, we are not forced to take or leave any œuvre as a whole. We have the right, and even the duty, not only to hem and haw and wrangle, but to finger the stuff of thoughts, to test their solidity, and to expose to the light of interrogation inspirations, concepts, and prospects. And so it will be in the discussions that follow, and principally in regard to Jean-Luc Marion's *Reduction and Givenness,* where our objections will be directed not at the theological as such, but at certain of its translations or intrusions into the phenomenological field.

PHENOMENOLOGY AND METAPHYSICS

Whereas, until Wolff, and still today in neo-Thomism, rational metaphysics played the role of a propaedeutic to theology, its scope was inverted by Heidegger. For him, access to the "God most divine" depends on a disengagement from the metaphysical mode of thinking. In *L'idole et la distance* and *God without Being,*[3] Mar-

---

[2] Wassily Kandinsky, *Du spirituel dans l'art* (Paris: Denoël-Méditations, 1969), trans. P. Volboudt, pp. 59–60; English trans., *Concerning the Spiritual in Art* (New York: Dover Publications, 1977), trans. M. T. H. Sadler, pp. 53–55. Cf. Michel Henry, *Voir l'invisible. Sur Kandinsky* (Paris: François Bourin, 1988). For Henry, the abstraction of "inner necessity" that Kandinsky liberates has nothing to do with geometrical abstraction. We will return to this thesis and to the phenomenological interest of Henry's book in chapter 5.

[3] Marion, *L'idole et la distance* (Paris: Grasset, 1977), and *Dieu sans l'être* (1982; Paris: Presses Universitaires de France, 1991); English trans., *God without Being* (Chicago: University of Chicago Press, 1991), trans. Thomas A. Carlson.

ion, for his own part, took this Heideggerian reversal in the direction of a nonontological, nonrepresentative theology of Christly love. *Reduction and Givenness* is infinitely more discreet in this regard, and for this discretion we can only praise its author: this work is presented as an ensemble of phenomenological investigations. This presentation does not, though, rid it of all difficulties. What is questionable, from the methodological point of view, is the status of phenomenology—and of the phenomenological—between a metaphysics that has been "overcome" (or challenged) and a theology that has been made possible (at once prepared and held in reserve).

Not only has Marion lucidly perceived this problem, but he has resolved it in his own manner, putting in place in 1984 (in the "Foreword" to the collection *Phénoménologie et métaphysique*) a framework by means of which phenomenology becomes the privileged inheritor of philosophy at the era of metaphysics' completion.[4] He writes: "Clearly, since metaphysics found its end, whether in fulfillment with Hegel, or in twilight with Nietzsche, philosophy has been able to pursue itself authentically only under the figure of phenomenology."[5] This thesis is reaffirmed and even emphasized when Marion suggests that we have thus swung "toward a thought [that is] perhaps already postmetaphysical."[6]

These affirmations call for, at first, a kind of head-on examination. What is their validity; are they acceptable in themselves? If they are not self-evident, but instead dubious, we must ask why the thesis of the "metaphysical extraterritoriality of phenomenology" has been pushed so far and what it permits or authorizes.[7]

Chiefly contestable is the "evidence" concerning the end of metaphysics and the historicist form given to this Heideggerian thesis (that we have entered into the "postmetaphysical" era). Admittedly Marion nuances this thesis with a "perhaps" and concedes its "unilateral violence," its dogmatic massiveness. It remains the case, nonetheless, that this schema is adopted as quasi-evident. Here we encounter a twofold series of difficulties. On

---

[4] *Phénoménologie et métaphysique* (Paris: Presses Universitaires de France, 1984), ed. Jean-Luc Marion and Guy Planty-Bonjour.

[5] Ibid., p. 7.

[6] Marion, *Réduction et donation*, p. 7; trans., p. 1.

[7] *Phénoménologie et métaphysique*, p. 7.

the one hand, must the Heideggerian thesis of the accomplishment of metaphysics be so completely accepted? And on the other hand, and more importantly, is it a question here of a *historiale* thesis—not only a historical one? The response to the second point will permit us to clarify our first objection. If Heidegger never employs the expression "postmetaphysical," this is because its use would lead us to believe that the exit out of metaphysics has already been reached. In truth, he thinks the contrary: planetary technique brings metaphysics to its "unconditional rule."[8] "Experienced in the dawn of its beginning, metaphysics is, however, at the same time past [*vergangen*], in the sense that it has entered into its ending [*in ihre Ver-endung eingegangen ist*]. The ending *lasts* longer than the heretofore history of metaphysics."[9] We do indeed, then, have to do with a *historiale* thesis in whose name we cannot at all justify presenting a philosophical current as escaping the *Ver-endung* of metaphysics.

Given as much, the attitude to adopt before the first question must not be unilateral, insofar as Heidegger's thinking on the "overcoming" of metaphysics is, paradoxically, both complex and simplifying. Complex, because it requires us to make a double connection between the *Vollendung* and the *Verwindung*—to comprehend, and even to make our own, the contemporaneity of the accomplishment of metaphysics and the withdrawal this means for it. Simplifying, however, to the extent that this thesis unifies under the same term 'metaphysics' *metaphysica generalis* (as condition of the articulation of the senses of being [*sens de l'étant*]) and *metaphysica specialis* (as principled foundation of being [*l'étant*]) to respond to one and the same injunction, both epochal and destinal. The onto-theological structure accedes to a credit so large and so enveloping that it suffocates or minimizes all exceptions or marginalities. So attests the case of Nietzsche, concerning whom contemporary research doubts more and more (and with justification) that he "led to its end and accomplished all the possibilities—even inverted—of metaphysics" (to cite, once more, a formulation of Jean-Luc Marion).[10]

---

[8] Martin Heidegger, *Vorträge und Aufsätze* (Pfullingen: Neske, 1954), p. 63; English trans., *The End of Philosophy* (New York: Harper & Row, 1973), trans. Joan Stambaugh, p. 85.

[9] Ibid. (trans. modified).

[10] Marion, *Réduction et donation*, p. 7; trans., p. 1 (trans. modified).

It is evident that this discussion, bearing on the purported end of metaphysics and directed at the Heideggerian thesis as well as the formulation Marion gives it, puts into play important stakes implicating phenomenology. For putting metaphysics into perspective by means of a historical schema (or, more grandly, a *historial* one) implies a complementary ordering of phenomenology. According to Marion, phenomenology would be, since Hegel, the place of an essentially antimetaphysical breakthrough: "Phenomenology does not introduce metaphysics, it exits from it [*elle en sort*]."[11]

The argumentation in regard to Hegel merits examination. It authorizes itself to deduce, from the renewed debate among interpreters on the relationship of the *Phenomenology of Spirit* to the ensemble of Hegel's System, a "conflict with the knowledge of metaphysics."[12] But this argumentation rests on an altogether illegitimate elision (in any case, one not justified in Marion's text) between System and metaphysics. No one will contest that there is a divide, if not a distortion, between the masterpiece of 1807 and section III, I B, of the *Encyclopedia*. But it does not follow that there is a question here of a "conflict" between phenomenology and *metaphysics*. Even if the *Phenomenology* is detached from the System—whether from the anthropological point of view, as by Alexandre Kojève; in a Marxist sense, as by Herbert Marcuse; or in an existential sense, as by Jean Hyppolite—the Heideggerian question of the metaphysical status of Hegelianism nevertheless arises. There is nothing more metaphysical than the final chapter of the *Phenomenology* on *Geist*, and it is the same for the initial chapter on "Sense Certainty" as for the conceptual armature of the whole work. Heidegger himself, in the remarkable commentary he devoted to the introduction, interpreted the "science of the experience of consciousness" as an inspired tissue of ambiguity, within metaphysics (that is to say, the parousia of the absolute), between the present and presence. He affirms this quite clearly: "At the time of the first publication of the *Phenomenology of Spirit*, science is for Hegel the onto-theological knowledge of what truly

---

[11] *Phénoménologie et métaphysique*, pp. 10–11.
[12] Ibid., p. 10.

is insofar as it is [*wahrhaft Seienden als Seinden*]."[13] The tension between the *Phenomenology* and the *Logic* is in no way interpreted by Heidegger in terms of a decisive break with metaphysics (in the first work), but in terms of a change in emphasis (from ontology to speculative theology) within onto-theology, that is to say, metaphysics. It is then illegitimate, even from the Heideggerian point of view, to hold that "the first entry of phenomenology in metaphysics came to its end, with Hegel, in [phenomenology's] being put aside."[14]

Must we go so far as to claim that phenomenology separates Hegel from metaphysics? With Husserl, the undertaking becomes more delicate yet. For how can we find support for the thesis of a conflict between phenomenology and metaphysics in an itinerary that, despite the breakthrough of the *Logical Investigations*, restores—by the admission of Marion himself—all the exigencies and structures of transcendental idealism? It is evident that, if Husserl brackets *metaphysica specialis* and initially dismisses ontology, he does not do the same in regard to *metaphysica generalis*. As eidetic, the reduction is an eminently Platonic act; as transcendental, it encounters the problem of foundation across that of autoconstitution (which Marion very justly notes).[15] These clear facts ought to lead to a revision of Marion's thus imperiled thesis. The example of Husserl shows quite clearly that a metaphysical phenomenology is possible; ought we to add, more categorically perhaps, that phenomenology, radically implemented and methodically conducted, can only be metaphysical (in the sense of *metaphysica generalis*)? Marion prefers to take a step back, to a position that does not altogether mask his discomfiture: "The strangeness, as troubling as fascinating, of the Husserlian institution inheres in its radical impuissance to take a position regarding the essence of metaphysics."[16] But is Husserl only interesting on ac-

---

[13] Heidegger, *Holzwege* (Frankfurt am Main: Vittorio Klostermann, 1967), pp. 183–84; English trans., *Hegel's Concept of Experience* (New York: Harper & Row, 1970), trans. anonymous, p. 142. Heidegger adds: "This truth is the essence of metaphysics [*Diese Wahreheit ist das Wesen der Metaphysik*]" (trans., p. 143; trans. modified).

[14] *Phénoménologie et métaphysique*, p. 11.

[15] Ibid., p. 12.

[16] Ibid.

count of his "impuissance"? This negative appraisal—paradoxical, if not disingenuous—of the Husserlian institution is only explicable, in fact, by the double presupposition that it is Heidegger who radicalizes and deepens the Husserlian reduction and that he does so by opening phenomenology to the ontological question and confronting it with the essence of metaphysics. But this retrospective unification, if it is not qualified by precautions, sets down a grid of interpretation that only prepares the way for further schematizations. Concerning the relation to metaphysics, if it is evident that Husserl does not explore its essence, it follows neither that we must neglect his refusal of *metaphysica specialis*, nor overlook or scorn the positive sense he intended to give to *metaphysica generalis* in reinstituting transcendental idealism. If the relation between phenomenology and metaphysics is more open and complex than Marion's presentation of the problem would have us believe, by the same stroke the linearity he projects onto the Heideggerian "radicalization" of the reduction must be called into question.

THE SCHEMATISM OF THE THREE REDUCTIONS

We have called into doubt the "postmetaphysical" character of phenomenology as Marion tries to unify it. But we must go further in dismantling a framework within which the "schematism of the three reductions" permits us to imagine a relation of inverse proportionality between reduction and givenness. The purpose of this framework is to establish an appearance of formal continuity between the best known nucleus of the phenomenological method and "the pure form of the call"[17]—a most elliptical operation that does not fear to disconcert us by announcing other "new and rigorous paradoxes,"[18] but whose brio cannot spare the author of having to warrant our belief. Let us review in order, then, the demands he makes of us. Let us examine the methodological solidity of the triad of reductions, their supposed relations with givenness, and, finally, the astonishing promotion of a pure givenness.

---

[17] Marion, *Réduction et donation*, p. 305; trans., p. 205.
[18] Ibid.

The schema of the three reductions is summarized at the end of *Reduction and Givenness*, but obviously we must refer to developments within the body of the text to appreciate its ramifications.[19] According to Marion, the first reduction is transcendental, the second existential, and the third pure, almost unqualifiable. These correspond quite simply to three signatures: Husserl, Heidegger, Marion. But is the situation so clear? Let us take a closer look.

Let us also immediately correct what was just suggested: for Marion, the transcendental reduction is not uniquely Husserlian, but "Cartesian" or even "Kantian" as well. "It matters little here," the author bizarrely specifies. On the contrary, it matters a lot, even ultimately, for the question is whether it is possible to amalgamate, for the needs of the cause, such different undertakings. The scare quotes, however, mean to make us set aside any historical suspicions, and so be it. But what is the relation between the "Cartesian" reduction and that of Descartes, and so on? The recapitulative movement of "phenomenological" truth, we are to believe, enables us to circumscribe the enterprise of reduction in four (hastily enumerated) strokes: constitution of objects [1] for a constituting I [2], the transcendental reduction opens onto only regional ontologies [3] and excludes all that exceeds the horizon of objectivity [4].[20]

But this unified presentation of the transcendental reduction fails to recognize the difference, introduced by Husserl in the *Ideas*,[21] between regional reductions and the *epochē* as such. The *epoché* is no longer simply directed at objects related to psychological events, but at pure lived experiences [*vécus*] in their intentional correlations.[22] While claiming Cartesian inspiration, Husserl shows in §10 of his *Cartesian Meditations* in what sense Descartes missed the transcendental orientation: he made the *ego*

---

[19] Ibid., pp. 304 and 97–103, 289–96; trans., pp. 204 and 62–66, 192–98.

[20] Ibid., p. 304; trans., p. 204.

[21] Husserl, *Ideen zu einer reinen Phänomenologie und phänomenologischen Philosophie: Erstes Buch*, Husserliana Band 3 (The Hague: Martinus Nijhoff, 1950), ed. Walter Biemel, §33, pp. 73–74; English trans., *Ideas Pertaining to a Pure Phenomenology and to a Phenomenological Philosophy: First Book* (The Hague: Martinus Nijhoff, 1983), trans. F. Kersten, pp. 65–66.

[22] Ibid., §36, p. 80; trans., p. 73.

a separate "*substantia cogitans.*"[23] This point is not a secondary one, for, if it is not appreciated, the very sense of the *epoché* and the radical novelty of intentionality will be misunderstood. In "the free and unlimited field of consciousness," it is the "world-phenomenon" itself that is disengaged, and not simply "objects" for a "constitutive I." The reference to Kant (to the "paralogisms of pure reason"[24]) in Marion's text equally obliges us to correct this idea. According to the "paralogisms of pure reason," the *I think* as liaison of representations is not substantially constitutive of objects, but is only the foyer—problematic and formal—of the transcendental correlation. Kant writes: "Through this I, or he, or it (the thing) which thinks, nothing further is represented than a transcendental subject of the thoughts = *x*, which is known only by the thoughts that are its predicates, and of which, apart from these, we could never have the least concept."[25] No more in Kant than in Husserl, the transcendental horizon cannot be diminished to an egology constituting objects. We must instead maintain the profundity of this field and the precautions (including those concerning the transcendental scope, or not, of the Cartesian *cogito*) that *Reduction and Givenness* seems to lack, and not only in its final pages. Throughout the book, the phenomenon in the Husserlian sense is systematically presented as "flat,"[26] which implies that the quest for integral and objective presence annuls the opening [*ouverture*] of the *epoché* onto the correlation with the world as such. More royalist than the king, Marion systematizes the Heideggerian critique of the Husserlian reduction (which Heidegger formulated, in particular, in the *Basic Problems of Phenomenology*[27]) to such a point that it becomes impossible to

---

[23] Husserl, *Cartesianische Meditationen und Pariser Vorträge*, Husserliana Band 7 (The Hague: Martinus Nijhoff, 1950), ed. S. Strasser, §10, p. 63; English trans., *Cartesian Meditations* (The Hague: Martinus Nijohoff, 1960), trans. Dorion Cairns, p. 24.

[24] Immanuel Kant, *Kritik der reinen Vernunft*, A-341/B-399ff.; English trans., *Critique of Pure Reason* (New York: St. Martin's, 1929), trans. Norman Kemp Smith, pp. 328ff.

[25] Ibid., A-346/B-405; trans. p. 331 (trans. modified).

[26] Marion, *Réduction et donation*, p. 90; trans., p. 56.

[27] Heidegger, *Die Grundprobleme der Phänomenologie*, Gesamtausgabe Band 24 (Frankfurt am Main: Vittorio Klostermann, 1975), ed. Friedrich-Wilhelm von Hermann, p. 29; English trans., *The Basic Problems of Phenomenology* (Bloomington, Ind.,: Indiana University Press, 1982), trans. Alfred Hofstadter, p. 21.

discern either the interest or the originality of Husserl. Let us turn, then, to the second reduction in order to discover the "true" meaning of phenomenology.

Basing himself, essentially, on the *History of the Concept of Time* and the *Basic Problems* (courses Heidegger gave in 1925 and 1927, respectively), Marion presents the Heideggerian ontology as a radicalization and revival of Husserlian phenomenology. And during the years of his elaboration of *Being and Time*, this was indeed how Heidegger opposed himself to Husserl. "*For us*," Heidegger writes in the *Basic Problems*, "the phenomenological reduction means leading the phenomenological regard back from the apprehension of the entity [*Erfassung des Seienden*]—whatever the character of this apprehension—to the understanding of the being [*Verstehen des Seins*] of this entity [*dieses Seienden*]."[28] To this extent, it is justifiable to interpret the Heideggerian "reduction" as a "redoubled reduction." As Marion writes: "The privilege of *Dasein* comes to it only from its disposition to undergo a redoubled phenomenological reduction. This [reduction] makes the transition from the entity [*l'étant*] to the 'sense of being' ['*sens d'être*'] only by working through *that* entity [*cet étant*] that being [*l'être de l'étant*] determines par excellence."[29] Being [*être*] is no longer understood as immanent to intentional consciousness, but inversely as the horizon of phenomenality, that is, in terms of the uncovering of the entity [*l'étant*]. Phenomenality will thus be interrogated, in a privileged manner, on the basis of the ontico-ontological articulations offered by *Dasein*, whose sense of being [*sens d'être*] no eidetic ever exhausts.

Only, to whatever extent it is true that Heidegger questions "the very appearing [*l'apparaître*] of the phenomenon,"[30] must we agree that his ontological soundings operate exclusively by the reduction and toward "reviving" phenomenology? This is what Marion would have us believe in his study "The Entity and the Phenomenon [*L'étant et le phénomène*],"[31] and by design: we discover the rationale of the schema of the three reductions, within which Heidegger's "way" is stylized in a manner so elliptical that

---

[28] Ibid. (trans. modified).
[29] Marion, *Réduction et donation*, p. 110; trans., p. 70 (trans. modified).
[30] Ibid., p. 99; trans., p. 63.
[31] Ibid., pp. 65–118; trans., 40–76.

it becomes unrecognizable. In effect, why pass over in silence, first, the fact that "fundamental ontology," as it is deployed in *Being and Time*, is already presented no longer as reduction, but as an analytic of *Dasein*; and, second, that Heidegger will later completely abandon all terminology of Husserlian origin? And why neglect this even more significant detail: Heidegger's relativization, starting with the *Basic Problems*, of the reduction itself? "The phenomenological reduction, as the leading-back of the regard from the entity to being [*vom Seienden zum Sein*]," Heidegger writes in that book, "is not, however, the unique *nor even central* fundamental part [*Grundstück*] of the phenomenological method."[32] He adds that the question of being [*être*] stands in need not only of the reduction, but of the destruction and reconstruction of the fundamental concepts of philosophy. Even reinterpreted in the ontological sense, the reduction is, for Heidegger, only a "part" or a phase of an ampler procedure that will require both a more and more thoroughgoing destruction of the history of metaphysics and its rereading in function of the ontological difference.

Following the internal logic of Heidegger's path from the *History of the Concept of Time* to *What Is Metaphysics?*, we find no evidence for the extension of the problematic of the reduction toward an existential or ontological reduction that would stand as an autonomous, philosophical finality. Still less do we discern, in the latter lecture, a "phenomenological framework" that would allow us to recognize in it "a sort of phenomenological reduction."[33] On the contrary, Heidegger immediately delimits the field of phenomenological reductions, transcendental and eidetic, within the horizon of intentionality.[34] Further, circumscribing this horizon in a critical manner on account of its idealist and Cartesian character, he more and more distances himself from what it implies. He retains from the reduction only its *ontological differenti-*

---

[32] Heidegger, *Die Grundprobleme der Phänomenologie*, p. 29; trans., p. 21 (italics added by Janicaud; trans. modified).

[33] Marion, *Réduction et donation*, p. 111; trans., p. 71.

[34] Heidegger, *Prolegomena zur Geschichte des Zeitbegriffs*, Gesamtausgabe Band 20 (Frankfurt am Main, Vittorio Klostermann, 1979), ed. Petra Jaeger, p. 137; English trans., *History of the Concept of Time: Prolegomena* (Bloomington, Ind.: Indiana University Press, 1982), trans. Theodore Kisiel, p. 100.

ation, whose proper accentuation will oblige him to pose the question of metaphysics still more radically. But at the epoch of fundamental ontology, Heidegger has recourse to the reduction only under implicit or explicit scare quotes—a recourse occasioned by his difficulty in settling upon a method proper to the mode of thought still trying to find itself across the existential analytic. The problem becomes more complicated yet if we consider that, as Jean-François Courtine has seen, the "ontological reduction" still remains burdened with transcendentalism.[35]

Over and against the claim that "Heidegger remains, therefore, a phenomenologist, since he resumes [*reprend*] the reduction,"[36] it is rather the inverse that is true: he directs himself toward the true sense of phenomenality, the "*ek-static*" horizon of time, only to the extent that the elaboration of the question of being [*être*] is substituted for the reductions. (Heidegger does not, then, focus on the phenomenon of being [*être*] "in itself" ["*en personne*"], as Marion writes, but on its mode of uncovering.[37])

The reader will perhaps excuse this detailed reappraisal when reminded that it allows us to understand the purpose (but also the fragility) of the framework by which Marion makes his way to the third reduction. In the end, this game is not hidden. We read, regarding this tertium quid, "[O]ur whole enterprise has tended toward nothing other than to render the recognition of it inevitable."[38] But it is obvious that this recognition cannot take place, nor certainly appear inevitable, if the path that was supposed to lead to it proves to have been too artificially flattened.

If it is difficult to linger for long with this pseudoreduction, of which we learn only what it is *not* (we shall return to this thinness), the strategy of the seizure of phenomenology must nevertheless see its assurance confronted by what it masks and risks.

---

[35] Jean-François Courtine, "L'idée de la phénoménologie et la problématique de la réduction," in *Phénoménologie et métaphysique*, p. 226.

[36] Marion, *Réduction et donation*, p. 102; trans., p. 65. *Translator's note*: Carlson translates "reprend" as "resumes," and I have followed him, though it might be argued that this translation misses the nuance and that "retakes" might be better—if it were not so awkward. As Marion sees it, Heidegger not only takes up the reduction, but both takes it back from Husserl and "retakes" it in the sense that a film director retakes a cut.

[37] Ibid., p. 117; trans., p. 75.

[38] Ibid., p. 305; trans., p. 204.

"[T]he transgression of the claim of being [*être*] by the pure form of the call," Marion writes, "belongs to the phenomenological field for exactly the same reason that would allow the analytic of *Dasein* to replace the constitution of the transcendental *I*."[39] We have here an admission of the mimetic methodology by which Marion wants to pass off the *salto mortale* toward the "pure call" as proceeding from the same rigor as Heidegger's deepening of the Husserlian reduction. But this trick has already been pulled off by Lévinas (whom it is not surprising to see cited on page 197 of *Reduction and Givenness* [page 295 of *Réduction et donation*]), as it will be again by more than one comrade: repeating, in displacing to advantage, the Heideggerian "overcoming" of idealist intentionality (or metaphysics, or ontology). Only here Marion raises the bar still higher in claiming that his transgression is rigorous and scrupulous, arising "eminently from phenomenology."[40] But what remains phenomenological in a reduction that, "properly speaking, *is* not,"[41] and refers back to "a point of reference [that is] all the more original and unconditioned as it is more restricted"?[42] Many pains have been taken, in purportedly methodological arguments, to lead us to this absolute and above all to make us believe in its phenomenological character. We must turn now to this pure givenness so as to specify how it is incompatible—for as much as it is utterable—with the astute detours by which Marion wants, at any price, to render phenomenological what cannot be.

What Givenness, What Call, and What Promise?

We have already seen that the more doubtful the phenomenological character of the procedure, the more emphatically this character has been affirmed. The passage from the second to the third reduction was as if hooked onto the model of the passage from the first to the second. But the trajectory of this first passage, given as a model for the second, seemed to us much too complex

---

[39] Ibid., p. 296; trans., p. 197 (trans. modified).
[40] Ibid., p. 297; trans., p. 198 (trans. modified).
[41] Ibid., p. 305; trans., p. 204.
[42] Ibid., p. 303; trans., p. 203 (trans. modified).

to be formalized as Marion did, thus imperiling the whole operation. What do we end up with? With a call, given as the "originary schema," whose pure form "plays before all specification,
even of being [*être*]."[43]

From here onward, whether it is a question of the reduction,
givenness, or the call, we find ourselves confronted by a *coinci-
dentia oppositorum* in the truly classical sense, on the theological,
mystical way. The more phenomenality becomes attenuated, to
the point of annihilating itself, the more the absolute inflates and
amplifies itself, to the point of apotheosis. We have to do, here,
with a rather dry mystical night; the superabundance of grace has
been put through the Heideggerian ringer. But the qualifying
terms, in any case, are neither human nor finite: pure, absolute,
unconditioned—such is this call. It addresses itself, it is true, to a
reader, an interlocutor [*interloqué*], however ideal. But voilà! the
interlocutor is in his or her turn reduced to his or her pure form,
to the interlocuted "as such."[44] Is not this experience, slimmed
down to its a priori sheathe, too pure to dare to pass itself off as
phenomenological? And will not the reader who is thus "interlocuted" be tempted to cede to the facilities of irony before sentences like these: "Literally, surprise prohibits the interlocuted
from comprehending the convocation that it nevertheless receives"?[45] Or again, "The imprecision, the indecision, indeed the
confusion of the claiming instance attests much rather that, at the
origin, is found the pure form of the call as such"?[46]

We want to believe that it is by design, and not without a
certain complaisance, that farewell is thus bid not only to common sense, but to the stuff of phenomena. In fact, the only tie
that binds these citations to whatever kind of experience is religious. When we read, "Listen, Israel, Jahweh our God, Jahweh
alone,"[47] we no longer doubt the nature of the call, nor that of
the promised givenness; as for the response, it depends on each of
us. But who introduces "imprecision, indecision, nay confusion,"
if not the philosopher who means to transform references of an-

---

[43] Ibid., p. 297; trans., p. 198.
[44] Ibid., p. 302; trans., p. 202.
[45] Ibid., p. 301; trans., p. 201.
[46] Ibid., p. 302; trans., p. 202 (trans. modified).
[47] Ibid., p. 295 (citation of Deuteronomy 6.4); trans., p. 197.

other order, as Pascal would have put it, into an a priori instance and general schemes?

Now Marion invokes none other than the leitmotif of Pascal to respond to the excellent question posed by the editors of the *Revue de métaphysique et de morale* concerning the very "problematic" character of the third reduction and the "equivocality of the very term givenness [*donation*]."[48] As much as his response is justified in relating the problematic of his *On Descartes' Metaphysical Prism* to the Pascalian destitution of the "vanity" of philosophy,[49] it becomes just as much acrobatic in claiming that *Reduction and Givenness*'s terminal point "beyond being [*hors d'être*]"— conceded "empty"—does not base itself on "external givens [*données*] admitted by hypothesis." The reasoning is strange: Marion admits that, since it is a question here of phenomenology (a point to which he clings), we need an immediate intuition. But he concedes that this intuition is absent: "Therefore *Reduction and Givenness* limits itself to a kind of negative phenomenology, following after the negative theology deployed by *God without Being*. Only derivative phenomena appear—the interlocuted, ennui, and others—and indices or effects of phenomena still indescribable as such—the call, nonindifferent assignation, and others."[50] We had to cite this sentence to its end; it makes a capital concession (the phenomenological element in *Reduction and Givenness* is "derivative," in any case when we come to the threshold of the third reduction), but immediately takes it back in a somewhat specious form. This consists, on the one hand, in playing on the notion of "negative phenomenology"—which calls for examination, as it is not evident that it coincides with the most founded phenomenology—and, on the other hand, in introducing the idea that there would be "phenomena not yet manifest"[51]—a strangely surreptitious displacement toward a kind of progressivism in phenomenality. If the "pure form of the call" appears empty in 1991, it

---

[48] *Revue de métaphysique et de morale* 1 (1991): 65.

[49] Trans. See Marion, *Sur le prisme métaphysique de Descartes* (Paris: Presses Universitaires de France, 1986), pp. 293–369; English trans., *On Descartes' Metaphysical Prism* (Chicago: University of Chicago Press, 1999), trans. Jeffrey L. Koskey, pp. 277–345.

[50] *Revue de métaphysique et de morale*, p. 68.

[51] Ibid.

seems that the happy, humming days to come of a phenomenology more and more negative will draw out the contours of, alas, a "more difficult" work.

In Marion's work, there is no respect for the phenomenological order; it is manipulated as an ever-elastic apparatus, even when it is claimed to be "strict." In the same way, his response concerning "givenness" [*donation*] makes use of the term's very ambiguity to avoid truly responding to the question posed, which did not contest the recourse to the notion of givenness, but the precise use (or misuse) the ultimate stage of *Reduction and Givenness* makes of it. Marion makes the argument, among others, that Merleau-Ponty gave a conceptual treatment of givenness, in spite of (or because of) its ambiguity: if we look at page 360 of the *Phenomenology of Perception* [page 413 of *Phénoménologie de la perception*] (which Marion cites), we will note that the givenness in question is that of a reflection "open on the unreflected [*irréfléchi*]." This is, par excellence, *situated* givenness, since it is that which unveils the tie between my subjectivity and the world. "My freedom, the fundamental power that I have to be the subject of all my experiences, is not distinct from my insertion in the world," Merleau-Ponty writes. Here the question is one of a totally phenomenal givenness, which is precisely not the case with the third, "Marionesque" givenness. The question then stands, and it does not suffice to displace it toward a hypothetical future, whether to exploit the ambiguity of the notion of givenness, or to use the "phenomenology of the unapparent" as a kind of talisman or alibi.

In fact, Marion's end point is clear, and its phenomenological emptiness can be explained only by a double reference, which the acute reader of his texts recognizes: to the problematic of the overcoming of ontology (or metaphysics), and to the properly theological or spiritual dimension. It is the running together of these two schemas under the cover of phenomenology that is contested here. Not only does this strategy afford itself no few rhetorical facilities, but it leads us back to an autosufficiency (pure givenness "gives *itself*"!) that restores *metaphysica specialis*—and its favorite trick, autofoundation—rather than giving it the boot.

If the paradoxes of *Reduction and Givenness* were restricted to questioning the notion of givenness and interrogating its phenomenological sense (such is the posture Marion adopts at the end of his first response to the *Revue de métaphysique et de morale*), we would have no objection.[52] But we must not let the "radicality" of Marion's interrogation prejudice us as to the radicality (real or pretended) of his furnished response. By now it is evident that *Réduction and Givenness* does not at all limit itself to interrogation: this book, by Marion's own admission, is destined "to lay the foundation platform available for a higher edifice."[53] The metaphor is revelatory, and we will see a comparable veering, both metaphoric and methodological, in the work of Jean-Louis Chrétien, *La voix nue. Phénoménologie de la promesse* [*The Naked Voice: Phenomenology of the Promise*].

This book is remarkable for many of its traits: the quality of its writing, the richness of its references, the fineness of its analyses. The criticisms that follow must not, then, be misunderstood: they are uniquely methodological and will concentrate, too briefly, on the sense of the book's subtitle, "phenomenology of the promise." Our challenge bears less on the intentions Chrétien acknowledges in his introduction than on their realization. His project wishes to be phenomenological: on the nakedness of the voice and of the body as well as on the lie, equivocality, admission, and testimony. His question is altogether legitimate: "Is it phenomenologically possible to think a body without secret and without reserve, whose glory would be full manifestation and perfect visibility?"[54] Likewise legitimate is his question about whether the study of the "oblique character of manifestation" is not preeminently phenomenological. The answer here is that it doubtless is—on condition one respects minimal rules that cleave to the spirit of phenomenology. Proclaimed on the first page of the introduction, the "critique of philosophies of presence" will be, we are led to believe, a leitmotif in this regard. We anticipate, then, that the intertwining of analyses and phenomenological descriptions will show up the metaphysical closure on the illusion of thoroughgoing transparence (as the title of the first part, "Critique of Transparence," indicates).

---

[52] Ibid., p. 69.
[53] Ibid., p. 67.
[54] Chrétien, *La voix nue*, p. 8.

Now, on the first page consecrated to "the glory of the body," and after several beautiful lines consecrated to the body offered to vision, the extended sleeper or twirling dancer, we read: "In rendering itself visible, the body does not render itself alone visible, but lets come into the light of the world the invisible soul that, in vivifying [the body], is its perpetual origin, without which it would show nothing."[55] In the following, recourse to this concept of soul is constantly made, as if it were self-evident; how it escapes from metaphysics—given that it is "perpetual origin" indispensable to corporal manifestation—is also not explained. Admittedly, the text criticizes the idea of a complete manifestation of the soul across the body, a criticism phenomenology upholds. But this critique of the glorious body operates to the advantage of a more secretive metaphysics where the soul wraps itself up in the "body's nights." From here flow the suggestive evocations of a body "haunting the distances," once more making sign toward glory, but a glory that is the "very assumption" of the secret and not a complete manifestation. From here also flows the conclusion on eternal life as "act of praise," and the firm hope that the secret of the body will be "finally given in glory, without our being able to retake it."

Let us be clear: it is not at all a question here of contesting the interest, for a Christian thinker, of rethinking corporeality, including in the perspective of the resurrection promised by the Scriptures. But we must observe, as a matter of fact, that in the text in question the recourse to phenomenology is constantly biased by both a "call" that is purportedly original and a reference, imposed on the reader, to religious experience. It is a question here, we might put it, of a Christian phenomenology [*phénoménologie chrétienne*], but whose properly phenomenological sense must fall away, for a nonbeliever, midway through the journey (assuming, even, that he or she accepts the reference, properly metaphysical, to the notion of soul).

This same kind of utilization of phenomenology recurs throughout the rest of this work, so rich in philosophical, theological, and patristic references. Chrétien apprehends and thinks the Christian sense of the Incarnation against (and on the basis of)

---

[55] Ibid., p. 13.

successive and insistent figures of the metaphysics of transparence: the nakedness of essence, the angelic horizon, the obliquity of the divine, freedom as transparent causality, the experience of paradise, the generosity of the One, God's purely speculative intelligence, the translucence of excessively intellectual love. He thus succeeds in writing up, often with touching grace, a spiritual experience whose corporal envelope gestures toward both the word's invisible ties and the exaltation of a promise in excess to itself. "The naked soul is the naked hand, the naked voice, the naked shadow of the promise that always already surrounds us."[56] A challenge to the metaphysics of transparence, this thought of the pure promise gives itself off as "phenomenology" only to reintroduce, subtly but with an altogether strategic constancy, a metaphysics of the secret divine and the transcendent call.

Our questions on the sense of givenness, the call, and the promise were, then, quite naïve: the "phenomenologies" of Marion and Chrétien, however different in their twists, turns, and qualities, are woven with the same immaculate thread. The theological veering is too obvious. And it does not suffice, in order to minimize it, to claim as a pretext that it "is obviously not a question here of invoking revealed authority in order to broaden phenomenology's field."[57] That has been, in a sense, clearer yet. In fact, and despite all the denials, phenomenological neutrality has been abandoned, just as the reasons that explicitly led Husserl to put the transcendence of God "out of circuit" have been put aside (or neglected). "Upon this 'absolute' and 'transcendent,'" Husserl writes, "we naturally extend the phenomenological reduction. It [the transcendence of God] must remain excluded from the new field of study we have to create, insofar as this field must be a field of pure consciousness."[58] This Husserlian methodological precaution applied itself not only to the explicit reference to God in the method's practice, but to reasons drawn from "religious consciousness,"[59] among whose number it is not,

---

[56] Ibid., p. 60.

[57] Marion, *Réduction et donation*, p. 295; trans., p. 197 (trans. modified).

[58] Husserl, *Ideen zu einer reinen Phänomenologie*, §58, p. 140; trans., p. 134 (trans. modified).

[59] Ibid., p. 139; trans., p. 134.

without doubt, illegitimate to count "the call" or "the promise" as figures of Transcendence.

A second characteristic of the theological veering is that it leads to analyses that verge on edification—if they do not succumb to it with delectation. Whether it is a question of a call always ready to claim a listening interlocuted, or of a promise that precedes itself and holds in reserve the unhoped-for, phenomenality knows the negative or the absurd only under the passable form of ennui or the lyrical evocation of a fear ready to be reassured. Would not a phenomenology whose dice have not been fixed have more attention for the atrocious, despairing, unqualifiable, or even only undecidable—where our condition is also woven? Does not E. M. Cioran reveal himself, then, to be at least as phenomenological as our authors, in many of his ruthless descriptions of our human condition? We borrow from him this conclusion: "For the unbeliever, infatuated with waste and dispersion, there is no spectacle more disturbing than these ruminants on the absolute. . . . Where do they find such pertinacity in the unverifiable, so much attention in the vague, and so much ardor to seize it?"[60]

---

[60] E. M. Cioran, *Précis de décomposition* (Paris: Gallimard, 1949), p. 196; English trans., *A Short History of Decay* (New York: Viking Press, 1975), trans. Richard Howard, p. 139 (trans. modified).

4

The Surprises of Immanence

THOUGH LÉVINAS DENIED building a properly theological discourse, he set the tone for the movement of thought whose methodological liberties we have followed and criticized. Phenomenology is used as a springboard in a quest for divine transcendence. If the intelligibility of this transcendence is not ontological, it still exploits the resources of the *logos* to destroy the *logos*. This is the strategy Lévinas exposes very clearly at the conclusion of "God and Philosophy":

> Transcendence owes it to itself to interrupt its own demonstration and monstration, its phenomenality. It requires the blinking and dia-chrony of enigma, which is not simply precarious certitude, but breaks up the unity of transcendental apperception, wherein immanence always triumphs over transcendence.[1]

Is it the same in Michel Henry? Going by the letter, the situation is just the opposite. "Immanence has been defined by reference to transcendence and through the exclusion of this latter from its internal structure," we read at the heart of *The Essence of Manifestation*.[2] In fact, in this book phenomenology is delimited and practiced as a radical return to the foundation of experience, with no other appeal than to its internal structure. Moreover, Henry's concern for methodology has been constant, to the point that an independent essay was recently devoted to this question.[3] What more to ask for? We must add that the publication date of *The Essence of Manifestation*, 1963, as well as the direct dialogue it initiated with Husserl and Heidegger, testifies to the singular

---

[1] Lévinas, "Dieu et la philosophie," in *De Dieu qui vient à l'idée*, p. 127; English trans., *Of God Who Comes to Mind*, p. 78. See also "God and Philosophy," in *The Lévinas Reader* (Oxford: Blackwell, 1989), ed. Séan Hand, trans. Richard A. Cohen and Alphonso Lingis, p. 186.

[2] Michel Henry, *L'essence de la manifestation*, p. 349; trans., p. 281.

[3] Henry, "La méthode phénoménologique," in *Phénoménologie matérielle*, pp. 61–136.

originality of a kind of thinking that has long been unique and only recently been turned into a school of thought. So it is only right to be surprised to see Michel Henry appear at this detour of our "theological turn." This surprise is also not foreign to me; indeed, I have not ceased to be surprised since I started frequenting Henry's œuvre, and the perplexities that have given birth to this essay have only given my surprise renewed life. Incontestably, Henry's phenomenology is organized around the question of immanence; that is also where our questions will be articulated, and what we must interrogate first.

THE STRUCTURE OF IMMANENCE

In the ordinary sense, *immanence* designates what is comprised in a being [*être*] and does not involve any principle of explanation outside of this being. Formally, *The Essence of Manifestation* does not change this definition. The question that must at once be asked, however, is what is the subject of this immanence. Is it consciousness? This hypothesis is very quickly overcome. The being [*être*] of the *cogito* is related back to the universal phenomenological horizon in which it appears. Phenomenological immanence cannot be reduced to the autoreference of self-representation, nor to transcendence in the Sartrean sense (to the annihilation [*néantisation*] of the entity [*l'étant*]); immanence, in the essential sense, does not limit itself to merely reversing a simply ontical transcendence. But do we come closer to its sense by relating it to the transcendental horizon itself? Since we mean to do away with every ontical comprehension of phenomenality, must we not go back to being [*être*] as the ultimate horizon of all phenomenal donation? Once again, this hypothesis is challenged, and for the following reason: being [*être*], isolated by Heidegger as the "appearing [*l'apparaître*] of what appears," remains marked by the exteriority of the horizon from which it is extracted. Transcendental thinking, even when ontologically radicalized, is always conditioned by objectivity (in the broad sense), that is to say, by a presupposition going back to the Greeks and consisting of comprehending manifestation not as a function of its internal structure, but on the basis of the phenomenon. If it is true that "[t]he pure horizon of being [*être*] considered in itself is abstract,"[4] we must attain a yet more originary grasp that pushes the investigation into the very heart of manifestation.

Such is the radical immanence that it is a question of thinking here: not the reversal of perceptive transcendence, but its first condition—a receptivity every going-beyond toward a horizon supposes. "Immanence is the originary mode according to which is accomplished the revelation of transcendence and hence the originary essence of revelation."[5] Henry integrates the Husserlian *epochē* and the Heideggerian ontological difference into what he claims to be a more fundamental return to the things themselves, that of manifestation as revelation. The rest of the work will explain this as autoaffection: the essence of manifestation reveals itself in affectivity, not that of an individual subject, derisively subjective, but of revelation itself, absolute in its inner experience.

It is evidently going out on something of a limb to summarize thus, in a brief sketch, investigations that extend for hundreds of pages and spare themselves none of the constraints (nor, perhaps, the academic delights) of a truly impressive summa, pursuing phenomenological seriousness even to the imitation of a singularly germanic scholarly style. The important thing here is not to fail to recognize the incontestable philosophical élan animating this project and to follow it as closely as possible, so as not to lose the thread of our methodological question. It would be easy to fly directly to the end and to exhibit this project's essentially religious character: the revelation of absolute being [*être*] "is not separated from [this being],"[6] but is itself absolute; the autoaffection is that of life, nonhistorical, nonfinite, but eternally and mysteriously bound to itself. But what matters here is to understand and to make understandable how a phenomenological problematic that presents itself as rigorous, coherent, and radical terminates in such metaphysical conclusions. In this complex montage—which the reader insufficiently initiated in the study of phenomenology will be only too ready to consider an inextricable labyrinth—what thread will allow us to find our way out again?

---

[4] Henry, *L'essence de la manifestation*, p. 242; trans., p. 197.

[5] Ibid., pp. 279–80; trans., p. 227. *Translator's note*: I have rendered "originaire" as "originary" rather than Etzkorn's "original."

[6] Ibid., p. 859; trans., p. 683.

We have tried to follow the guiding thread of immanence and its internal structure. But now it appears that this immanence no longer qualifies any phenomenon or subject, since the "reduction" to it was intent on being as originary as possible. Does immanence, then, concern phenomenality? Only so far as phenomenality is related to the essence of manifestation. Now just as immanence thus becomes "a pure ontological category,"[7] essence is considered in itself, isolated in "radical independence."[8] It is a question here of going back to a receptivity so fundamental that it escapes, while conditioning, every phenomenal grasp. Its reserve—unless it is actually poverty—is to be discovered and confessed.

What is coherent in this project is assuredly its pursuit of the originary. "Always more fundamental! Always more intimate!" So might be summarized the return to the things themselves in *The Essence of Manifestation*. Only this formal coherence can, in its rigid and systematic character, turn against its own intention if its attention to the "thing" in question is insufficiently adapted. A first observation, relevant to immanence, leads us to remark that its purported "internal structure" is not a structure at all. A structure, whether formal or empirical, has identifiable characteristics or relations; if it had any consistency, the structure of immanence would be phenomenologically determinable. But this is not the case: "phenomenology," having dismissed every phenomenon, retains no more than the originary and the internal. The structure of immanence, then, is its pure autoreference. Let us underline, though, that this is not a structure: it is a tautological interiority.

Henry supplies his work with all the appearances (and titles) of phenomenology in order to achieve the most fantastic restoration of essentialism. But the methodological process by which he does this is, finally, rather simple. By means of the originary, he installs himself in the essential, autonomizes it, even celebrates it. The play on the word "essence" in *The Essence of Manifestation* is patent. Henry authorizes himself, from the investigation of a (determined) *eidos*, to go back to a purely autoreferential foundation. Likewise, immanence becomes the strict contrary of what it

---

[7] Ibid., p. 323; trans., p. 259.
[8] Ibid., p. 160; trans., p. 130.

claims to mean: not adherence to phenomenological experience, but absolute autorevelation.

Phenomenology has thus served as a crutch for a return to the originary. But this return gives proof of an extreme attenuation of experience. Phenomenology is turned into its contrary, the most idealist metaphysics—a metaphysics of life and sentiment, one quite close to that of the young Hegel in Frankfurt. Among others, these concluding lines to *The Essence of Manifestation* (where, by the way, the ontological horizon is not absent) testify as much: "In the absolute unity of its radical immanence, being [*être*] affects itself and experiences itself in such a way that there is nothing in it that that does not affect it and which is not experienced by it, no content transcendent to the experience of self that constitutes it."[9] The phenomenologist, having become the spokesperson for the absolute, calmly reveals to us its transparence in categorical terms. But if it is true that this transparence comes to us in sentiment, how is this possible? For our thesis to receive all its content, we must delve into specifics here: a theology that, though negative, is more structured than the immanence from which it emerges.

THE NONKNOWLEDGE OF DIVINE LIFE

The tautological circularity we have begun to identify is this: The essence of manifestation constitutes the manifestation itself. This immanent autoreference to manifestation is expressly designated as absolute. "The absolute . . . , which founds every possible manifestation in general, founds it in manifesting itself and precisely in this manifestation of itself."[10] In this immanence, life benefits from attributes that seem to make it equal to God: autoaffection, eternity, absence of finitude, omnicompleteness (it is all reality). We look in vain, however, for the positive attributes setting off the God of Catholic orthodoxy as such: all-powerfulness, personality, infinitely good will, and the like. Though Henry rejects Hegelian monism, which he reduces to an objectivism of

---

[9] Ibid., p. 858; trans., p. 682 (trans. modified).
[10] Ibid., p. 597; trans., p. 478 (trans. modified).

consciousness, he reaffirms, on this point, the immanence of absolute spirit to its phenomenal manifestations. But with one fine
difference, which is capital: divine immanence escapes not only
representation, but knowledge [*savoir*]. If affectivity is the essence
of life, life must be felt, must allow itself to be penetrated by its
radical passivity. And we must give ourselves over to a doubly
paradoxical experience respecting knowledge and the universality
of life. Knowledge terminates in nonknowledge: having con-
quered the essence of manifestation by a progressive renunciation
of all ontical appearances, Henry must lay down his arms when
he comes to the threshold of life itself. But strangely, life—which
supports each of us and in which all of us stand in common—
refers back only to its essence and to the unity of this essence. By
force of being exalted, it finds itself isolated. "That which has the
experience of self, that which enjoys itself and is nothing other
than this pure enjoyment of itself, than this pure experience of
self, is life. Solitude is the essence of life."[11] This is a strange solitude, which "constitutes an absolutely universal structure"[12] yet
is absolutely set apart in a Parousia that relates only to itself! This
coincidence of opposites recurs in the totally paradoxical scission
between the essentialism of knowledge and the nonknowledge of
sentiment: "The reunion of the essence with itself is none other
than the essence itself."[13]

To this precision, we cannot help but object that it is a question, here, of a fantastic metaphysical essentialism autopromoting
itself. Certainly it will be countered that this essentialism of
knowledge finds its real content and proper phenomenality in the
invisible and unutterable experience of joyful or painful feeling,
life's primordial *pathos*. But this is to admit that, under the cover
of phenomenology, a system is put in place that has its own coherence, but on condition of pushing to the extreme the paradoxical
scission by which it glorifies itself.

It is not appropriate here for me to pronounce as theologian on
the Christian character of this paradoxical teaching. (The Rever-
end Xavier Tilliette expresses satisfaction in an orientation that is

---

[11] Ibid., p. 354; trans., p. 285.
[12] Ibid., p. 355; trans., p. 285.
[13] Ibid.

"far from disappointing its expectation."[14]) What alone matters to us, but which is already a lot, is to show that the conceptual analysis just performed permits us to situate what passed itself off, at the beginning, as "pure phenomenology" within a spiritual movement. This movement is perfectly identifiable, if rather secretive, as the mystical thinking of Meister Eckhart, itself in consonance with many of the words of Jesus, and such as Hegel rethought them in "The Spirit of Christianity and Its Fate."[15] These references are altogether explicit in *The Essence of Manifestation*;[16] Henry has no reason to have to hide them, as they are noble and magnificent. But we must return persistently to our methodological question: To what extent are they compatible with a phenomenology?

Following a path to which Heidegger had shown him the way, Henry perfectly understood the spiritual part he could draw from Eckhart (without, however, making explicit in his own thinking the consequences of Heidegger's mediation).[17] The fundamental point of anchorage Henry justly retained from Eckhart's teaching is the immanence to our soul of divine revelation, an immanence that is so intimate that the essence of the soul merges with that of God. This profound unity is the uncreated tie that Eckhart names "Godhead" and in which all representation must be stripped, even that of God as substance or person. The exclusion of all relation of transcendence within the divine life opened to us goes together, thus, with a moment of atheism.[18] We know that this audacity, joined with criticism of the faith, rendered Eckhart suspect to the Church of his time. But to Henry's eyes these traits make him, to the contrary, a master of immanence, and allow the latter-day philosopher to find in him both an exceptional annun-

---

[14] Xavier Tilliette, "Michel Henry: La philosophie de la vie," in *Philosophie* 15: 20.

[15] G. W. F. Hegel, "The Spirit of Christianity and Its Fate," in *Early Theological Writings* (Philadelphia: University of Pennsylvania Press, 1975), trans. T. M. Knox.

[16] See Henry, *L'essence de la manifestation*, §§39, 40, and 49 on Eckhart, and pp. 359–60, 367, and 511 (trans., pp. 289–90, 295, and 407) on the young Hegel.

[17] Heidegger, *Der Feldweg* (Frankfurt am Main: Vittorio Klostermann, 1956), p. 4.

[18] On this last point, see Henry, *L'essence de la manifestation*, p. 538; trans., p. 429.

ciator of the essence of manifestation as Parousia and a systematic critic of knowledge. Eckhart gestures toward the nonvisage of the affective essence of reality. He makes us understand, and make our own, that the invisible "determines the essence of immanence and constitutes it."[19]

If a phenomenological reality subsists in this spiritual itinerary, it is that of evangelical love: "I could never see God, if it were not there that God sees himself."[20] This saying of Eckhart is shocking for a spirit respectful of Transcendence, in the sense of the Old Testament or even the canonical teaching of the Church. But it is undeniable that the Gospels introduce the idea of a Kingdom of God accomplishing itself *hic et nunc*, of whose spirit of love the Son is the bearer. This incontestable inspiration remains, however, in the background in *The Essence of Manifestation*, where the explication of affectivity as absolute revelation of the absolute founds no prescription, no moral nor even spiritual rule. If it is affirmed that "[a]ll thought is essentially religious,"[21] this orientation remains general and does not receive any positive determination. By spirit and by terminology, however, it reveals itself quite close to the thinking of Christian love as reconciliation with life and in life, such as Hegel evoked and analyzed it in the fragments gathered under the title "The Spirit of Christianity and Its Fate." "I am the truth and the life": the young Hegel knew how to evoke this communion as a living union, a full and innocent harmony, where the exteriority of observances founds itself. Henry found there, but also in Kierkegaard, the affective and spiritual tonality that seems to justify the abandonment of all exteriority, the extreme withdrawal into an essential and pathetic unity of human and divine.

It is for all that significant that, even in the texts of the young Hegel, Henry does not take seriously into consideration a problem Hegel there circled, but did not yet resolve by means of a systematic dialectic: the question of fate. The withdrawal into the absolute interiority of life leaves Jesus totally disarmed before the effective Kingdom, that is, the persistence of the Law and the

---

[19] Ibid., p. 553; trans., p. 441.
[20] Citation given by Henry, ibid., p. 542; trans., pp. 432–33 (trans. modified).
[21] Ibid., p. 897; trans., p. 727.

action of the political power whose logic goes on to crush him. The love where this sublime soul confines itself leads to the tragic scission par excellence. As Hegel notes, "[T]his removal of itself from all fate is just its supreme fate."[22] Henry's indifference to this problem corresponds more generally, in his mystical phenomenology, to a complete scorn for all of life's actual determinations. His concern for the fundamental and the originary drives out every other concern, thereby disincarnating the affectivity he wanted concrete. It follows that the split between knowledge and life's actual determinations is completed. By Henry's own admission, life's monumental knowledge annuls itself in the nonknowledge of affectivity. But to reach this result—at bottom more mystical than properly theological—was it necessary to deploy such heavy conceptual machinery in the quest for essence? Could not affectivity have pierced in advance the apparently phenomenological armor that was supposed to lead to it? The response is again paradoxical: the nonknowledge of divine life knows at least that archoriginal affectivity absolutely adheres to itself, is absolutely transparent to itself. There is a new presupposition here that all life, in its folds and its hierarchical teleonomies, seems to give the lie to. For phenomenology still has its word to say, if its sense of complexity is stronger than this too metaphysical fascination with the originary.

One result can be seen from this discussion: the religious dimension of these investigations into the essence of manifestation leaves no doubt; it also leads Henry's thought, in our eyes, out of the strict domain of phenomenology. But this observation is only the starting point for new perplexities: in the meanwhile, Henry has pursued and developed his path of thinking, but without abandoning the ambition to radicalize the question of phenomenology.[23] In recent texts where the Husserlian heritage is once again taken into consideration and discussed with precision, Henry so seriously examines questions of method that he raises an objection rejoining our interrogations: "Is not a phenomenology of the invisible a contradiction in terms?"[24] Have our critiques

---

[22] Hegel, "The Spirit of Christianity and Its Fate," p. 281.

[23] Henry, *Phénoménologie matérielle*, p. 6.

[24] Ibid., p. 8.

thus been rendered useless, since they were foreseen even before being formulated?

THE NEW DISCOURSE ON METHOD AND ITS PARADOXES

In a dense text, "*La méthode phénoménologique*," which makes up the substance of *Phénoménologie matérielle*,[25] to justify his own method Henry develops a systematic critique of the presuppositions of what he names "historical phenomenology." Commenting first on the five *Lessons* delivered by Husserl at Göttingen,[26] then on the celebrated §7 of *Being and Time*, he means to demonstrate, in the two cases, a radical failure: the plenitude of the revelation of life is reduced to the phenomenality of the world, which is to say, to the visible. But the object of phenomenology (the original appearing [*apparaître*]) is lost on a method wrought from the ontical and "worldly" concept of the phenomenon. Husserl is the victim of a generalized "eidetism," unable to palliate a deep-seated impossibility. It is impossible, writes Henry, to constitute "a rigorous and precisely eidetic science of absolute subjectivity when this subjectivity steals away in principle from every grasp of this kind."[27] Heidegger, for his part, did not liberate himself from a trivial and superficial concept of the phenomenon, "purely and simply borrowed from ordinary perception."[28] The one and the other, in postulating the identity of the object and the method of phenomenology, presuppose a homogeneity in principle between "bringing to sight" (*logos* in the Greek sense) and the phenomenon (reduced to the visible). They thus consummate the failure of all of Western philosophy to grasp life in its pathetic autorevelation.

Reversing the fundamental presupposition of this "historical phenomenology," Henry's phenomenology founds itself on the

---

[25] Ibid., pp. 61–136.

[26] Husserl, *Die Idee der Phänomenologie*, Husserliana Band 2 (The Hague: Martinus Nijhoff, 1958), ed. Walter Biemel; English trans., *The Idea of Phenomenology* (The Hague: Martinus Nijhoff, 1964), trans. William P. Alston and George Nakhnikian.

[27] Henry, *Phénoménologie matérielle*, p. 100.

[28] Ibid., p. 120.

originary datum of a radical heterogeneity between transcendental life and the eidetic method. This heterogeneity is so radical that it seems to run right into an impossibility: If there is an irreducible difference separating affectivity and our essentially descriptive methods, must we not renounce "bringing to sight" affectivity in itself?[29] The response presents itself as paradoxical: the autoexplication of life renders possible its auto–objectification. "I can represent to myself my life, and this possibility in principle is included in life."[30] A re-presentation that no longer founds itself refers back to the pathetic and invisible plenitude of life. Material phenomenology stretches "bringing to sight" to consciousness of its limit: method cannot hand over its "object," which offers itself originally, invisibly, as *pathos*. The bitter destiny of phenomenology is that of every vision that claims to penetrate reality "in person," but can only surprise it in "oblique directions" once it has recognized that "life retains itself in the invisible."[31]

This recapitulation, though brief, has at least the interest of highlighting the extraordinarily paradoxical character of Henry's methodological procedure in the text we have been analyzing. We immediately note a strange distortion between the double critical commentary on the two masters of "historical phenomenology" and the "positive" part of the text concerning material phenomenology. The content of this latter is indicated only in points and dots—an implicit admission that the proclamation of the positivity of the new method is immediately given the lie by the impossibility of putting it to work. The only logical conclusion to draw from a text that presents itself as logical and rigorous is that, "true life" being absent, the phenomenology that directs itself at it proves to be strictly impossible as a scientific discipline. Material phenomenology professes itself to be "altogether other" and issuing from another type of thinking than eidetic-logical phenomenology, like the second Heidegger tracing a clean line in the sand between metaphysics and "thought." Now Henry at once mimes this Heideggerian distancing from the Greek *logos* (while making short shrift of the historial interrogation of meta-

---

[29] Ibid., pp. 122–23.
[30] Ibid., p. 129.
[31] Ibid., p. 134.

physics that it implies) and restores a positive phenomenology—as loftily proclaimed as it is fragile and paradoxical.

We end up, then, with a complete disjunction between form and content. From the point of view of form, we obtain only a program condemned, in fact, to the indefinite reiteration of the absolute autoreference of life (the Archi-revelation reaffirmed without end). On the other side, that of content, we effectively discover, if we only pay a little attention, the *pathos* of a theology in larva. The effectivity of God, at first only named,[32] lets itself be more distinctly identified as "the Verb that comes into this world."[33] The language becomes that of the "Word of Life,"[34] and the method molts into a "Way."[35] We would truly need to have no knowledge of the Gospels, and especially that of John, not to understand where this disjunction between the object and the method of phenomenology comes down.

There would be no reason to object to this mutation if it presented itself as what it is, a conversion or leap toward an experience more secret than that of any phenomenology. We have no intention, certainly, of ridiculing this radical and explicit passage to another dimension (for example, by caricaturing it as romantic mysticism). But Henry turns paradox into a lure. Why claim, against all the evidence, that in material phenomenology "the phenomenological plenitude of life" is attained "in its infrangible positivity"?[36] To keep the phenomenological robe and its academic dignity? The very expression "infrangible positivity" testifies to the self-contradiction where this new "phenomenology" inextricably entraps itself. On the one hand, a reality posed as "infrangible" could not be known positively, unless we are to understand by "positivity" the opposite of a determined procedure, the pure intuition of a thing in itself. On the other hand, Henry has himself recognized, in the text occupying us and at the high point of his trajectory, the fundamentally aporetic character of the split in the appearing [*l'apparaître*] itself.[37] If this aporia is

---

[32] Ibid., p. 127.
[33] Ibid., p. 131.
[34] Ibid., p. 133.
[35] Ibid., pp. 132–33.
[36] Ibid., p. 132.
[37] Ibid., p. 122.

fundamental—and we believe it is—why minimize the fact that Husserl and Heidgger were its first witnesses, explicitly taking it up, deepening it phenomenologically? Why does Henry want, at any price, to give himself the lead, quasi-miraculous role of realizing the impossible: a phenomenology whose materiality would be life "crushed against itself in the invincible implosion of its pathos"?[38]

These objections can be shored up by reexamining Henry's critique of Husserl's and Heidegger's phenomenological positions. At a preliminary, still general level, Husserl sees himself reproached for a "capital error," thinking "the reality of the *cogitatio* as transcendence."[39] This led him to make the eidetic the essential support of his method. Now, however, we must ask if this objection is sufficiently specified or if it does not rather have in its sights, across Husserl (as well as Heidegger), a characteristic tendency of the whole Western tradition. This hypothesis proves to be correct since, at the end of this long text, Henry calls into question the "bringing to sight" proper to the *logos* in the Greek sense. But it is illegitimate to play cards with two decks at once. If the generalized "eidetization" to which Husserl gave himself stems in a direct line from the Greek *logos*, then Henry ought to attack this *logos*. But in this case it is fallacious to tax this orientation with "error." In it is active the destiny of Western philosophy, as the basis for *epistēmē* and as the support for the "vulgar" conception of the phenomenon. It is not possible to want to correct an "error" and, at the same time, to impute it to a fundamental deflection in the history of thought. Here we must choose. If Henry does not, the reason is that he apparently wants to avoid having to take into consideration the second Heidegger's interrogation of metaphysics as such. But only this interrogation allows us to understand the metaphysical logic still governing Husserlian phenomenology and, no doubt, the conceptual framework of *Being and Time*'s existential analytic.

It is strange for Henry to fall silent on this antecedence and to present his challenge to the "bringing to sight" of the Greek *logos* as original. For it was precisely Heidegger's shock, relayed and

---

[38] Ibid., p. 132.
[39] Ibid., p. 108.

displaced by Lévinas, Derrida, and several others, that permitted the opening up of so many breaches in the eidetic project and the classical vision of essence. This silence appears all the stranger when, in the text we are rereading, Heidegger's thinking is beaten back onto the most ordinary conception of the phenomenon. The fact is, however, that §7 of *Being and Time* takes this conception into account only as a point of departure, just as Heidegger reexamines the vulgar conception of time precisely to call it into question. Apart from a brief allusion to the Zähringen seminars,[40] the ensemble of Heidegger's questioning bearing specifically on the privilege of "bringing to sight" (as well as intentionality and truth) is ignored. In fact, Henry fails to note that Heidegger signals very clearly, and several times over,[41] that he is exposing, at the beginning of *Being and Time*, only the "foreconcept" (*Vorbegriff*) of phenomenology—as the title of §7C indicates. Explicitly distinguishing vulgar, formal, and phenomenological concepts,[42] Heidegger turns toward the *possibility* of phenomenology.[43] It is beyond bold, then, to claim that phenomenology designates for Heidegger, even at the beginning of *Being and Time*, only "the most ordinary experience,"[44] when the ontological difference is straightaway indicated and in a way that has not ceased to disconcert "the most ordinary experience." Here as elsewhere, Henry wants, at any price, to reduce the Heideggerian ek-static to the "worldly" (or visible), which comes down to caricaturing Heidegger's thinking while drawing on its resources for this operation.

Reexamining the criticisms addressed at Husserl will also enable us to reach another level of discussion concerning phenomenology as, more specifically, a method and a discipline. Is it true that

---

[40] Ibid., p. 109.

[41] Heidegger, *Sein und Zeit* (Tübingen: Max Niemeyer, 1967), pp. 28, 34, and 357; English trans., *Being and Time* (New York: Harper & Row, 1962), trans. Joan Macquarrie and Edward Robinson, pp. 50, 58, 408; and *Being and Time* (Albany: State University of New York Press, 1996), trans. Joam Stambaugh, pp. 24–25, 30, 326–27.

[42] Ibid., p. 35; Macquarrie and Robinson trans., p. 59; Stambaugh trans., p. 31. See also the whole of §7.

[43] Ibid., p. 38; Macquarrie and Robinson trans., pp. 62–63; Stambaugh trans., p. 34. "Understanding phenomenology lies uniquely in seizing upon it as possibility." Trans. modified.

[44] Henry, *Phénoménologie matérielle*, p. 120.

Husserl reduces "the *cogitatio* to the evidence that gives it"[45] and thus completely "noematizes" thinking? In fixing on Husserl's *The Idea of Phenomenology*, Henry makes things easy for himself, for in this text the reduction is still only "gnoseological." It is not difficult for Henry, from there, to show that the "pure phenomenon," for example, red, is essentialized. But if there is no denying the privilege Husserl never ceased to accord to the eidetic (from the particular *Wesenschau* to the idea of a universal, apodictic science), does this mean that the sense of the transcendental reduction exhausts itself in the essentialism of the eidetic? The *epoché* allows us to attain the absolute *Urregion*,[46] and Husserl neatly distinguishes the reduction from eidetic intuition.[47] The bracketing of the "thesis of the world" makes the visible vacillate in a more radical way than the Cartesian *cogito*. Despite Henry's affirmations concerning the self-givenness of the *cogitatio* in Descartes, "the purely methodological sense of the transcendental *epochē*"[48] in Husserl is something new, as his *Cartesian Meditations* underlines. Add to these considerations that, in minimizing the primordiality of the *epochē*, Henry makes it difficult for himself to justify his recourse, in his book *La barbarie*, to the Husserlian comprehension of life as transcendental subjectivity in the *Crisis*. This last work by Husserl shows quite well that essentialism is not the last word of his phenomenology.

Ultimately, this discussion obliges us to pose the basic problem of the scientificity of phenomenology, a problem central to Husserl. In presenting the self-givenness of the *cogitatio* (or of life) as a winning substitute for essentializing representation, does Henry respond to this problem? He would if, ceasing to elevate the self-givenness of life into an absolute and separate principle, he recognized that phenomenology can only think of itself as a "rigorous science" (in a specific sense to which we will return) if it postulates a homogeneity in principle between its method and its object. If this methodological postulate (rendered ontologically possible by the Parmenidean sameness of thinking and being [*être*]) is challenged, no science (in the Western sense) is able to

---

[45] Ibid., p. 82.
[46] See Husserl, *Ideen zu einer reinen Phänomenologie*, §76, p. 174; trans., p. 171.
[47] See Husserl, *Cartesianische Meditationen*, §34, p. 106; trans., p. 72.
[48] Ibid., §13, pp. 69–70; trans., p. 31.

be either founded, or practiced. Henry seems ready to admit this when, referring suddenly to his Marx, he envisages the substitution of the noematic essence of work by living work (to which would correspond, in Husserl, the substitution of his noematic theory of representation by the self-givenness of living thought).[49] But in the case of political economy as phenomenology, returning to living subjectivity and originary *pathos* is no sufficient basis for claiming a new foundation. For this to be the case, the space of thinking thus disengaged must allow us both to determine the minimal presuppositions for every discipline of a scientific type and to account for the inevitable, destined character of this rational determination of experience.

In other words, gesturing toward the invisibility and inexpressibility of life is a high task of poetry and thought that Henry often pulls off quite well (for example, when he evokes the white of Kandinsky, "the color of the before of things, the place of the possible," or again the red of the Resurrection in Matthias Grünewald's "Isenheim Altarpiece").[50] But it does not at all follow that phenomenological discourse, in making itself "material," can say "*in all rigor* in what phenomenologically consists the phenomenality of . . . this pure phenomenality."[51] It is not the intention here we call into question—whether it be theological or purely poetic—but the peremptory postulation of rigor when its essential condition, the correspondence between the method and the object of phenomenology, has been eliminated. (Henry nowhere demonstrates, moreover, that phenomenology must uniquely concern itself with life in its pathetic unity.)

Phenomenology cannot afford to skimp on the question of method. Husserl and Heidegger insisted on this point. And Henry himself recognized as much at the beginning of his essay on "*La méthode phénoménologique*." He has also lately consecrated special attention to the principles that must guide phenomenology.[52]

---

[49] Henry, *Phénoménologie matérielle*, p. 134.

[50] Henry, *Voir l'invisible*, p. 226.

[51] Henry, *Phénoménologie matérielle*, p. 122 (italics added).

[52] Ibid., p. 61, and the foreword, p. 5. See also "Quatre principes de la phénoménologie," in *Revue de métaphysique et de morale* 1 (1991): 3–26. This text makes manifest, once more, the theological end point of Henry's thinking. Two citations: (1) The original "appearing" [*apparaître*] is "this infinite Life that does not cease to give us to ourselves and to engender us as it engenders itself in its eternal

What, then, in the final analysis, do we object to? Precisely the use of the flag and the cloak of the phenomenological method to invert it or compromise its effective insights—to transform precise, limited, clarifying procedures into incantory preludes to the absolute autoreference of life and its pathetic sacredness. Phenomenology is not all of philosophy. It owes its interest and its scope to the respect of its proper rules as well as to the audacity of its breakthroughs. But we must sharpen this point, this time more positively than critically.

---

autoaffection" (p. 11); (2) "Thus there would be nothing without this triumphal eruption of the revelation of the Absolute" (p. 20). What phenomenological sense can the notions of infinity, eternity, and the absolute receive here? None. But Henry inverses the first rule analyzed (as much appearing [*apparaître*], as much being [*être*]) to lead to a position totally contrary to its neo-Kantian spirit: ontical appearing [*apparaître*] does not give over anything of the ontological and vital Archi-revelation. The second methodological rule, which concerns intuition, is equally rejected. Qualified (like the first) as "murder" (p. 12), it does not warrant any positive attention under the pretext that life subtracts itself "by nature" from the types of evidence isolated by Husserl. The commentary on the third principle (*zu den Sachen selbst*) pretends to believe that this principle is directed at "things in themselves" (p. 6), which permits disqualifying it without demonstrating this point. Thus Henry deliberately abandons three essential rules of "historical phenomenology" in favor of the principle recently formulated by Jean-Luc Marion: "the more reduction, the more givenness." While affirming that everything about this principle is phenomenological (p. 23), Henry acknowledges the "stupendous" character of the problematic of the call in Marion, and does not mask the separation between the "pure form of the call" and the pathetic drunkenness of life.

To begin to show the contradictions and indeterminations of the principles of "historical phenomenology" was interesting. But we must observe that the principle of the "new" phenomenology remains totally unjustified itself. This is above all the case as to the relation of proportionality on which it is suspended and about which we can say precisely what Henry writes about the first principle of "historical phenomenology." The terms at hand have changed from appearing [*apparaître*] and being [*être*] to reduction and givenness; the question, however, remains the same. "What sense to give to the relation of proportionality that unites them?" Does it not "become forever enigmatic, between two equally unknown terms" (p. 9)?

5

Reorientation

How can we reconcile the demand for rigor with a positive project for phenomenology? Conjuring the theological "temptation" away is not enough; nor is restoring Husserl's programmatic ardor in its aporetic tension between an infinitely unfinished work and the dream of a totally renewed scientific corpus. "[T]he greatest step our age has to take," Husserl wrote, "is to recognize that, with the true sense of philosophical intuition, the *phenomenological grasp of essence*, an infinite field of work opens itself up and a science [presents itself] that . . . acquires a plenitude of perfectly rigorous and decisive knowledge for *all* subsequent philosophy."[1] We must make several distinctions here. The opening up of the horizon of sense is profoundly respectable and authentically philosophical; so, too, is the consciousness of an infinite task reactivated by phenomenology's methodological institution. But can we say as much of the resolve to make *all* philosophy pass through the Caudine Forks[2] of a scientifically rigorous project? We do not believe so. Indeed, there is a pretension in this resolve that we must identify and criticize, without caricaturing it. That is what we will try to do in the following pages, keeping in mind that we find in Husserl a foundational hope as ambitious and ambiguous as that in Bergson.

"We must break with the frameworks of mathematics," Bergson wrote, "take stock of the biological, psychological, and sociological sciences, and on this wider base build a metaphysics capable of rising higher and higher, by the continuous, progres-

---

[1] Husserl, *Aufsätze und Vorträge (1911–1921)*, Husserliana Band 25 (The Hague: Martinus Nijhoff, 1987), ed. Thomas Nenon and Hans Rainer Sepp, pp. 61–62; English trans., "Philosophy as Rigorous Science," in *Phenomenology and the Crisis of Philosophy* (New York: Harper & Row, 1965), trans. Quentin Lauer, p. 147 (trans. modified).

[2] Translator's note: Caudine Forks (*fourches caudines*) is the name of a narrow mountain pass in Southern Italy. It was the site of a battle in 321 B.C.E., when the ancient Samnites defeated and captured a Roman army.

sive, and organized effort of all philosophers associated in the same respect for experience."[3] But between the demands for "precision" (or rigor) and opening, equilibrium is not easy to establish. And if it is always a delicate task to anticipate the possibilities of a discipline as "comprehensive" as philosophy, this difficulty is doubled in this case by the inclusion of the concern for scientificity in the wrapping of philosophical inquietude. Certainly, both Husserl and Bergson escape the positivist illusion they know so well how to criticize: it is not a question, here, of modeling philosophical method on the procedures of the exact and positive sciences, nor of limiting the scope of philosophical interest to enregistering science's results. The inverse failing, which consists in wanting to restore the supremacy of philosophy over the sciences *directly*, is equally avoided. Husserl and Bergson share, however, the conviction that a profound renewal of philosophical methodology can enable philosophy to enter into a dialogue with the positive sciences and thus retrieve and reevaluate the question of the very sense of the whole of human knowledge. This reform of knowledge comes to pass, for Bergson, by apprenticeship to intuition at all levels where the work of intelligence operates; for Husserl, it goes by the double exercise of the transcendental reduction and eidetic vision (also an intuition, but in a non-Bergsonian sense).

The fact that Bergsonian intuition is a "sympathy" whereas Husserlian intuition is a vision of essence no doubt matters less than the distance taken, in both cases, in regard to logical or mathematical formalism (the ensemble of "indirect methods" for Husserl, the excessively "intelligent" procedures for Bergson). What we have here is an extremely paradoxical situation: a marked, almost ceremonial effort on the behalf of scientificity (and of the refoundation of the relation to scientific rationality) finds itself thrown back toward irrationalism or pure idealism. In both cases, intuitionism has played the role of a "false friend" of science. Certainly, in the first instance (within philosophy), it permitted Husserl and Bergson to affirm their originality and to rearticulate the philosophical enterprise. But subsequently it betrayed both men. Their view of science is too unifying and too

---

[3] Bergson, *Mélanges* (Paris: Presses Universitaires de France, 1972), p. 488.

constraining *not* to appear like a new philosophical attempt to restore the "originary" or the "foundational." And the consequence is clear: despite the nobility of their projects, neither Husserl nor Bergson succeeded in spanning the breach, first opened with the Galilean institution of an autonomous mathematical physics, between the operative formalism of the positive sciences and the philosophical claim for the unity of sense. The bridge they would have built by the role of argumentation (which Plato found already in dialectics) had been booby-trapped from the start by intuitionism (whether eidetic or vitalist).

The parallel between Husserl and Bergson cannot be pushed too far, but it is instructive to the extent that their methodological diversions did not prevent them both from running into the same fundamental misunderstanding: philosophy cannot claim both to have a sui generis rigor and to play a prescriptive role for all the other scientific disciplines. Bergson's empiricism (in the larger sense) should have, in principle, made the task of integrating philosophy and science easier: "Let us work then to fasten onto experience as closely as possible," he wrote in 1901. And who would not agree with such a praiseworthy intention? But he adds something that is less innocent: "Let us take science with its current complexity, and let us begin anew ourselves, with this new science for our matter, an analogous effort to that which the ancient metaphysicians exerted on a simpler science."[4] The problem is that the sciences do not allow themselves to be modeled like docile matter, and the interplay between science and metaphysics is much subtler than Bergson allows. Does not metaphysics already intervene within scientific activities? For example, is the very exercise of formalism in the natural sciences possible without an implicitly philosophical presupposition of the "calculability" of physical things? Bergson's controlling interest in the life sciences made him believe that the distribution of roles he imagined was possible. But it must be acknowledged that the evolution of the biological sciences toward a more and more thoroughgoing formalism (in particular, with the notions of code, program, and information) renders the Bergsonian ambition to "give form" to science from the metaphysical point of view more unsatisfactory still.

---

[4] Ibid.

These considerations might seem to take us away from phenomenology, but on the contrary they bring us back to it. The eventual Husserlian retreat from the concrete sciences and his critique of naturalism and of psychologism can be explained by a resolve less subtly formulated than in Bergson, but not less decided, to "give form" to scientific activity. Now, if we must agree that the Husserlian project fails to stand up before the positive sciences and even in regard to logic (for it would be foolhardy to claim that his confrontation with Frege turned to Husserl's advantage), its standing is equally contestable in the properly philosophical field. What is contestable is not the fact of proposing a method (among others); it is undeniable that the eidetic vision has its rigor and its fecundity. But can we accept a prescription like this: "Pure phenomenology as a science can . . . only be an investigation of essence and not at all of existence"?[5] Let us be clear: our objection does not ring against the rule phenomenology imposes on itself insofar as it wants to be pure; it sounds against the extension of this rule (and of its methodological implications) to the rest of the philosophical field. It is not at all self-evident that philosophy, open onto the world, must let itself be exclusively captured by the "phenomenological grasp of essence."[6] No more is it given that all philosophy must be phenomenological and that, if it is, it cannot be relayed by other methods, such as the genealogical return to foundations or argued analysis.

In principle, we should be able to accept the Husserlian prescriptions inside the phenomenological domain and challenge them when they become excessively rigid or abusively totalizing. Thus philosophy could guard its freshness of interrogation, without being enclosed in a neo-Cartesian project. In fact, though, the phenomenological movement very early saw its own project contested from within (by Heidegger in his Marburg courses[7]): an effort was made to disengage it from the rationalist and Cartesian conception of intentionality in which it tended to enclose itself. Likewise, thereafter, from Merleau-Ponty to Henry (and even in Lévinas, in a more complex manner), the preference has been to

---

[5] Husserl, *Aufsätze und Vorträge*, p. 36; trans., p. 116 (trans. modified).

[6] Ibid., p. 62; trans. p. 147 (trans. modified).

[7] See Heidegger, *Prolegomena zur Geschichte der Zeitsbegriff* [*History of the Concept of Time*], §13.

open up phenomenology from within, without entirely abandoning it to the Husserlian exigencies.

That the destiny of phenomenology escaped the intentions of its founder is neither surprising nor scandalous; every heritage knows such misadventures. The philosophical fecundity of a mode of thought is not, moreover, measured by the strict respect accorded its orthodoxy—quite the contrary! But phenomenologists' creative ardor has perhaps made them neglect what there was to respect in the Husserlian concern for rigor, and a specific rigor at that. The risk was a methodological slacking off, of which we have noted several of the effects in following the theological turn of French phenomenology. In Husserl himself or in his "inheritors," close or distant, phenomenology opens its way *between* the objectivism of the sciences and the most speculative metaphysics. But this double distancing does not result in any method; it obliges thought to turn itself toward the "thing itself" out of the abyssal liberty of the *epochē*. We have seen that Husserl never claimed to model his method on those of the exact sciences; he even goes so far as to write, in *The Crisis of the European Sciences and Transcendental Phenomenology*, that "the 'unscientificity' of philosophy is unmistakable."[8] But in trying to invest phenomenology with its own rigor, he never turned his attention away from the progress of these sciences and the course of scientificity. Even in moments of doubt, Husserl never disassociated phenomenology from the rational teleology assigned to the sciences. Philosophy, as transcendental phenomenology, must "show the way" to the excessively objectifying or naturalist sciences, and restore their faith in the rational ideal. Beyond the rules of the reduction and the eidetic, Husserl therefore maintained a still higher norm: the ideal of a unifying-totalizing reason, purveyor of sense.

This guarded relation with scientificity and this constancy to the rational ideal both kept Husserl from any regression to the *metaphysica specialis* of the tradition and equally safeguarded his capacity to pose the problem of the sense of the lifeworld. It is no

---

[8] Husserl, *Die Krisis der Europäischen Wissenschaften und die Transzendentale Phänomenologie*, Husserliana Band 6 (The Hague: Martinus Nijhoff, 1954), ed. Walter Biemel, p. 2; English trans., *The Crisis of European Sciences and Transcendental Phenomenology* (Evanston, Ill.: Northwestern University Press, 1970), trans. David Carr, pp. 4–5 (trans. modified).

longer the same, though, when the originary and the fundamental serve as a cover for a speculative or theological restoration (reducing phenomenology nearly to the role of a manuscript illustrator). But rather than stick with critiques, it is more interesting to show how other ways open up to phenomenology so long as it does not stray out of its proper limits. Before laying out the field that experience offers to phenomenology, let us return to our methodological question to get a better sense of the ambiguous status of this field. It is neither altogether disciplinary nor altogether doctrinal, neither completely scientific nor wholly metaphysical.

The Phenomenological Estate

Confronting our effort to introduce a little more methodological clarity in the field of phenomenological studies, resistance will come not only from the "spiritualist camp," which will not easily agree to see itself roped off from such potentially fertile lands, but likely from a skeptical and "analytic" rationalism as well. It would not be surprising were its proponents to charge that lack of rigor has always been phenomenology's lot, even in Husserl, whose quest for scientificity remained largely rhetorical. From the moment this concern was overtly abandoned by his successors, was it any wonder that the phenomenological movement became the shelter for all the metaphysical questions "continental" thought still has not succeeded in throwing off? The shelter also for the summit of all metaphysics, the inevitable mirage of the absolute?

The most severe judgment in this matter was formulated in a most British style by Gilbert Ryle: "It is my personal opinion that *qua* First Philosophy Phenomenology is at present heading for bankruptcy and disaster and will end either in self-ruinous subjectivism or in a windy Mysticism."[9] Without tumbling into such an alarmist dramatization and in a more argumentative fashion, Vincent Descombes has exposed the laxity of phenomenology in

---

[9] Cited by Herbert Spiegelberg, in *The Phenomenological Movement* (The Hague: Martinus Nijhoff, 1965), vol. 1, p. 347. *Translator's note*: Ryle made this remark at the conclusion of his 1929 review of *Being and Time*. For a reprint of this review, see the *Journal of the British Society for Phenomenology* 1, no. 3 (1970): 3–13.

matters of *meaning* [*sens*], which phenomenologists do not submit to any preliminary grammatical inspection: "We recognize a philosopher whose primary formation has been phenomenological in that his uses of *meaning* do not give him any qualms."[10] From these critical judgments, the temptation is strong to draw the conclusion that the self-correction of phenomenology is impossible, the ambiguity of its presuppositions and its terminology serving as "cover" for unforeseeable rhetorical sleights-of-hand permitting its brilliant, regenerative, and curious feats and recirculating the speculations, or dreams, of its new visionaries. There is no more to do than wait, then, and let all these symptoms manifest themselves until phenomenology, having disgorged all its humors, definitively wastes away into inconsequence. . . .

We shall not choose one scenario against another (Michel Henry imagines phenomenology triumphing as the sole great and authentic philosophical movement of the century), but simply keep ourselves from completely despairing of a movement of thought that has already revealed itself to be so fertile, even if it has not followed the Husserlian prescriptions to the letter and seems not to have exhausted all of its potentialities. We do not despair since, if phenomenology supposes before all else a "concept of method," as the early Heidegger saw, this does not at all imply that this method consists of a series of rules or principles fixed once and for all. Even the procedures of the so-called exact sciences, especially once we go beyond the stage of logical-mathematical formalization, cannot be deduced from a methodological code functioning a priori; Paul Feyerabend scored several points on this question. Now there is no sidestepping the fact that phenomenology came into its own, with Husserl, only by inventing a new mode of intersection between two domains that have not ceased, since the Greeks got such things going, not only to overlap, but also to redefine one another's topology conflictually: philosophical questioning and the scientific quest for invariants. The sui generis novelty of the Husserlian mode of intersection between philosophy and science must now be defined.

We must recall, first of all, that Husserl never conceived of the

---

[10] Descombes, *Grammaire d'objets en tous genres*, p. 56; trans., p. 50 (trans. modified).

dialogue between philosophy and science as the analysis of the *results* acquired by human knowledge, but as a tension within one and the same project—what the Greeks named *epistēmē*, and which is far from being brought to completion even in the positive sciences. "All sciences are incomplete, even the much-admired exact sciences."[11] Being then assumed that the essence of science does not find its effective realization in any science,[12] it falls to philosophy to take up the project of true, universal, and disinterested knowledge, precisely where the sciences lack it, at the level of the foundations of knowledge and the principles of phenomenality. "Philosophy is in its essence the science of veritable beginnings."[13]

We have seen that this project is not shielded from old misunderstandings in the history of Western thought, that is, the desire to assign philosophy a prescriptive role in relation to the sciences, to nourish the illusion of holding the key for a future encyclopedic corpus of scientific idealities. But even if Husserl was not totally liberated from these excessive and recurrent hopes, the program he fixed for phenomenology was new in that, not directly taking for its model any already constituted science, it took up *both* the philosophical project and the concern for scientificity while putting classical metaphysical problems aside. The bracketing of the natural attitude is rightly underscored, but it should not be forgotten that the *epochē* equally concerns the positions and propositions of *metaphysica specialis*—the nature of the soul, of the world, and of God.

Thus disengaged by the *epochē* is an attentive, positive, and curious neutrality in search of truth. The space of intersection between philosophy and scientificity is white [*blanc*]; it is a space of possible truths. Concerning what domain? This is a specification of capital importance that is not at all self-evident: the open field

---

[11] Husserl, *Aufsätze und Vorträge*, p. 4; trans., p. 74 (trans. modified).

[12] See translator Quentin Lauer's comment in Husserl's *La philosophie comme science rigoureuse* (Paris: Presses Universitaires de France, 1955), p. 127, n. 9: "To understand the Husserlian notion of philosophy, it is first of all necessary to understand his notion of science. To understand this notion is needed a complete phenomenological analysis—the sciences serving as examples from which is drawn the essence 'science,' which is not completely realized in any positive science."

[13] Husserl, *Aufsätze und Vorträge*, p. 61; trans., p. 146 (trans. modified).

is that of the entire human experience. We must not forget, in this regard, all that Husserl owed to Locke and to Hume—how essential both attention to the genesis of "sense data" and the return to the immanence of perceptive experience were to his phenomenological project.[14] The abandonment of the metaphysical mode of thinking (in the sense of *metaphysica specialis*) is then a condition of possibility for constituting the new intersection between philosophy and science.

Phenomenology is totally philosophical in Husserl, never reducing itself to what it could be in the physical or chemical sciences. It is never, that is to say, a simple, methodical description of the appearances offered by bodies in the natural world—a description preliminary to the experimental and formal interventions that permit scientists to disengage constant, determined, and (in principle) verifiable relations among phenomena of a particular order. But we see here that "philosophical" does not mean metaphysical in the sense of the search for Transcendence and interrogation of the last things. The return to the appearing [*l'apparaître*] of phenomena as they give themselves and as they can be recollected in certainty—such is the open, totally programmatic space of intersection in which Husserl goes to work with two sui generis methodological instruments, the reduction and eidetic description.

If there was a Husserlian "shock" whose creative tremor has not ceased to surprise and inspire, it is in this new intersection between philosophy and science. For a vision that has purified itself, returning to the quick of experience, without presupposing anything metaphysical, out of experience itself as it gives itself, here everything is again possible, both worthy of question and determinable. In its very novelty, this intersection is fragile—easily broken by Husserl's successors. The transcendental-empirical pairing gets thrown out of balance, usually from the transcendental side (for it is on the originary and fundamental side that philosophers believe they find their vocation). The theologi-

---

[14] See Ricœur, *À l'école de la phénoménologie* (Paris: Vrin, 1987), p. 8, and Descombes (citing Spiegelberg), *Grammaires d'objets en tous genres*, p. 56; trans., p. 49. In his fundamental book, *Le sens du temps et de la perception chez E. Husserl* (Paris: Gallimard, 1968), Gérard Granel equally insisted on this point: "Phenomenology is a reflection on the perceived [*perçu*]" (p. 104).

cal turn, we have seen, pushes this accentuation of the transcendental to the Archi-revelation, the pure call, originary alterity. The eidetic is abandoned, decried as superficial, essentializing, ontic. It is publicly denounced and shamed. But its accusers forget that, however modest it was in its intentions and in its "fulfillments," it brought balance to phenomenological research in the interests of determined, stable, and universal knowledge.

It will be objected that the eidetic method remains descriptive whereas contemporary science has revealed the extraordinary applied and operative power of formalizations. Without any doubt!—and that is exactly why Husserlian phenomenology does not occupy, vis-à-vis the positive sciences, a role corresponding to its ambitions. But science is not all of one piece (as Christ's tunic was); it has its levels and its folds, its dominant axes and its potentialities in reserve, following the swaths it cuts in experience. It would be going a little far, then, to claim that the eidetic method has brought nothing and cannot be fruitful still for determined knowledge of experience. At the same time, reducing phenomenology to an empirical method of investigation—a simple, typological technique—and thereby sacrificing its power of interrogation would be totally to mistake its philosophical scope. Just because the concern for the originary has been recently and cleverly mortgaged by ulterior, theological motives is no reason for junking it. At the intersection of its possibilities, is not phenomenology capable of assuming the richness of ambiguity that was already its own in Husserl: between the transcendental and the ideal, the conditions of the possibility of experience and experience's determined faces?

AT THE INTERSECTION OF POSSIBILITIES

If phenomenology is less a doctrine than a source of inspiration and less a school than an abundance of heresies, it owes this first of all to the contradictions in Husserl's own œuvre, "unresolved, embarrassed, scratched out, arrested in its development."[15] To divert this source to the benefit of an exterior ideology can only

---

[15] Ricœur, *À l'école de la phénoménologie*, p. 156.

dry it up; so, too, to try to impose on it an artificially unifying discipline, or further to make it the rallying point for the philosophical "good fight" against this or that fashion. So the methodological critique we have undertaken cannot terminate, without betraying the point of its own project, in a Manichaean censure of the authors studied. If our interventions have been precise and delicate enough, no misunderstanding is possible. We have inscribed these interventions within problematics whose philosophical interest is not contested; our signs of contradiction were meant to introduce a kind of interrogative intensification.

If now we turn toward the "possibilities" of the phenomenological method, we discover a "too full" rather than a void. Though contested on one side (especially since the "linguistic turn" has made inroads into francophone climes), phenomenology nevertheless finds itself claimed, solicited, even flattered. To make a list of this network of influences and fascinations holds only limited interest. We could certainly compose a kind of inventory of present-day phenomenological work. Following the progression of the Husserlian œuvre, we would begin with the heritage of the *Logical Investigations*, establish what might subsist of a transcendental logic, and widen our scope to take note also of the project—limited but pertinent—of a descriptive grammar of the true.[16] Turning then to the noetic-noematic correlation, this inspection would establish to what extent a descriptive theory of idealities and objectivities is still possible; how the studies of pure lived experiences and "mundanities" by which French phenomenology has distinguished itself can be enriched; and where phenomenological studies of space (and corporeality), internal time consciousness, and symbolic institution all stand. Finally—but can there be an end to this theoretical fiction?—we would have to reckon with "questions of reentry" to the evidence of the lifeworld and the status of such evidence in this Western world in the thrall of the crisis (of sense) of the sciences.

But the possibilities of phenomenology would be perhaps more profoundly sounded were we to undertake an altogether different investigation, one detached from the Husserlian œuvre. This

---

[16] See Descombes, "La phénoménologie pour nous," in *Critique de la raison phénoménologique* (Paris: Le Cerf, 1991), ed. J. Poulain, pp. 34–35.

investigation might cross borders and effect unforeseen methodological grafts and fertilizations: between transcendental phenomenology and the semantics of action; between the morphogenesis
of mathematical idealities and the foundation of a universal phenomenology; between eidetic intuition and the theory of the essence of the political; between the reevaluation of the question of
intentionality and the quest for new cognitive models. Heidegger
himself, in our opinion, became phenomenological once more
(and just when it was least expected) when he turned to a fourth
dimension of time, and its very givenness, in his lecture "Time
and Being."[17] And not to forget our new theologians, let us acknowledge their suggestive incursions into the phenomenology
of aesthetic experience. Henry's *Voir l'invisible* permits us to understand the internal tonality of color as the primordial ecstasy of
an emotion that, paradoxically, allows itself to be totally seen
while retaining itself in the invisible.[18] Marion's *La croisée du visible*, analyzing the paradoxes of perspective and opposing the modern idolatry of the image to the sacredness of the icon, enables us
to understand modern painting as a kind of square dance [*chassé-
croisé*] between lived experience and the intentional object.[19]

   These breakthroughs open onto other investigations. They are
not, without doubt, ultimately unifiable, and certainly not sys-
tematizable; but they all at least maintain, so long as they remain
phenomenological, attention to both the appearing [*l'apparaître*]
as such and what it offers. As Paul Ricœur has shown—and whose
itinerary "at the school of phenomenology" has been exemplary—phenomenology is born when we "treat the manner of
appearing [*apparaître*] of things as an autonomous problem."[20]
Phenomenology remains itself so long as it does not desert this
appearing and its manifestations, and so long as its critique of this
appearing does not lead it to deny its own essential finitude, but

---

[17] Heidegger, *Zur Sache des Denkens*, pp. 16ff.; *On Time and Being*, pp. 15ff.

[18] Henry, *Voir l'invisible*, pp. 26–42, 68–80.

[19] Marion, *La croisée du visible* (Paris: La Différence, 1991), pp. 31–35 and pas-
sim. The phenomenological interest of this book nevertheless does not allow us,
it will be divined, to approve of the explicit subordination of phenomenology
to theology, the clearest formulation—to this day—of the theological turn. We
read on p. 8: "Theology becomes, in this situation, an irrecusable instance of
every theory of painting."

[20] Ricœur, *À l'école de la phénoménologie*, p. 77.

draws out the lines of its self-limitation, in particular before the practical imperative, whose motivations escape sensibility and without doubt every theory of the pure appearing. There follows a double consequence, positive and negative. Positive: just as it is at every instant possible for the *epochē* to "convert" the natural attitude, the phenomenological opening is an a fortiori (and desirable) possibility for every philosophical interrogation. But the negative consequence is, for phenomenology, the renunciation of being the whole of philosophy. This point has been more and more clearly affirmed over the course of this essay. Here again, Ricœur has given us a felicitous expression: phenomenology is "not philosophy, but only its 'threshold.' "[21] Since Hegel at least, we know how much the crossing of the threshold engages the fate of all knowledge.

Phenomenology and Theology Make Two

In delimiting the theological turn of French phenomenology historically, then critically, we have wanted to effect a precise methodological work. We have not at all wanted to pass it off for what it is not: a synoptic and systematic study of the relations between phenomenology and theology. But in virtue of this limitation (in keeping with the logic of our subject matter), our reticence might be interpreted unfavorably in regard to theology itself. Is the hermeneutic indetermination in which we leave it the mask of scorn? Does ruling the question of God out of phenomenological legitimacy lead us, in fact, to the restoration of an atheist phenomenology in the manner of Sartre?

We must guard ourselves here against a new confusion that threatens to condemn every critical undertaking to a kind of perpetual "double frenzy." The above suspicion, if it appears, is of an ideological order and is the symptom of a constant contamination of the methodological by the ideological, including in discourses practicing an apologetic idealization of phenomenology to make it a countercurrent to neopositivism or scientistic reductionism. Refusing all ideologizing of this manner, we reaffirm the

---

[21] Ibid., p. 159.

uniquely methodological-critical character of this present study, and thus leave voluntarily out of our horizon the ensemble of questions concerning the legitimacy of the theological domain, its concepts, and its "contents."

In this regard, perhaps not enough attention has been lent, on either the phenomenological or the theological side, to the interest of a text little known in France, *Phenomenology and Theology*, a lecture given by Heidegger in 1927 in Tübingen but published only in 1970.[22] Postulating that theology is a "positive" knowledge absolutely different from philosophy, insomuch as its *positum* is Christian faith, Heidegger affirms that it has nothing to expect from philosophy as to *Christlichkeit* itself. Faith explains itself essentially out of itself, that is to say, in terms of the historicity proper to Christian revelation. It has need of philosophy only when its "scientific" character is to be taken into consideration. Thus faith can and even must do without philosophy to understand sin, which is not at all deducible from the existential phenomenology of the debt (*Schuld*) such as §58 of *Being and Time* explains it. But if theology undertakes to situate sin in the existential-ontological horizon and to generate a descriptive knowledge of it, then it cannot dispense with phenomenology, whose lights will play the role of "corrective for the ontic and so pre-Christian content of basic theological concepts."[23] If there can be no "phenomenological theology"—which would be a new version of that "circle squared," Christian philosophy—this is because only existential phenomenology can be both the guardian of the ontological difference as such and its formal indicator.

From this reference to Heidegger's text, we mean to retain only its methodological relevance, in the notions of "corrective" and

---

[22] Heidegger, *Phänomenologie und Theologie* (Frankfurt am Main: Vittorio Klostermann, 1970). *Translator's note:* See also *Wegmarken* (Frankfurt am Main: Vittorio Klostermann, 1967), pp. 47–67, and *Pathmarks* (Cambridge: Cambridge University Press, 1998), ed. William J. McNeill, trans. James G. Hart and John C. Maraldo, pp. 40–54.

[23] Ibid., p. 32; see also *Wegmarken*, p. 66, *Pathmarks*, p. 53 (trans. modified). In a remarkable book, with an overly modest title, *Note sur le temps* (Paris: Presses Universitaires de France, 1990), Jean-Yves Lacoste seems to us to have worked in this spirit. He defends and illustrates a theological mode of thought putting in place a "system of differences" that, while "phenomenologically inevident" (p. 125), is respectful of the finitude of being-in-the-world.

"formal indicator" it introduces on behalf of phenomenology. This "corrective" (and not "rectifying") aptitude appears to us essential for both the reduction and the eidetic description. In this sense, phenomenology does not cease to "cut its teeth" anew—to effect a reciprocal adjustment of its procedures and its unfolding horizons. The question of the phenomenological pertinence of the notions taken on and critiqued in this study (pure alterity, autoaffection, the call, givenness) must be posed from the moment they are introduced into the field of investigation, and certainly not in terms of "all or nothing." Thus, for givenness, the distinction must be made between the *Selbstgegebenheit* of a determined essence, the givenness of a temporal dimension or of time itself as a dimension, and finally givenness "in itself" (which is without doubt no more than a limit-concept on which nothing can be constructed, no more than it is legitimate to transform the invisible or the "unseen" into substantial realities, even under the form of fixed referents).

In this case—as in the usage of metaphor, self-reference, or the overdetermination of a concept (such as the Other [*Autre*], at once empirical, generic, and transgeneric, at least in Lévinas)—it is tempting to establish an ultimate court of appeal to pronounce on the question *quid juris* in things phenomenological. Is it a question here of a philosophical grammar to keep phenomenology in line? Without contesting the useful and even indispensable role of semantical elucidations, it is imperative to recognize that, with this question, we encounter the aporia all philosophy must assume as both judge and interested party in weighing the legitimacy of its propositions. The responsibility of the philosopher corresponds to this abyssal liberty. Grammar itself, if it is philosophical, will know this trouble in its new sovereignty.

Another site of investigation concerns the relation between phenomenology and metaphysics, whose complexity we have measured. We do not claim to have done away with this question, but on the contrary to have made it once more accessible. Can the theological dimension, essentially metaphysical, find in phenomenology a kind of propaedeutic exorcising the pitfalls of ontotheology? Let us indicate, one last time, the reasons for our skepticism. The question is asked whether a deconstructive enterprise is adequate to overcome metaphysics or can only, at most, displace it toward a still metaphysical meta-discourse, be this on the level of general ontology or thought of the Highest Being. Decentered toward an indescribable, inconceivable, indeed inutterable originary, phenomenology seems ready to take the place (occupy the site and fulfill the functions) of a *metaphysica generalis*: a methodical interrogation of the conditions of possibility of presence. Jacques Derrida has shown, in particular in *Speech and Phenomena*,[24] that the thinking of Husserl himself is liable to such a radical deconstruction. But at this point the problem of the restoration of *metaphysica specialis* within phenomenology does not yet arise.

The subtlety of this restoration comes from the fact that its artisans mean to exploit the deconstruction of the metaphysics of presence by appropriating and extending the Heideggerian contestation of Husserlian intentionality. Hence the distance explicitly taken and loftily proclaimed in regard to ontology, the dismissal of being [*être*], and the concern to avoid any return to the *onto*-theological structure. The critical determinations of this present study, however, have led us to doubt the success of these extraordinary precautions. And if it already appears unsure that the critique of the metaphysics of presence leads to the overcoming of all metaphysics, then it is more doubtful yet that this same critique can serve as a basis—indeed, assurance—for restoring the tension to the "beyond." Lévinas acknowledged the properly metaphysical character of this tension; Jean Greisch, for his part, has had the merit of underlining that Jean-Luc Marion's leap "out of being" cannot get away from having to think its relation (and its debt) to the Platonic *agathon* in its transcendence vis-à-vis the *ousia*.[25] This is all to say that the strategic step back from the transcendental analytic to the appearing [*l'apparaître*] as such (or even

---

[24] Derrida, *La voix et le phénomène. Introduction au problème du signe dans la phénoménologie de Husserl* (Paris: Presses Universitaires de France, 1967); English trans., *Speech and Phenomena* (Evanston, Ill.: Northwestern University Press, 1973), trans. David B. Allison. See also *Le problème de la genèse dans la philosophie de Husserl* (Paris: Presses Universitaires de France, 1990). I am well aware that Derrida's contribution to French phenomenology is not at all limited to these two titles. But the question equally arises whether, and to what extent, this œuvre exceeds phenomenology—a determination which, to be sure, goes beyond the subject matter of this essay.

[25] Jean Greisch, "L'herméneutique dans la phénoménologie comme telle," *Revue de métaphysique et de morale* 1 (1991): 63. This question is, in fact, put to Heideggerian thought across the work of Marion.

to a yet prior givenness) leaves open the difficult question of the relation between phenomenology and metaphysics.

These clarifications and reorientations will amount to something only if the phenomenological project assumes its specificity and autonomy in inscribing itself within a double limitation. The first limitation is, fundamentally, that of a critical and postcritical philosophy of finitude: renouncing metaphysics (as *metaphysica specialis*) to explore experience in its phenomenal limits. The second, more day-to-day, limitation is everything inherent to a methodological attention capable of articulating the transcendental regard in the patient quest of invariants and in the complexity of being-in-the-world.

We have not had any other design than to draw out these several traits and to recall an insurmountable difference: phenomenology and theology make two. To see as much and to understand it better, certainly it is not out of place here to draw attention, finally, to two thoughts equally worthy of being meditated upon in their very divergence. On the theological side, Luther: "Faith consists in giving oneself over to the hold of things we do not see."[26] On the phenomenological side, Gœthe: "There is nothing to look for behind the phenomena; they are themselves the doctrine."[27]

---

[26] Cited by Heidegger, in *Phänomenologie und Theologie*, p. 19. *Translator's note:* See also *Wegmarken*, p. 53, *Pathmarks*, p. 44 (trans. modified).

[27] Cited by Heidegger, *Zur Sache des Denkens*, p. 72; *On Time and Being*, pp. 65–66 (trans. modified).

Part II

Phenomenology and Theology

By Jean-Louis Chrétien, Michel Henry,
Jean-Luc Marion, *and* Paul Ricœur
Edited by Jean-François Courtine
Translation by Jeffrey L. Kosky *and*
Thomas A. Carlson

Translator's Preface:
The Phenomenology of Religion:
New Possibilities for Philosophy
and for Religion

WHEN A BOOK is translated from one language to another, not only does it find a new home in a new language, it also finds itself welcomed, hopefully, by a new audience. Those who have compared any translation with its original know that much is lost in the passage from one language to another; but it is equally obvious that, in the best of cases, the target language is invaluably enriched by the translator's struggle to find appropriate words and phrases to say what can only be said in a foreign tongue. The same is true for the target audience and its discourse. Once a work is translated, its new readers bring new expectations and new demands to the ideas contained in that work. As with the passage from one language to another, this is nothing to hide from or to shrink before; it releases many new meanings, and exposes heretofore unimagined possibilities. What is more important, however, is that the confrontation with a newly translated book can compel its audience to reconfigure their own interpretive frameworks and intellectual horizons. The translated work should be allowed to exercise its own intentions over its new audience in the hope that it will offer not only new perspectives on old questions but perhaps even wholly new questions.

My hope in writing this preface is to help English readers find their way to a place where they might experience the new questions and challenges posed by this book and others from the contributing authors. My task was made easier by the fact that the French edition of the work already had its own introduction, written by Jean-François Courtine, which is translated here. Since

Courtine has outlined the project that unites these thinkers, as well as the central issues involved in determining the relation between phenomenology and theology, I have chosen not to summarize the essays contained here. Instead, I want to suggest the familiar debates and questions of which they might partake, and those unfamiliar that they might incite.

Since its first reception in the middle of the twentieth century, phenomenology has been the single most important force driving French philosophy. While much of philosophical reflection veered toward Marxist criticism in the 1960s and 1970s or literary theory and poststructuralist debates in the 1970s and 1980s, phenomenology alone still staked a claim to a unique terrain for philosophy. Many of the greatest, most well-known philosophers from this period—Emmanuel Lévinas, Maurice Merleau-Ponty, Paul Ricœur, and Jean-Paul Sartre, to name some of the most well known—began their careers with work on Husserl, the founding figure of phenomenology. Even Jacques Derrida's earliest works were confrontations with Husserl; indeed, it was in and through readings of Husserl that Derrida worked out his earliest critiques of metaphysics and presence. Looking at this list of names, therefore, it would not be extravagant to suggest that, throughout the twentieth century, it has been the reception of Husserl that has again and again stimulated and fertilized new advances in French philosophy—even if these authors eventually left phenomenology for Marxist engagement, literary theory, or perhaps more generally the structuralist/poststructuralist debates.

The authors included in this volume (Paul Ricœur, Jean-Louis Chrétien, Jean-Luc Marion, and Michel Henry) participate, to a greater or lesser degree, in a return to phenomenology that has brought it back to the forefront of philosophical debate. Some have even hailed this retrieval of phenomenology as the first viable contender to the dominance of structuralist discourse in philosophy. Like all returns, however, this return enacts a difference. Many previously central phenomenological concepts have been displaced or revised, such that they no longer hold the importance they once had; and conversely, many previously overlooked or marginalized concepts and passages have now assumed central importance. The passages relating to the original impression and affectivity, passive synthesis, and givenness, for instance, have been brought out of the obscurity in which previous interpretation had left them and received lengthy development.

It is as if the return to phenomenology claimed to go back to the idea, or ideal, of phenomenology glimpsed by Husserl, but which had been lost or suppressed by each of its historical manifestations—Husserl's own phenomenology included. As such, many students of phenomenology in English-speaking countries will be troubled by these essays on account of the challenge they pose to historically operative phenomenological principles. Most noticeably, the primacy of the I and the promotion of the horizon are put into question by this phenomenology. That a phenomenon is possible that is not reducible to the I of consciousness; that a phenomenon might give itself absolutely without regard for the anterior condition of a horizon; that there is a mode of phenomenalization that does not happen in ecstatic openness, be it the ecstasy of *Dasein* or of intentionality; that affectivity might underlie constitution and that the first affection might be self-affection— these possibilities are precisely what this phenomenology attempts to establish. Nearly every key concept in phenomenological practice, therefore, finds itself reversed, put into question, or thoroughly revised. It should not be surprising, then, that new readers with a background in phenomenology will find themselves shocked by the version of phenomenology they find here.

In France, this shock was transformed into a debate as to whether this phenomenology is a recovery of or a turning away from Husserl's original insight and the idea of phenomenology. Is this a question of phenomenology pushed to its utmost possibility, or of an abandonment of phenomenology? No doubt, this question will and should be pursued by its English-speaking audience as well. Without making a decision about matters that should be debated elsewhere and at greater length, I want to point out that this phenomenology and its definition of phenomenon are, at the very least, worked out through a reading of Husserl's text. The texts to support these claims do exist in Husserl, and readers can consult a growing bibliography of works in which they are cited, interpreted, and commented on. Of the authors collected here, Jean-Luc Marion and Michel Henry have done the most to articulate the concepts belonging to this version of phenomenology;

in a sense, they are its theoreticians, developing a new phenomenological vision through careful interpretations of Husserl's texts.[1]
The readings they develop are precise and very close, so close that
at times they follow threads admitted but not pursued by Husserl
in the course of his own phenomenological analyses. It is often a
matter of making advances in possibilities that Husserl glimpsed
but before which he recoiled. Any decision about the phenomenological status of these analyses must be supported by equally
close readings of Husserl and decisions about the idea of phenomenology.

At the same time, this is a book about theology—as its title indicates. As such, its publication in English joins a growing list
of work concerned with religion and religious issues. Across all
the humanistic disciplines of the English-speaking academies,
throughout the print and televisual media, and in major represen-
tatives of artistic and literary culture, a renewed interest in
thinking about, discussing, and seeking out religion and the significance of religious themes can easily be tracked. While the academic interest in religion has no doubt been supported by and
manifested in the creation of religious studies departments in
major institutions of higher learning, it has also impacted departments of literature and philosophy, and influenced the research of
students of cultural studies throughout the academy. The translation of this book clearly both reflects and contributes to this
growing interest in religion.

One of the most popular methods or movements among students of religion has been the phenomenology of religion. This

---

[1] For a thorough appreciation of this phenomenological vision and its articulation in and through the reading of Husserl, see works by each of these authors.
For example, Michel Henry, *L'essence de la manifestation* (Paris: P.U.F., 1963),
English trans., *The Essence of Manifestation* (The Hague: Nijhoff, 1973), trans.
Girard Etzkorn; and *Phénoménologie matérielle* (Paris: P.U.F., 1990). The latter
work represents a more accessible articulation of Henry's vision of phenomenology and is notable for its close and careful readings of Husserl, indicating precisely where the author believes Husserl himself turned away from the idea of
phenomenology. See also Jean-Luc Marion, *Réduction et donation* (Paris: P.U.F.,
1989), English trans., *Reduction and Givenness: Investigations of Husserl, Heidegger,
and Phenomenology* (Evanston, Ill.: Northwestern University Press, 1998), trans.
Thomas A. Carlson; and *Etant donnée. Essai d'une phénoménologie de la donation*
(Paris: P.U.F., 1997).

branch of the academic study of religion was made popular in America by Mircea Eliade, though it has predecessors in the work of Gerardus van der Leeuw and others. In brief, for the American proponents of the phenomenology of religion, religious phenomena are to be described as they appear to the believers themselves. This phenomenology of religion assumes the position of the believer so as to describe the meaning of the religious acts in which he participates and the religious experience that he undergoes. It is, in short, the classic example of a hermeneutics of belief or recovery. In contrast to the suspicious discourse often adopted by students and scholars who assume a psychological or sociological perspective, the proponents of phenomenology of religion assume that the believer himself is capable of offering an account of the acts and experiences that engage him, that he alone knows their true meaning.

Since being adopted in America, however, the phenomenology of religion has foundered and no longer enjoys the popularity it once had. Several reasons have been responsible for this decline. First of all, Eliade and his followers were often criticized for being so-called theologians of the sacred, that is to say, they were faulted for not having assumed a critical standpoint that sought to explain religious phenomena, choosing instead to speak of the sacred (no longer the God of Western religion) as a real and irreducible event. According to the critics, this meant that the phenomenology of religion belonged less to the academy and its critical discourse than it did to the growing number of temples and cults meant to satisfy the spiritual quest of a growing number of seekers. A second, related reason also accounts for why the phenomenology of religion was gradually pushed out of favor in university settings. Quite simply, it lacked the ability to critically examine the foundations of its method. It was unable to justify its naïve acceptance of the believer's own account of religious phenomena, and its drift toward empiricism meant that it could not treat problems in the study of religion beyond a mere description of what it could only point to. Consequently, the phenomenology of religion became something like an anthropological typology, creating categories into which it placed various religious phenomena. What this phenomenology of religion could not address were fundamental questions, questions pertaining to its very possibility, questions such as: What is religion? What justifies assuming the various phenomena described under the heading Religion, a category that was created by and large by Western scholarship of the nineteenth century? How is it possible or what method makes it possible to describe phenomena as they appear to the *homo religiosus*, the religious phenomena as such?

Students of religion will therefore find themselves attracted to this work that seems to bring together phenomenology and religion and will at the same time will be surprised by what they find in it. "Surprised" because the phenomenology operative here mobilizes vocabulary, concepts, and methodological procedures that are absent from what they have been accustomed to expect from a phenomenology of religion. Here they will find a phenomenology of religion that is aware of itself as phenomenology and that has elaborated the concepts that make it possible to address the very foundation of a phenomenology of religion. In the essays by Henry and Marion, readers will discover critical reexaminations of the principles of phenomenology and of the meaning of phenomenality such that a religious phenomena might appear within the rigorous framework of a phenomenology. In the essays by Ricœur and Chrétien, in contrast, readers will find descriptions of religious phenomena (respectively, the Scriptures and prayer) that they might recognize as phenomenological. In short, here they will find a group of philosophers (and isn't it strange that philosophers should here be joining the American phenomenologists of religion!) who share their passion for a phenomenological description of religion and who are at the same time concerned about the very thing that adherents to the American phenomenology of religion have been unable to address, namely, establishing the possibility of a phenomenology.

This project, philosophically establishing the possibility of a phenomenology of religion, has raised its own set of questions and concerns. In fact, the relation between phenomenology and theology—a relation left undecided by a title, *Phenomenology and Theology*, which merely juxtaposes them—has been the subject of intense debate, even polemic, in French philosophical circles of the 1980s and 1990s. Are they two distinct, separate terms? If not, how are they connected? Does one exert a primacy over the other, determining it and guiding its discourse? Which one? Is this primacy conceptual or historical? And what is the significance of such a primacy for practitioners or devotees of each?

These authors all suggest that the phenomenology of religion belongs within philosophy, not within theology. As Courtine indicates in his introduction, they all claim to practice a philosophy of religion. Now, the philosophy of religion has classically confronted a seemingly unavoidable dilemma: Either philosophy constitutes religious phenomena and so has objects to study but thereby loses sight of what is specifically religious about such phenomena. Or it maintains the religious character of phenomena (their absoluteness, their unconditionality, in short, their claim to be irreducible to human constructions), but thereby is without objects, leaving religious phenomena to silence or unintelligibility—that is, to faith. In a direct challenge to these unsatisfactory alternatives, this book is premised on the idea that philosophical discourse can admit and describe religious phenomena through the discovery of a new phenomenological principle or a new mode of phenomenality. That is to say, a phenomenology that rejects the anterior condition of a horizon and that challenges the primacy of the I and its intentionality—more specifically, a phenomenology of *donation* (givenness) or a phenomenology of life—is able to describe religious phenomena without sacrificing their claim to absoluteness and irreducibility. In short, religion becomes admissible in philosophical discussion.

From a different perspective, it can also be said that for the authors of this volume the religious phenomenon represents a trial for phenomenology: more than posing a question *for* phenomenology, it poses the question *of* phenomenology itself—of its limits and the criteria it uses to determine phenomenality. The religious phenomenon marks a limit beyond which previous phenomenology had feared to tread, and consideration of the form of phenomenality claimed by the religious phenomenon points out the inadequacy of previous determinations of phenomenality. The religious phenomenon is not constituted and so is not susceptible to the criteria of objectivity. If nevertheless the religious phenomenon is to appear, as it certainly has been claimed, then phenomenology is compelled to admit a new determination of what it means to appear. Thus, passing through the crisis or trial posed by the religious phenomenon, phenomenology emerges in a new form. Whether or not the new form of phenomenology, a phenomenology open to other modes of phenomenality, betrays the idea of phenomenology or leads phenomenology back to its fundamental insight and guiding principle, is a question that can and should be asked by future students of phenomenology—as it has already been asked by these authors.

To help focus and encourage future discussion, I would like to outline four points that seem essential for the debate about the phenomenology of religion proposed here. These questions are meant to guide future discussion about method and principles, but also seem essential to the actual practice of the phenomenology of religion.

1. *Does this phenomenology of religion remain true to the phenomenological principle that philosophy is deployed in immanence?* For Husserl, the reduction was the royal road to the beginnings of a new philosophy because it eliminated the source of all doubt, uncertainty, and illusion by suspending all transcendence. Phenomenality could be defined broadly as the appearing that remains in and for consciousness when all ecstatic openness to transcendence has been shut down or closed by the reduction. It is, in short, the field of immanence. As such, any phenomenology of religion, if it is to respect the criterion of phenomenality and merit the name philosophy, must be deployed in the field of immanence.

It might be imagined, then, that the reduction would put phenomenology in an irresolvable conflict with religion. The phenomenological respect for immanence would oppose the religious claim of a given transcending the constituting I or the religious acceptance of the phenomenon as absolute, unconditioned, having its own meaning. In particular, the phenomenality of God would be forbidden, or at least subject to reduction, insofar as it reestablishes a transcendence subject to the reduction.

Readers will have to judge for themselves whether or not the essays collected here fall prey to this abandonment of immanence. I would like to suggest, however, that the mention of God and transcendence is not enough to indicate that the principle of immanence is not being respected. Might it be that the meaning of God or transcendence is recovered precisely through the reduction and a radically immanent analysis? This certainly was the case for the founding figure of modern philosophy, Descartes, when he discovered a God beyond the *I* and the *cogito* in and through the reflective analysis of the idea of infinity in him. Nothing prevents it from being the case here, too. Likewise, it has been the case for theological figures such as Augustine, others in the Augustinian tradition, and especially the mystics that God is not found by transcendence toward things, but by an inward turn that leads to a God more deeply within than I myself am according to the figure of the *Intus Deus altus est* (*Hom. on Psalms*, 130.12) and *interior intimo meo* (*Confessions* 3.11). The immanence described by these phrases would merit careful phenomenological consideration, and a comparison between it and the immanence of consciousness promises to be a fruitful research.

Finally, one should not let the historical construction of the philosophy of religion as a discipline lead one to assume that transcendence is absolutely foreign to it. If one had to pinpoint a time when the meaning of transcendence was thrown out of philosophy, it would have to be in the nineteenth-century philosophy of religion starting from Kant and running through Hegel to Nietzsche. This short history was worked out within a set of boundaries: either philosophy operates within the limits of phenomenal immanence and a transcendent God is wholly consigned to faith (Kant) or else philosophy steps beyond these limits to include God within the field of a now extended immanence (Hegel), with the eventual result that God is no longer God (Nietzsche). The challenge posed to the phenomenology of religion, then, is to overcome the nineteenth-century figure of philosophy that banished transcendence and at the same time to respect the principle that philosophy be deployed in immanence. That is to say, it is to recover the meaning of transcendence in immanence—a project that certainly was ever in the background of Husserl's own work.

2. *Is knowing or the constituting ego all there is to subjectivity?* For appearing to give phenomena, the reduction must lead back not infinitely but to a term. In Husserl, this term was consciousness, and ultimately the *ego* whose constitutive activity made phenomena appear. Phenomena therefore appear within the limits of what can be experienced by an *ego* or I. These limits include the horizon of the past and future lived experiences of this I, as well as

the finitude of human intuition. In general, if every phenomenon is to be reduced to the constituting I or *ego*, then absolute, irreducible, or unconditional phenomena are excluded at the very outset. Since this is precisely what the religious phenomenon claims, it would seem that the religious phenomenon cannot appear—unless there is more to subjectivity than the *ego* or the constituting I.

The phenomenology operative in the phenomenology of religion, therefore, demands a new understanding of subjectivity. In contrast to Husserl's focus on the active, constitutive role played by the *ego*, this phenomenology probes radically passive levels of subjectivity. The primacy of the *ego*'s intentional activity is challenged in favor of an analysis of passive states, that is, the subject's nonintentional immanence (the autoaffectivity of life or the body in Henry) or a reversed intentionality where the *ego* finds itself subject *to*, not the subject *of*, a gaze (the givenness of saturated phenomena in Marion). The I no longer precedes the phenomena that it constitutes, but is instead called into being or born as the one who receives or suffers this intentionality. As called into being by what precedes it, the I always misses the present of the given that therefore happens in an immemorial oblivion (a point developed at length by Chrétien[2]). Whether or not a new understanding of subjectivity can be developed phenomenologically therefore seems essential to the future elaboration of a phenomenology of religion. And inversely, the consideration of religious phenomena seems to lead to new possibilities for probing the depths of subjectivity.

3. *What distinguishes the phenomenology of religion from theology?* Each of the authors collected here is careful to emphasize that what he is doing is phenomenology and not theology. In Marion, for instance, the first examples of saturated phenomena are aesthetic (a painting or Kant's sublime) and philosophical (Plato's Good beyond Being and Descartes's idea of infinity). The properly religious phenomena of revelation, theophany, comes up only as one phenomenon in a list that includes these others. Mari-

---

[2] The notion of the Immemorial, though operative in many of these authors, is developed at length in Jean-Louis Chrétien, *L'inoubliable et l'inespéré* (Paris: Desclée de Brouwer, 1991).

on's discussion of revelation therefore belongs not to properly theological considerations but to considerations of the various modes of phenomenality, in particular the phenomenality of saturation. With regard to the essay that is most indicative of a phenomenology in practice, that is, Chrétien's essay, on what basis can it be accused of a theological drift? Is it theological because it cites recognized theologians? Is it theological because it is describing the experience of prayer? It needs to be emphasized that this essay puts forward no doctrine or pronouncement about the existence, the essence, or the attributes of God. Instead, the essay claims to be a description of the lived experience of prayer, an experience that is perhaps not shared by everyone but that is nonetheless testified in certain cases. It thus takes up the challenge posed to philosophical discussion by the particularly difficult phenomena of religion.

In other texts, Marion has put forward distinctions that help clarify the relation of phenomenology and theology. In determining this relationship, a clear distinction must be made between two theologies: a philosophical theology and a revealed theology. The first would be a branch of special metaphysics or the science that considers God in terms of real transcendence, causality, and substance; it is where the arguments for the existence of God are made. With its supposition of transcendence and its positing of existence, this theology is clearly subject to phenomenological critique, and any evidence that it is still operative would disqualify the phenomenological status of these considerations. Revealed theology, on the other hand, is based on given facts, on appearances and manifestations described in the Scriptures, which come up within the field of phenomena and have their own way of phenomenalizing themselves. Considered strictly as such, the phenomena of revealed theology could not *not* be an issue for phenomenology.[3] In fact, Marion argues, they pose the question of phenomenology itself —of its limits and its principles. Husserl's "principle of all principles" claims that everything offered in intu-

---

[3] See Jean-Luc Marion, "The Other First Philosophy and the Question of Donation," *Critical Inquiry* 25, no. 4 (1999). On this point, one can also consult an earlier article, "Metaphysics and Phenomenology: A Relief for Theology," *Critical Inquiry* 20, no. 4 (1994), where Marion's position is articulated in slightly different terms.

ition has the right to be taken as it gives itself (*Ideas*, §24); its Heideggerian revision claims that "phenomenon" is to be understood as what gives itself from itself (*Being and Time*, §7). To reject the religious phenomenon's claim to appear would therefore be something highly contrary to the principles of phenomenology, seeing as these principles mean to extend the right to appear to all that claims to appear. Stated positively, insofar as revealed theology, the Scriptures, claims to describe certain appearings and manifestations, theophanies, it belongs within phenomenology.

4. *What is the relation of the phenomenology of religion to historical religions and culture?* While most of the polemic surrounding this phenomenology of religion has centered on the claim that a theological agenda or prior determination by theology betrays its phenomenological status, an entirely different set of questions concerns the relation between this phenomenology of religion and actual historical religions. In Paul Ricœur's contribution, Ricœur suggests that the religion or religious phenomena elaborated by this phenomenology in fact cannot be found in any historical actualizations. Like language, religion is realized only in different historical and particular acts, and phenomenology is essentially a gaze on essences or the general. As such, for Ricœur, the description of religion calls not so much for a phenomenology as for a hermeneutic that can interpret the texts and practices of different particular religions.

Without denying Ricœur's claims, I would like to suggest that we understand this according to distinctions made by Jean-Luc Marion and Jacques Derrida.[4] What phenomenology can attest to is a possible religion, never a historically actual religion. The "possibility of religion" here does not mean the conditions for the possibility of an actual religion or a possibility that would then become actual, but religion considered as a possibility, purely as possible. The possibility of religion would be subject to phenomenological description, but for the description of actual religion

---

[4] See, first, Jacques Derrida, "Donner la mort," in *L'éthique du don. Jacques Derrida et la pensée du don* (Paris, 1992), ed. Jean-Marie Rabaté and Michael Wetzel, esp. pp. 52–53; English trans., *The Gift of Death* (Chicago: University of Chicago Press, 1995), trans. David Wills, esp. p. 49. Also see Jean-Luc Marion's reference to Derrida's position in "Metaphysics and Phenomenology: A Relief for Theology," *Critical Inquiry* 20, no. 4 (1994): 590.

one would follow Ricœur and have recourse to a textual herme-neutic, perhaps along lines exemplified here by Chrétien.

This is by no means to denigrate the accomplishment of this phenomenology, but it does open another set of questions about the relation between phenomenology and historical religions. Everything seems to happen as if phenomenological analysis of the subject—be it the subject of the call or the subject of autoaffection—were enough to open religion as a pure possibility. The possibility of religion thus seems wholly divorced from the events of revelation, and phenomenology, without the authority of religious tradition, could recover the significance of religious notions. But one might well wonder if this notion of the subject was already produced by a historical religious tradition such that its phenomenology produces, in a circular fashion, a possible religion that repeats an actual, historic religion. That is to say, is the figure of the phenomenological subject transmitted as part of a historical inheritance, and can historical research into religious traditions establish this? I suspect that some or much of future scholarship in religion and continental philosophy will investigate these matters more fully.

Finally, at this time, the newly revived phenomenology of religion has, to my knowledge, considered only religious phenomena belonging to Western religious traditions. In the American context in which it is now being received, it seems inevitable that one will address its relevance to the religious phenomena of other traditions. Can this phenomenology be part of a comparative study of religion, and can it help expose the intelligibility of religious phenomena belonging to the experience of Eastern religious traditions? To fail in this task would not necessarily be grounds for blame or criticism. It might, however, point out the limits of this phenomenology.

The success of any work cannot always be measured by the degree to which it has fulfilled its stated or unstated intentions. It remains for the recipients to testify to the value of a work, not so much by their critical appraisal or trenchant critique as by what they are able to do in the wake of having received it. From this perspective, the success of this volume will be to have made religion and the divine a question for philosophy, to have created a space within philosophical discourse where religious phenomena can be discussed. This success was already witnessed, no doubt, in the intense polemic leading to and resulting from the publication of this book in France, and it has continued to be registered in the many subsequent works of philosophy that have taken up the challenge of a phenomenology of religion. Whether or not one sees this as a wrong turn unfortunately taken by philosophy or as a next step toward the genuine idea of philosophy, it cannot be denied that religious phenomena have assumed a place in current philosophical investigation—and this marks the achievement, whose value is still being debated, of the present work.

To conclude, I'd like to add a few words of thanks, words that perhaps belong at the beginning since they acknowledge something without which beginning would be impossible. The idea for this translation came to me through Jack Caputo, who has an admirable eye for spotting works that deserve attention and an admirable skill for seeing that they receive it. I thank him for entrusting me with a task whose importance to him was clear from the beginning. Thanks of a different sort are also due to a friend who is more than a friend, Stephanie Hodde, whose presence in my life during times of loss and separation and absence tells me where my home is to be found.

Jeffrey L. Kosky
July 1999
Chicago, Illinois

Introduction:
Phenomenology and
Hermeneutics of Religion

THIS TITLE captures the theme of the seminar conducted at the "Centre de recherches phénoménologiques et herméneutiques—Archives Husserl de Paris" during the two academic years 1990–1991 and 1991–1992. The contributions collected in this volume, if they can be said to close this cycle of studies,[1] obviously do not mean to propose something like a conclusion; this would be even more improbable here than in any other question. This is also why this short introduction does not pretend to be some sort of definitive assessment. It is instead an attempt to elucidate certain motifs within the collective seminar in the form of some preliminary remarks.

In setting this general theme for the seminar, we did not want merely to enlarge or to renew the field of investigation for works that march under the banner of phenomenology and are still open to its inspiration. This field admits expansion and renewal thanks to the diversity of its agents and its orientations and by integrating as completely as possible the criticisms or the crises that could befall it historically and systematically, and from which it continually draws nourishment. For these criticisms arise from within the "movement"—either by plumbing the depths of this or that theme or guiding concept, in and through a more precise assessment of some inaugural decision, or by reinscribing it in a more general metaphysical context—or else they come from without, from the confrontation with some domain of objects or givens of experience.

In any case, what in general appeared interesting or worthy of

---

[1] Within the framework of a daylong series of studies organized at the École normale supérieure, 15 May 1992.

question to the researchers at the Center—whether it concerned, as it did some years ago, the examination of the work of art and its specific mode of Being or, more recently, the investigation of subjectivity, of the intersubjective alteration, or even of the melancholic or in general "pathologically" affected subjectivity[2]—was to lead phenomenology to its limit or to confront it with limit phenomena, ones able to serve as touchstones for assessing the pertinence and the rigor of phenomenology's fundamental principles and the methodic procedures that constitute it. In a word, it still and always was a matter of leading phenomenology back to the idea of its possibility, in accordance with Heidegger's celebrated directive in *Sein und Zeit*: "Higher than actuality stands possibility. We can understand phenomenology only by seizing upon it as a possibility." The same was true when we approached the order of "religious" phenomena, by examining at one and the same time how Husserl, in the esoteric or thematic movement of his own thought, determined the idea of God as entelechy and how the philosophy of religion was able to appropriate phenomenological and hermeneutic orientations.[3]

The first guiding question that supported the choice of this theme (still stated in a provisional and insufficient way) could be formulated thus: Can phenomenology, in a specific way, that is to say, at the apex of its possibility—if it is still an issue of its possibility—treat religion? And what does "religion" signify here? Roughly put, we were aiming at an order of phenomena characterized by a unique modality of appearing or a determinate type of givenness (the "sacred," "God," the "gods," whether they be considered dead or in flight). Or, to pose the question in another way: Is there, in religious experience, a specific form of phenomenality, of appearance or epiphanic arising, that can affect phenomenology itself in its project, its aim, its fundamental concepts, indeed its very methods? Is there, more generally, some part of

---

[2] See the volume *Figures de la subjectivité* (Paris: CNRS, 1992), ed. J.-F. Courtine.

[3] Taking into account as rigorously as possible what Heidegger thematized as methodic or principled "a-theism" in all phenomenology. In the "*Natorpbericht*," he clearly noted in 1922: "Atheistic here means: freed from all preoccupation and any temptation to speak simply of religiosity. The very idea of philosophy of religion, especially if it does not let the facticity of man enter into consideration—is it not pure nonsense?"

the phenomenal that leads to or compels redefining phenomenology's task, which was presented in these terms in Husserl's *Krisis*: "To carefully examine the how of the appearing of a thing in its actual and possible alterations and to pay consistent attention to the correlation it involves between *appearing* and *that which appears as such*." It is this discovery of a "universal a priori of correlation between experienced object and manners of givenness"—which Husserl says he discovered while working on the *Logische Untersuchungen*—that constituted phenomenology's "breakthrough": "My whole subsequent life-work has been dominated by the task of systematically elaborating on this a priori of correlation."[4]

Our initial question can therefore be reformulated more rigorously in these terms: Is there an order of phenomena, a type of appearance, and a determinate "manner" of appearing that can put into question or crisis this correlational a priori? Or, if not, and at the very least, is there an "object" whose modes of being given and appearing would disturb the classic phenomenological procedure? If this is the case, as we will see, the "phenomenology of religion" might not be simply an ontic, regional science toward which one would be free to "turn" or not. Rather, it would affect the central aim of phenomenology itself, considered in terms of its own task and style.

In terms of what idea, experience or, better, ordeal of truth do we assess or interrogate the "evidence" of the religious phenomenon thus apprehended in its greatest generality possible? At the very least, we can say: Beyond the evidence of the intended as such—"I can simply look at that which is *intended as such* and grasp it absolutely. There is no evidence that could ever be superior to this," Husserl declared in the sketch that serves as preface to the 1913 edition of the *Logische Untersuchungen*. At the same time, he reminded us of the fundamental necessity that phenomenology "give that which is clearly seen its due as that which is originary" and also emphasized that it is "the return to seeing which both ultimately clarifies and fulfills," at least officially (Preface to *Logische Untersuchungen*).[5]

There is no doubt but that it is now necessary to address a first

---

[4] *Krisis* [English trans., p. 165; 166 n.].

[5] Preface to the 1913 edition of *Logische Untersuchungen* [English trans., p. 24].

question, which has the form of an objection, and to add some needed clarification. It will be asked: Concretely, to what experience do you refer here? Once again to the experience (plural, multiform, essentially heterogeneous, no doubt theological and atheological) of the divine, of the passage of the god (that is to say, negatively, of the retreat, disenchantment, flight, of the *Entgötterung*), indeed to "aesthetic," "cultural" experiences or to prayer, even praise—however extraordinary (indeed fantastic, phantasmagoric) these experiences might be, seen here only with regard to their possibility. A cardinal experience, in a Christian milieu and according to a dominant tradition, would naturally be that of the Disciples, or of the Apostles when faced with the appearance of Christ, or, better, of God in Christ. But the relation to the Other or to the world (θεωρία) could be thought of as its vehicle, since of such an experience there is *on principle* no paradigm.

The second question, in the background of our work during these two years, could thus be stated in the form of an alternative: To what degree does the philosophy of religion, when it appears historically, and in fact after a long delay,[6] repeat an old and influential undertaking: namely, natural theology; and does it obey a structural constraint not expressly recognized as such, but which can be called, to come quickly to the point, the onto–theological constitution of metaphysics? What, then, is it that boils down to natural theology in the form of philosophy of religion?—The other hypothesis would be that the philosophy of religion constitutes a decisive element in the destruction (deconstruction) of onto-theology, owing to the possible resurgence of a more ancient thematic of the φαίνειν which phenomenology would recall forgetfully.

Within such a perspective, it seems opportune, indeed necessary, to bring about a more direct confrontation between phenomenology and the philosophy of religion, such as it was widely deployed in the nineteenth century, with and starting from the Hegelian completion of metaphysics. This can be done by examining how, in Hegel and Schelling, the key concepts of all

---

[6] Cf. K. Feiereis, *Die Umprägung der natürlichen Theologie in Religionsphilosophie. Ein Beitrag zur deutschen Geistesgeschichte des 18. Jahrhunderts* (Leipzig, 1965).

philosophy of religion (phenomenon, manifestation, revelation), concepts that phenomenological reflection is obliged to pass through, are determined in contrasting ways.

Naturally, it is on principle difficult to move between corpuses, landscapes as different and clashing as those of German idealism (dialectic and speculative) and those of phenomenology, whether it be Husserl himself, the phenomenological movement, or the phenomenological dissent. In any case, one must first of all be on guard against any hasty assimilation or rapprochement and be content most often with homologies or analogies. But, it seemed to us, that with philosophy of religion on the one hand and phenomenology of religion on the other, the confrontation (call it a structural one) could prove to be fruitful. That is, the questions could be elaborated according to the lead provided by a comparative perspective on the Hegelian (metaphysical, onto-theological) project in the *Lectures on the Philosophy of Religion*, the later Schelling, centering on the diptych (philosophy of mythology—philosophy of revelation), and finally the possibility and the principal difficulties of a phenomenology of religion (within a Husserlian horizon). These questions could be formulated in this way: (1) To what degree does the philosophy of religion (in the wake of Kant, according to the redistribution of the transcendental dialectic[7]) remain the vehicle for *theologia naturalis*? (2) To what degree does a renewed critical study of the order of religious phenomena (one independent of dogmatics or religious philosophy, as well as of the claim to constitute a Christian philosophy) open the space for a new approach to phenomenality, susceptible of overturning a classically metaphysical (onto-theological) edifice or balance? (3) Finally, how can phenomenology, envisioned in its possibility, profit from this confrontation, according to whether it is oriented toward absolute idealism (this is the slippery slope traveled by Husserl, according to R. Boehm)[8] or keeps a meaning—by running the perhaps permanent risk of "mysticology" or "theosophy"—for Schellingian positivity, in other words, for factuality, within the framework of a higher empiricism?

---

[7] Transcendental dialectic, final section of chap. 2 ("Critique of All Speculative Theology Based upon Speculative Principles of Reason").

[8] R. Boehm, *Vom Gesichtspunkt der Phänomenologie* (The Hague: Nijhoff, 1968), pp. 18ff.

It is no doubt important to emphasize, as Stanislas Breton has done in a suggestive study[9], that the fundamental aim of phenomenology and its principle, the principle of the absence of presuppositions—conveyed in the *Ideen* of 1913 by the principle of principles, regulated by the ideal of a complete *donation* that would adequately fulfill an intention or a signification—in reality refers to the more ancient experience of hierophanies or theophanies for which phenomenology would harbor a secret nostalgia when it dreams of a "return to the things themselves," such as they appear in truth. Up until its penultimate Heideggerian transformation, phenomenology let itself be fascinated by a Greek experience that lifts the opposition of appearance and appearing, and thanks to which the thing ends up perfectly coinciding with the light of its manifestation, in a total presence, excluding all mediation. But one may immediately add, by reversing the consequence from an obvious rapprochement to a critical point, that the aforementioned theophany can equally permit one to make phenomenologically evident the essential connection that unites appearing to spatiality and to temporality, to historicity, and in general to the "passage"—that is to say, in a word, to the conditions of the sensible and of sensibilization. If the appearing of the god could be the precise figure of phenomenalization κατ ἐξοχήν, when the face of Heaven—void of attributes—has ceased to veil some unknown god, it could still be reserved for a phenomenology of the inapparent to explore the Nameless through mediations, caesurae, divisions, and disseminations—no doubt at the risk of blurring the difference of the horizon or the backdrop against which figure, face, image, or icon would appear or come detached, indeed of striking out the difference between Being and beings, between the object and the clearing (*Lichtung*).

JEAN-FRANÇOIS COURTINE

---

[9] "Révélation, médiation, manifestation," in *Manifestation et révélation*, Institut Catholique de Paris, fasc. I (Paris: Institut Catholique de Paris, 1976), pp. 41ff.

6

Experience and Language in Religious Discourse

Paul Ricœur

THE DIFFICULTIES THAT CONFRONT A PHENOMENOLOGY OF RELIGION

TO BEGIN WITH, I would like to examine what seem to me to be the difficulties that confront a phenomenology of religion, by which I mean the religious phenomenon grasped in its historical and geographical universality.[1]

The most serious difficulties are not those that could be associated with the theme of intentionality, on the pretext that intentionality would forever be a tributary of representation, therefore of objectivization, therefore of the subject's claim to mastery over the meaning of its experience. Feelings and dispositions that can be called "religious" do indeed exist, and they can transgress the sway of representation and, in this sense, mark the subject's being overthrown from its ascendancy in the realm of meaning. Names have been given to these feelings: the feeling of absolute dependence (Schleiermacher); the feeling of utter confidence, in spite of everything, in spite of suffering and evil (Barth and Bultmann); the feeling of ultimate concern (Paul Tillich); the feeling of belonging to an economy of the gift, with its logic of overabundance, irreducible to the logic of equivalence, as I suggest in my essay *Amour et justice**; the feeling of being preceded

---

[1] This text was presented for the first time within the framework of an international colloquium organized in January 1992 by the Philosophy Faculty of the Institut catholique de Paris.

* *Translator's note*: English translation as "Love and Justice." In *Figuring the Sacred* (Minneapolis: Fortress Press, 1995), trans. David Pellauer, pp. 315–29.

in the order of speech, love, and existence (Rosenzweig). These are so many absolute feelings, ab-solute, in the sense of detached from the relation by which the subject would preserve its mastery over the object called religious, over the meaning of this presumed object. These feelings, consisting in ways of being absolutely affected, are test cases that bear witness to phenomenology's inability to open the intentionality of consciousness onto something completely other. To these feelings and these absolute affections correspond fundamental dispositions that can be placed under the general heading "prayer" and that range from complaints to praise, passing through supplication and demands. Prayer actively turns toward this Other by which consciousness is affected on the level of feeling. In return, this Other who affects it is apperceived as the source of the call to which the prayer responds.

No doubt, a phenomenology can propose to describe this structure (of call and response), one that seems to organize the feelings as well as the dispositions, in terms of its most universally widespread characteristics. Such a phenomenology would have as its essential task distinguishing the structure call/response from the relation question/response in light of the equivocity clinging to the term *response* common to both pairs of correlative terms. Just as the relation question/response implies, as Gadamer following Collingwood reminds us, a *prior* field of common understanding, so too does the relation call/response serve to engender the common field through obedience, on the level of absolute feeling, and through invocation, on the level of the disposition prayer. Here is where the difference between the response to a question and the response to a call shows up. The first must be understood as the resolution of a problem, thereby establishing a close correlation between the singularity of a problematic situation and the singularity of a resolution. (Granger calls this correlation between two singularities, a correlation that is itself singular, "style.")

From this sort of correlation between the problematic situation and the resolution of the problem, it is important to distinguish the relation between response and call. It should not be said, for example, that religious faith and theology offer responses to the questions posed but not resolved by scientific or philosophical knowing. Such a way of understanding the religious idea of response—be it in its arrogant and triumphant posture or in the apparently modest, indeed ashamed, posture of a stopgap faith, in the sense denounced by Bonhoeffer—rests on a misunderstanding of the cardinal difference that distinguishes the epistemological relation between question and response from the specifically religious relation between call and response. The religious response is obedient, in the strong sense of an "I hear" where the superiority of the call—by which we mean its position as Most High—is recognized, avowed, confessed.

I therefore grant unreservedly that there can be a phenomenology of feelings and dispositions that can be qualified as religious by virtue of the disproportion within the relation between call and response. This phenomenology would not be merely descriptive but critical, as I just suggested.

The difficulty to which I would like to devote this study does not, therefore, concern the obstacle that the constitution of intentionality, of the intentional consciousness, would pose in the degree to which it is not suitable for actually breaking the circle that consciousness forms with itself under the sway of representation and representative objectivity. And if one takes intentionality to be the prisoner of representation, then one would have to say that the feelings and dispositions evoked above mark the beyond of the intentionality imprisoned by its representative limit.

The biggest difficulty according to which a phenomenology of religion must be assessed lies elsewhere. It concerns the status of *immediacy* that could be claimed by the dispositions and feelings allied with the call-and-response structure in a religious order. If it were only a matter of taking into account the *linguistic* mediation without which feelings and dispositions, left in silence, would remain unformed, the difficulty would be minor, and not much of a rebuttal would be required. It has been a long time now since phenomenology stopped considering language as an "unproductive" layer superimposed on the properly eidetic layer of lived experiences, be they feelings or dispositions. Just as one cannot deny that in the absence of the above-named fundamental feelings, there is no occasion to speak of religion, so too one must hasten to concede that one cannot advance very far in the description of these feelings and dispositions without taking into account the verbal expressions that have given them form. The short enumeration of feelings that I just broached evokes the *Sitz-im-Leben* of a religious culture, subtly but precisely dated, whether it be romantic, post-Hegelian, post-Nietzschean, or other. As for the dispositions adjoining these basic feelings, they take form only as they are conveyed by determinate discursive acts, which themselves fall within a precise typology. I alluded to such a typology of linguistic acts when I earlier evoked the spectrum that prayer encompasses between complaint and praise, passing through supplication and demands.

These last remarks lead us to the threshold of the most significant difficulty that a phenomenology of religion must confront: to the *linguistic* mediation a *cultural* and *historical* mediation is added, of which the former is a mere reflection. To speak of "linguistic mediation" is already to summon up the grand edifices of speech and writing that have structured the memory of events, words, and personalities—all equally endowed with a founding value. To put it briefly: religion is like language itself, which is realized only in different tongues. The comparison can be pushed farther, to the degree that the difference between religions duplicates that of different tongues, sometimes fixing and consolidating it, if it does not serve to establish it. This weighty fact condemns phenomenology to run the gauntlet of a hermeneutic and more precisely of a *textual* or *scriptural* hermeneutic.

It is by deliberate choice that I just used the word "condemns" and that I speak of phenomenology's passage to the stage of a hermeneutic as "running the gauntlet." For the fragmentation of textual collections and scriptural traditions makes it such that the continent of the religious stands out like a detached archipelago, where one cannot locate anywhere the universality of the religious phenomenon. This state of affairs is easy to observe: the fundamental feelings and dispositions evoked above are nowhere visible in their naked immediacy, but are always already interpreted according to the canonic rules of reading and writing. We cannot even be sure that the universal character of the structure call/response can be attested independently of the different historical actualizations in which this structure is incarnated. If one persists in the task of stripping away, one will soon see that it is each time in a different way and with a different signification that what we above called obedience to the Most High is felt and practiced. Height: immanent or transcendent? Anonymous or personal? Obedience passively submitted to or actively missionary? Solitary or communal?

From this uncomfortable situation, I draw a series of consequences. The first is that we must renounce the idea of creating a phenomenology of the religious phenomenon taken in its indivisible universality, and that we must be content, at the outset, with tracing the broad hermeneutic strands of just one religion. This is why in the analysis that follows I have chosen to confine myself within the limits of the Jewish and Christian Scriptures. That being said, the listener is not being asked to adhere explicitly to the convictions proper to the Jewish or Christian use of the terms Word★ and Scriptures, but to assume them in the imagination and with sympathy, in a way compatible with the suspension of believing engagement. This suspension, and the descriptive tone that results from it, makes the hermeneutic such that it still deserves to be called "phenomenological," even though it cannot occupy the place of a phenomenology of religion in general.

Second consequence: the internal hermeneutic of a particular religion can approach equality with a universal phenomenology of the religious phenomenon only with the help of a second extension, organized by a process of analogizing transfer, progressing one step at a time, starting from the place where one stands at the outset. I oppose this procedure to that of the comparative history of religions, which presupposes—ideally at least—the adoption of a placeless place, a surveillance point, from which the uninterested epistemological subject considers with a neutral and simply curious eye the dispersed field of religious beliefs. If a certain external description is accessible to this

---

★ *Translator's note*: What is here being translated "Word" is the French term "Parole." This French term can also be rendered "Speech," as when rendering the distinction made, in French, between *langue* and *parole*, language and speech. As such, it should be borne in mind that "Word" and "word" connote speech or a spoken word. Occasionally, context will dictate that *parole* be translated "speech"—in which case the reader should remember that this is the same term elsewhere translated as "word."

"gaze from nowhere," the comprehension of what is in question, what is at stake, the *Woraufhin*, is not. I will not busy myself here with this way of analogizing transfer and step-by-step comprehension that the latter authorizes. I will instead limit myself to grounding its mere possibility on the attitude of a phenomenological suspense practiced with regard to my own convictions. What is thus demanded of me is the following: with regard to religions other than my own, I should practice the same imaginative and sympathetic adoption that I demand of my listeners when, in their presence, I proceed with a hermeneutic of the Hebraic and Christian faith.

Third and final consequence: if, in opposition to the claims of a rootless comprehension, the only option is an analogizing transfer proceeding step by step, the *idea* of a phenomenology of religion as such, the Religion, remains just an idea—by which one is to understand a regulative ideal projected on the horizon of our investigations. This idea is not, however, inert; it teleologically motivates what I would like to formulate as the wish for an interconfessional, interreligious hospitality, comparable to the linguistic hospitality that presides over the work of translating one tongue into another.

At the moment of entering into the field of significations delimited by the Jewish and Christian Scriptures, I would like to bring to the fore the greatest enigma that the hermeneutic status of the phenomenology of this religion poses for us. It is, quite precisely, the hermeneutic circle, or rather the hermeneutic circles, inherent to the scriptural constitution of the Jewish and Christian faith. About this circle—or about these circles—we will never cease to ask ourselves if it is, or if they are, vicious or favorable.

First circle: the Jewish religion and the Christian religion are said to be founded on a word received as the Word of God; but this word is nowhere accessible outside the writings considered to be holy, in the sense of separate from all the rest of literature. Now, the relation between the divine Word and the Holy Scriptures appears circular to the extent that such a Word is held to be the founding instance of Scripture and Scripture to be the place where the Word is made manifest. In other words, the Word cannot attest to its foundational function without recourse to the

Scriptures that give it something like a body (the comparison with the Incarnation is frequent in the conciliar documents of the Catholic Church); but Scripture would not be counted as manifestation unless it is deemed the trace left by the Word that founds it. Thus we have the circle of the living word and the scriptural trace.

In turn, this circle of Word and Scripture appears to be inscribed in a wider circle that puts in play, on the one hand, the pair Word-Scripture* and, on the other, the ecclesial community that draws its identity from the acknowledgment of these Scriptures and the Word that is supposed to have founded them. One can designate this wider circle as that of the inspired word and the interpreting and confessing community, by virtue of which a relation of mutual election is established between one and the other, as soon as the community understands itself in the light of *these Scriptures* rather than *those other Scriptures*. This is the second circle in which the previous one is inscribed.

An important corollary to this circle is the one that concerns the rule for reading the Scriptures. On one hand, the primacy of Scripture over tradition can be proclaimed, indeed the exclusive *position* of the Scripture supposedly capable of interpreting itself according to the well-known formula of the Reformers: *sola scriptura!* On the other hand, it must be admitted that a Scripture free of all interpretation is properly speaking impossible to find. This admission must not be taken as a confession of weakness; rather, it must be said that the history of their interpretation and that of the diverse traditions that result from it is constitutive of the very meaning of the Scriptures. From this, there results a certain competition between fidelity to the original text and the creativity at work in the history of interpretation. This circle determines the status of tradition, according to whether one sees in it the simple transmission of an unchangeable deposit or the dynamism of an innovative interpretation without which the letter would remain dead.

A second corollary to this circle of scriptural foundation and

---

* *Translator's note*: In other contexts, the distinction *Parole/Ecriture* could be rendered "Speech/Writing." It has been translated "Word/Scripture" because of the theological or religious context in which Ricœur uses it.

ecclesial identity concerns the considerable segment of the tradition that is made up of debts to neighboring cultures. Concerning the Jewish Scriptures, there is the many thousand years' old collection of cultures of the ancient Near East, from Egypt to Mesopotamia and Persia passing through Canaan and Ugarit. Concerning the Scriptures of Second Temple Judaism and of nascent Christianity, there is the encounter with Hellenism, an encounter sealed by the septuagental translation of the Hebrew Bible into the Greek tongue. From this major event was born the long dialogue between Jerusalem and Athens, whose heirs we are, whether we accept or reject this reality. I have placed this confluence, to which we owe the works of Augustine, Maimonides, Avicenna, Thomas Aquinas, and Duns Scotus, beneath the sign of the circle, insofar as in it one can detect a Hellenization of Judaism, of Islam, or, concerning Christianity, a Christianization of Hellenism, as wise contemporary medievalists have asserted. Everything happens as if the mutual election discussed above between the scriptural basis and the tradition was prolonged within the tradition itself between Hebraic thought and the conceptuality of Greek origin—Jews, Muslims, and Christians interpreting the Greek source in order to better understand their own scriptural sources. One would therefore be wrong to consider these mutual explications as regrettable contaminations, still less as perversions. It is rather an issue of an unsurpassable historical destiny for whomever lives and thinks only by understanding himself through his other. Another Logos besides that of the Jewish, Christian, and Islamic Scriptures has always come between the believers and the living Word of their God. This is the place to repeat—with Pier Cesare Bori, author of the important book that he entitles *Interprétation infinie*—the words of Albert the Great: "Scripture grows with those who read it." This growth does not stop with the great medievals; it is carried on in and through the intermediacy of Descartes and other Cartesians, of Kant and all German idealism, not to mention the Jewish post-Hegelians at the beginning of the twentieth century, from Hermann Cohen to Rosenzweig.

I would like to conclude this meditation on the circle by evoking a final circle, one that encompasses the preceding ones, and their corollaries too, at the level of each individual believer.

This believer is, in effect, confronted with the preaching by which the meaning of the Scriptures is actualized for him in each instance; but, this happens only on condition that he lay hold of this meaning and understand himself through it. Thus is repeated, on the miniature scale of the believing soul, the circle that the Scriptures and the confessing communities together sketch on the level of world history. Thus miniaturized, the hermeneutic circle of the Word and Scripture, that of the Scriptures and the tradition, that of the scriptural tradition and the cultural and conceptual mediations, are transformed into existential questions. In distinction from adherence to a philosophical school, an adherence that can be argued for and justified, at least up to a certain point, adherence to a religious confession bears a unique character. In the first place, it is, for the majority, an issue of an accident of birth, for others, of the risks of a conversion. Along the way, the contingency is transformed into a rational choice and culminates finally in a sort of destiny, leaving its stamp on the global comprehension of others, oneself, and the world, beneath the sign of the reception of the Word of an Other, gathered in its historical and mediated traces by long chains of interpretations. Such is the existential circle: an accident transformed into destiny through an ongoing choice. The believer wagers that this circle can be not vicious, but indeed favorable and enlivening.

INTERLUDE: THE "GREAT CODE"

Before undertaking a more precise analysis of the texture of what are for the most part Hebrew Scriptures, I propose as a transition that we first take a detour and follow the instructions of Northrop Frye in his *The Great Code*. Without ignoring what the historical-critical method has established, but neglecting the questions of authorship, sources, the history of redaction, and faithfulness to historical reality such as it can be established today, we will use only the resources of literary criticism applied to the Bible considered as a work of literature. In other words, we will simply ask how this text produces significations on the basis of textual structures. If I am interested in this book that is foreign to the main

trends of exegesis, this is because it shelters the text from a subject's claim to determine meaning; it does so by emphasizing, on
the one hand, the strangeness of its language in relation to that
which we speak today and, on the other hand, the internal coherence of its configuration in terms of its own internal criteria of
meaning. These two characteristics have the most admirable virtue of decentering anything concerned with the *ego*'s project of
self-constitution.

   Biblical language, Frye emphasizes first, is completely strange
in relation to ours in that to reconnect with it one must fight
one's way back up the slope of language—which being metaphorical in the epoch of Homer and the Greek tragedians, became
argumentative with the Neoplatonic theologies, and especially
with the apparatus of the proofs for the existence of God from
the Scholastics to Hegel, and finally became demonstrative with
mathematics and the empirical sciences. Poetry alone testifies
today, in the midst of our language, to the power of metaphorical
language, which says to us not "This is *like* that," but "This *is*
that." Only through the channel of poetry can one draw closer
to the kerygmatic language of the Bible, when the latter proclaims, in a metaphoric way: the Lord is my rock, my fortress; I
am the way, the truth, and the life; this is my body, and so on.
This language has in addition a complete internal coherence, but
this coherence is that of a metaphoric or premetaphoric language.
It results first from the extreme consistency of the biblical imagery
that the author of *The Great Code* sees distributed on two levels,
one paradisiac or apocalyptic (but we will see in a little while
that the two adjectives are typologically equivalent), the other
demonic. One can thus move from high to low and back again
by traversing the ladder along which are arranged the celestial
powers, heroes, humans, animals, plants, and minerals. The
"imaginative" (and not imaginary) unity of the Bible is assured
much more decisively by the thoroughly typological function of
the biblical signified. Frye sees in the Bible a highly ramified network of correspondences between types and antitypes, to use the
language of Saint Paul, correspondences that cause the intersigni-
fication of, for example, the Exodus of the Hebrews and the Resurrection of Christ, the Law of Sinai and the New Law of the
Sermon on the Mount, the Creation in Genesis and the Prologue

to the Gospel of John, indeed the figures of Joshua and Jesus. This typological interpretation does not circulate merely between the Old and the New Testament, but within the Hebrew Bible itself where the covenants between God and Noah, Abraham, Moses, David, and so on follow and mutually interpret each other. It thus turns out that the Bible deploys a series of figures in the form of a "U," of peaks and abysses, each described in terms of the grand metaphor, in turn apocalyptic or demonic, and linked together according to the typological rule that assures their cumulative character. On the chain of peaks, the author places the figures of Eden, then of the Promised Land, then of the Gift of the Law, then of Zion, then of the Second Temple, then of the Kingdom proclaimed by Jesus, then of the Messiah awaited by the Jews and of the Second Coming awaited by the Christians; on the chain of the abysses, he places the lost Paradise and Cain, the captivity in Egypt, the Philistines, Babylon, the profanation of the Second Temple, Rome and Nero, and much more. The typological correspondence is thus spread over a temporal sequence without the inner line of affinity connecting the terms of any single series ever being broken.

If I have given Frye's *The Great Code* such an important place in this essay, this is to emphasize the coherence of a symbolic field determined by purely internal laws of organization and development: what Frye characterizes as the "centripetal" structure that the Bible shares with all the great poetic texts.

This self-constitution and self-sufficiency of *The Great Code* finds an important echo in the theory of the self that corresponds to it. To the extent that one brackets the possible representation of real historical events, and therefore brackets the "centrifugal" movement of the text—a movement that prevails in argumentative language and still more in demonstrative language, which, in our culture, have covered over and suppressed metaphorical language—what is important is neither the relation to nature, as in a book of cosmology, nor the relation to the actual unfolding of events, as in a book of history, but the power of the biblical text to arouse, in the listener and the reader, the desire to understand himself in terms of "the Great Code." Precisely because the text does not aim at any outside, it has us as its sole outside—us who, in receiving the text and assimilating ourselves to it, make

of the book a mirror, according to the well-known patristic metaphor of the Book and the Mirror (*Liber et Speculum*). From this
moment on, the language, poetic in itself, becomes kerygmatic
for us.[2]

THE BIBLE: A POLYPHONIC TEXT

In the third part of our investigation, I would like to propose, as
a corrective to the preceding approach, a fairly different vision
of the biblical text, one that, like the other, has nonnegligible
consequences for the passage from the text's internal configuration to its effect of refiguring the self. This vision of the text is
still close to literary analysis in that it accents the genres relevant
to the great biblical poetics: narrative discourse, prescriptive discourse, prophetic discourse, wisdom discourse, hymnic discourse,
letters, parables, and so on. But this approach differs from the
previous one in two important respects.

First, the principal accent is placed on the variety of discursive
genres, rather than on the "imaginative" unity of the Bible, as in
a typological reading. Without going so far as to fragment the
text, one can insist, as James Barr, Claus Westermann, and others
have done, on the absence of any theological center in the Hebrew Bible, thereby opposing systematizations as respectable as
covenantal theology and the theology of *Heilsgeschichte*. If some
unity can be recognized in the Bible, it is more of a polyphonic
than of a typological order.

The second point accentuates the difference between the approaches without opposing them radically. While the typological
unity is maintained at a pre- or hypermetaphorical level, the
articulations by genre are raised to the rank of *theologoumena* by
a favorable conjunction of historical-critical exegesis and biblical
theology. Likewise, the search for *theologoumena* appropriate to
the literary genres of the Bible is itself also displaced and de-

---

[2] The English exegete James Barr, to whom I owe much, says something close,
without giving so considerable a role to typological coherence: in the Bible,
events, characters, institutions do not follow one another in a linear way, where
what follows would simply replace what precedes; rather they accumulate and
mutually reinforce one another.

centered in relation to the theological constructions of a more recent past, which would impose on the Bible our own way of questioning, as much on the anthropological and cosmological levels as on the theological level. Since the time of my presentation at Louvain on the idea of revelation, where I adopted the distinction between narrative, prescriptive, prophetic, wisdom, and hymnic genres, I have found in Paul Beauchamp's *L'un et l'autre testament* a typology that avoids the endless division that an analysis by literary genres cannot resist. This learned exegete proposes that we return to the great triad of the rabbis: the Torah, the Prophets, and what is called the Writings. This distinction does not, properly speaking, concern literary genres that can be infinitely subdivided, but three different ways of articulating Scripture and the Word. This approach seemed the most appropriate to an investigation into the relations between religious experience and language. It is not insignificant either to recall that the first generation of Christians constantly referred to this fundamental typology: every time there is a question of "fulfilling the Scriptures," this is basically a reference to the Law and the Prophets. Taken together, Torah, Prophets, and Writings form the Book—about which, soon enough, we will have to ask in what sense it is open and in what sense it is closed. But, considered separately at first, they are—for a synchronic, and in this sense structural reading—three Scriptures, according to Beauchamp's excellent expression.

It seems wise to begin with the first term, *Torah*, rather than with the second, *Prophets*. And this is so for two reasons. First, the prophetic word risks casting us unprepared into a confrontation with a short circuit in the connection between the Word of the Other and the human word, a short circuit in which the mediation of Scripture seems superfluous, to the extent that inspiration seems to be identified with another voice being breathed into one's own voice: thus says YHWH. That prophecy strongly suggests this interpretation will be seen a little farther along—which is one more reason not to divorce it from the pair that is formed by Torah and Prophets together. As to the second reason for following the order imposed by the rabbis, the Torah as Scripture is itself twofold, being divided into law properly speaking and story. Together the legislative and the narrative bring about the transfer from Scripture, that is writing, to the originary word. On one side, the giving of the Law is recounted as an event woven into the fabric of a history of liberation: "Hear O Israel: YHWH our God is the sole YHWH" (Deuteronomy 6.4). On the other, this history is such only because it frames the promulgation of the Law: "I am the Eternal your God who brought you up from Egypt, from the house of servitude." How is the relation of the Word and Scripture, speech and writing, played out here?

Let us start from the legislative pole of the Torah, the one privileged by the rabbinic tradition. It is a spoken word, to be sure—an injunction, more precisely, that calls for hearing, as the utterance of the *shema* has just reminded us. But what a strange word spoken! First of all, we know it only through the written story that is made from its promulgation; next, the totality of laws that the exegetes distinguish and lay out in detail is assigned to an intermediary, a messenger, Moses, who—whatever his historical character might have been, and it was probably considerable—is not the author of the Law as it is said that Jeremiah and Ezekiel were "the authors" of their prophecies. Moses is raised above all speaking voices, all hearing ears, as the eponymous subject of the Law, a Law that consists in the principle, the summation, and the result of all earlier legislation. It is immediately evident how their being joined to the story of founding events helps raise the instructions above all the other biblical speeches and legislative writings. The Law alone, without yet speaking about foundational stories, is already the immemorial, the origin, that is to say, the principle, of the historically situated commandments. A remarkable situation results from this. On the one hand, there is no scriptureless word at the origin of the Law. Inasmuch as it can be considered Scripture separate from the Word spoken, the Law, Beauchamp emphasizes, "is pronounced as a function of the legislator's absence." Augustine had already marveled at this in the *Confessions*: "Moses wrote and went away." On the other hand, Scripture is an orphan without the covenant forever reinstated by the reading which is a spoken word and the approbation of the people who commit themselves with an oath. We are touching on the circle evoked above: here, between Sinai and the people that receives its identity from it. Put otherwise, the circle is the bipolar covenant. Thus it can be said that the Law is a word or speech with regard to the origin of the call, the convocation, the injunction, but Scripture or writing inasmuch as the legislator has absented himself.

Here is where the conjunction between Law and story—a conjunction constitutive of the Torah—makes its decisive contribution to the dialectic of Scripture and the Word. The narrative core of the Pentateuch, we know, is Exodus. Exodus stands out against the background of the continuous history as an event without equal, one that serves to institute, to found. To speak truly, it is part of a chain of primordial events, all of which have inaugural and, to leave nothing unsaid, creative value—for the identity of the people, its ethical vocation, its geopolitical destination. This chain of founding events, if one heads back toward the origin of origins, leads to the story of Creation and, through this story, to the coincidence between the Word and the emergence of all things. This primordial story proclaims that the Word is the origin and that, opposite our own speech, "it puts words before things," as Beauchamp has nicely put it. But this story speaks of an event witnessed by no one. That means it can be signified only by reconsidering and correcting immemorial writings (for example, Babylonian, Canaanite, Egyptian myths) which were themselves already there when the biblical writers— the Yahwist and the author of the priestly document (P)—wrote. On the basis of these earlier writings, the latter can in turn write: "God said: let there be light. . . ." A palimpsest of writings is thus necessary to tell of the origin which is the origin of the discourse.

After the Torah, we come to the *Prophets*. We have already come across the famous words spoken by the messenger: "Thus says YHWH." The prophecy that follows is something like a citation from the mouth of YHWH. We have also cautioned against an overhasty exegesis of the messenger's words, where it seems two voices coincide, that of the Lord and that of his messenger, or better, of his representative, in the sense of *Stellvertreter*. Isn't this the model for every conjunction between the Word of God and the human word? In a sense, yes: "No man is as present in the words he speaks as the one who says: thus says an other, namely God. While someone speaks of Abraham, Hosea speaks of Hosea and Isaiah of Isaiah," Beauchamp notes. But this happens only on certain conditions that complicate the model a bit. First of all, it is not possible for the Prophet to pronounce the name of YHWH without evoking the Lord of the Torah and to do so in his twofold function: legislative and narrative. This is enough to bridge the gap between two levels of the Word; for, we have seen, it is the writings, the Scriptures, that collect the tales of origin as well as the laws. As a result, the present voice crying out in the desert echoes he who is absent from all law and all history. And if we turn away from the voice of the Prophet, we find that it is prey to contestation: who says that the Prophet is not a false prophet? This is why his speech sums up the frailty of our own: it is dated and it appoints a date. "While biblical law causes its actuality and its own date to be forgotten by referring itself to the archetypal era, prophecy puts to the fore the precise moment of its production" (Beauchamp, *L'un et l'autre testament,* p. 75). And it is in writing that the Prophet appoints a date. Thus the word of YHWH, put into the mouth of the prophet, has the fragility of all words that Scripture alone saves from destruction. Thus one hears Jeremiah calling the scribe Baruch "who, listening to his dictation, wrote on a scroll all the words which YHWH had spoken to his prophet" (Jeremiah 36.4). And the danger that even the written trace would disappear could be so urgent that Ezechiel, we learn, considered himself summoned by the voice to devour his book, as if the very mouth that speaks and eats could offer a body to the writing already deprived, as writing, of assistance from the living voice.

How does the genre of writings referred to as *Wisdom* come to be added to the pair Law and Prophets, which is the sole thing that the New Testament seems to know? Likewise, the rabbinic classification, with the label "other writings," seems to suggest a certain disquiet. It is nonetheless in the wisdom writings that the work of Scripture is the most remarkable. This work becomes visible if one considers, with Beauchamp, wisdom's position in relation to time. It can be said that wisdom is at once timeless and daily. As immemorial, wisdom joins the beginning celebrated in the creation stories, and through them, it joins the creative word. This is the meaning of Proverbs 8, where wisdom personified speaks in the first person and declares itself older than creation itself. Thus, by virtue of immemorial Scripture, this word is uprooted from the everyday course of our words, the Jewish hypostasis of wisdom placing itself along the trajectory of this vertical elevation of speech. But this elevation, this hypostasis, does not put Scripture out of a job. It is the miracle of Scripture to convert the fleeting today into the persistence and perdurance of "all the days," of the "daily," whose nauseating repetition is deplored by *Qohelet*.

In relation to the Law and the Prophets, wisdom seems at first glance to be one genre too many, since it is not named in the Evangelic revival. Perhaps wisdom has another function, that of articulating the singularity of Israel together with the universality of cultures. Through it, Israel competes with the nations: "Israel," Beauchamp observes, "here accepted the same terrain as that where the idolators arose, when it considered the other side of the idea of a unique God to be the idea of the divine in the world" (p. 117). And: Israel, here, "adopted a figure steeped in gentleness, the figure of wisdom, but not because she was seduced" (p. 117). "With wisdom, Israel rejoiced in being universal, but it is still Israel" (p. 118).

This declaration could not be without an echo among the Christian gentiles: its ecclesiology is invited to assume the new singularity from which it proceeds, the Christic singularity, but by relocating it within the horizon of this new universality expressed in the terms of the Greek Logos.

What remains to be discussed in our conclusion is the way in which these three Scriptures contribute to articulating the moment of call and that of response, each with the other.

On the side of the call, we must, I believe, insist, as Claus Westermann does throughout his work, on the absence of a theological center in the Hebrew Bible. In this regard, it is perhaps not necessary to valorize, as the generation of von Rad and Karl Barth did, the *Heilsgeschichte* or the covenantal theology. The Bible is a library. This way of putting it will take on its full importance when we characterize the reply of the self responding to this polyphony of the call: it is perhaps a polycentric, rather than a monocentric, self that these fragmented Scriptures suggest. To be sure, we have the guide of the three Scriptures. But these three Scriptures suggest a plural naming of God. God is named differently in the narration, where he is designated as supreme Agent; in the code of prescriptions, where he is designated as source of the imperative; in the prophecy, where he is designated as divine I doubling the human I; in the wisdom, which searches for him as the meaning of the meaningful; and—we are at fault for not having spoken of it earlier—in the hymn, which expresses in turn complaint and praise.

To complete this polycentrism of the *theologoumena*, we should add what could be called the *withdrawal of the Name*. The name of God is at once what circulates between genres and between Scriptures, belonging to none of them, but intersignified by all, and what escapes from each and every one of them, as a sign of the incompleteness of all discourse on God. God is named in turn as the target of and the vanishing point outside each discourse and the whole of them. In this regard, the decisive text could be Exodus 3.14: "I am who I am." Of course, one can take this as a sort of biblical ontological proposition, and in this way coordinate it with the Greek tradition, as Gilson did when he spoke of the "metaphysics of Exodus." But one can also think that the redoubling of "I am" places the secret of an *incognito* at the margins of all discourse. Likewise, Exodus 3.14b says: " 'I am' sent me." "I am," become the subject of a sending, lets appear only the sending power that proceeds from this very withdrawal.

Corresponding to this polyphony of a decentered text some typical figures of a responding self are provided. In his small book *Que dit sur Dieu l'Ancien Testament?*, Claus Westermann shows that each figure of God, the God who saves, the God who punishes, the God who blesses, the God who suffers with men, and so on, calls for a different response. A plurality of figures of response would correspond to this polycentrism of the naming of God.

And now, if one takes as a guide the distinction among three Scriptures, one arrives at this: The Torah, inasmuch as it is indivisibly law and narrative tradition, establishes what could be called the ethico-narrative identity of the people; and this identity is grounded in the security and the stability of a tradition. Prophecy, in turn, confronts this identity with the hazards of a strange and hostile history. Harbingers and witnesses of the destruction, the Prophets establish an essentially threatened identity. André Néher has said elsewhere that the Jewish culture alone knew how to integrate its own death into its self-understanding; he spoke of the captivity and the exile as a slice of nothingness breaking the continuity of a reassuring history. Opposite an identity that could be called well grounded, one finds an identity destabilized by prophetic speech, against the background of an agonizing question: Hasn't our God died with his people? It is to this serious question that Second Isaiah offered a passionate response; for it was necessary to call on the universality of a God of history and creation if one wanted to tear oneself away from the ghost of a vanquished God. As for the third form of Scripture, that of wisdom, it serves, as I suggested above, as the hinge connecting historical singularity[3] and universality. We are thus thrown at one fell swoop into more contemporary debates concerning the relations of the universal and the historical. I am thinking, of course, about the universality extolled by Habermas and the communitarianism that is opposed to him. Wisdom, in its relation to the Torah, anticipates this crisis. The Torah is addressed to a people, Wisdom to each individual.

It is in this way that the triad of the call—Torah, Prophets, Wisdom—is answered, on the side of the self, by the triadic rhythm of a grounded identity, a fragmented identity, and an identity at once singularized and universalized. This reciprocity between the triad of the call and that of the response is the concrete figure which, in the tradition of the Jewish then Christian Scriptures, is worn by the hermeneutic circle constitutive of the historically incarnated religious consciousness.

The problem that this deliberately fragmentary investigation leaves open is that of knowing how this religious consciousness, informed by the biblical Great Code, could be open to other religious consciousnesses, informed by other scriptural codes, and

---

[3] This part of my study sums up a paper, "L'enchevêtrement de la voix et de l'écrit dans le discours biblique," that I gave at the Colloque Castelli, in Rome, in January 1992.

how it could communicate with the latter within the horizon of the regulative idea evoked at the beginning of this study under the title interconfessional hospitality of one religion to another. A phenomenology of religion itself is purchased at the price of this *actual* opening and this *actual* communication.[4]

---

[4] I would like to say a few words about the point where the final two Gifford Lectures connect with *Soi-même comme un autre* [English translation, *Oneself as Another* (Chicago: University of Chicago Press, 1992), trans. Kathleen Blamey]. The connection would be located at the level of what I call "the ontology of action." Setting up a self through the mediation of the Scriptures and the application to oneself of the multiple figures of naming God happens at the level of our most fundamental capacity for action. It is the *homo capax*, capable man, who is interpellated and restored. I believe that I thus retrieve Kant's central intuition in *Religion within the Limits of Reason Alone*, at least as I have reconstituted it in the essay included in the book rendering homage to Father Geffré. The task of religion, according to Kant, is to restore in the moral subject the capacity for acting in accordance with obligation. The regeneration, which is at issue in this philosophy of religion, happens at the level of the fundamental disposition, at the level of what I am here calling "the capable self." This restoration, this regeneration, this rebirth of the capable self, stands in a close relation to the economy of the gift which I celebrate in the study "Amour et justice" [English trans., "Love and Justice," in *Figuring the Sacred*]. Love, I say in this presentation, watches over justice, to the extent that justice, the justice of reciprocity and of equivalence, is forever threatened with falling back, despite itself, to the level of interested calculation, of: *do ut des* (I give so that you give). Love protects justice against this slippery slope by proclaiming: "I give because you have already given to me." It is thus that I see the relation between charity and justice as the practical form of the relation between theology and philosophy. It is within the same perspective that I propose rethinking the theological-political, namely, the end of a certain theological-political constructed on the vertical relation domination/subordination. A political theology oriented otherwise would, as I see it, be obliged to stop constituting itself as a theology of domination and thereby set itself up as the justification for wanting to live together in just institutions.

This study has issued from the next to last lecture delivered within the framework of the Gifford Lectures. It was followed by the lesson published in the *Revue de l'Institut Catholique de Paris* (1988), with the title "Le sujet convoqué. A l'école des récits de vocation prophétique" [English trans., "The Summoned Subject in the School of the Narratives of the Prophetic Vocation," in *Figuring the Sacred*, pp. 262–75]. These two presentations were taken out of the collection whose revision ended up as my last work, *Soi-même comme un autre*. I would like, in the near future, to regroup these two studies in a collection where the text published in Tübingen with the title *Liebe und Gerechtigkeit (Love and Justice)* would appear after them. The collection would have as its conclusion a reflection on the destiny of the theological-political, in a confrontation with the problematic of "the disenchantment of the world."

7

The Wounded Word: The Phenomenology of Prayer

Jean-Louis Chrétien

PRAYER IS THE RELIGIOUS PHENOMENON par excellence, for it is the sole human act that opens the religious dimension and never ceases to underwrite, to support, and to suffer this opening. Of course, there are other specifically religious phenomena, but to their conditions of possibility prayer always belongs. If we were unable to address our speech to God or the gods, no other act could intend the divine. Thus sacrifice is an act that is essentially distinct, at least at first glance, from prayer, but one could not imagine sacrifice without prayer in some fashion or other accompanying it and constituting it as such. With prayer, the religious appears and disappears.

This appearing can, in some cases, open only onto the virtual, as when Supervielle, in his *Prière à l'inconnu*, speaks to a god whose existence he does not posit and who may or may not be listening—he does not know:

> How surprised I am to be addressing you,
> My God, I who know not if you exist.[1]

Nevertheless, this prayer to a virtual God, whatever religious or poetic appreciation one might have for it, is not itself a virtual prayer, but an actual and real prayer, and this poem belongs properly to the religious order, with the virtual character of the God to whom it says "you" constituting a moment in the meaning of its religiosity. This is an example of the weakest and most dilute form of a possibility that is given in particularly trenchant and

---

[1] This poem appears in the collection *La fable du monde* (Paris, 1950), p. 39, where Supervielle invokes elsewhere (p. 55) a "very watered-down God."

vibrant examples by the Evangelist—for instance, "Lord, teach us to pray," which is a prayer; or also "I believe! Come and help my lack of faith."[2]

The most diverse of thinkers emphasize this foundation of the religious in and through prayer. Novalis, for instance, writes in a fragment of his *Encyclopedia* "*To pray* is in religion what to think is in *philosophy*. To pray is *to make religion* [*Religion-machen*]. . . . The religious sense prays—as the mental organ thinks,"[3] and Ludwig Feuerbach, considering from a heuristic point of view what Novalis asserts genetically, asserts in *The Essence of Christianity*: "The ultimate essence of religion is revealed by the simplest act of religion—prayer."[4]

Simple? This is the question. And supposing it is, the simplicity, here no more than elsewhere, does not easily lend itself to being grasped. This fundamental, that is, irreducible, phenomenon is difficult to describe, so varied are the forms that it can take and the definitions that have been offered for it. The most widely accepted and the most traditional typologies and classifications can be phenomenologically impure and will veil the phenomenon instead of conforming themselves to it. This is the case with the distinction between vocal and mental prayer. This distinction seems clear when separating silent acts from acts where the prayer is uttered or pronounced. But it is more problematic as soon as one notices, as Saint Teresa of Avila has, that for the prayer to be mental, it is not simply an issue of keeping one's mouth closed (*tener cerrada la boca*). If the prayer is made only with one's lips (*solo cerrada la boca*), it will not be Christian, even though the practices of reciting a formula or repeating a word, to the point of drunken stupor, appears in various religions; but if the real vocal prayer is always paired with the mental prayer, as Saint Teresa affirms, this distinction can no longer be used in a rigorous description of the phenomenon of prayer.[5]

---

[2] Respectively, Luke 11.1 and Mark 9.24.

[3] Novalis, *Encyclopédie* (Paris, 1966), trans. de Gandillac, p. 398.

[4] *The Essence of Christianity*, p. 122. At the beginning of his important work on prayer, Friedrich Heiler qualifies it as the "central phenomenon of religion," and collects citations proving his point; see *Das Gebet, Eine religionsgeschichtliche und religionspsychologische Untersuchung* (Munich, 1923), p. 1.

[5] *The Way of Perfection*, chap. 22, text in *Obras completas* (Madrid, 1972), ed. Efren de la Madre de Dios, pp. 264–65.

Moreover—and this represents another and not the least difficulty with the description—in questions regarding the constitution of the meaning of prayer, the addressee is thoroughly essential. Even if, as a phenomenologist, the positing of existence is not achieved, it remains the case that the manner in which one addresses him, names him, speaks to him, the nature of what one asks and can ask of him, the fear or the confidence with which praying turns toward him—all this depends on the being of this addressee as it appears to the faithful one. One cannot describe prayer without describing the power to whom it is addressed. But, as a result, doesn't the description of prayer amount to explaining, in a nonpositional form, the different possible or real theologies? But then doesn't a phenomenology of prayer dissolve into an inventory of the different possible modes in which the divine can appear? For to each prayer, there is a face of the divine, and vice versa. What is more, each established religion has its *lex orandi*; its prayer has a norm that the phenomenologist can no more ignore, seeing that it makes up a part of the phenomenon, than adopt and make his own.

To cut through these difficulties, it seems wise to limit the study, which left to itself could be indefinite. Prayer will be treated only as a *speech act*, even if the history of religions describes all sorts of prayers that are not at all, at least not at first glance, speech acts. And the guiding question will be that of the *voice* in this act. Why and how, in prayer, do we lend voice, give voice, to our voice? What is the meaning of the different forms of utterance? This is not an arbitrary limitation, nor is it purely opportunistic, for these questions bear on the essence of prayer: Is vocal prayer merely one form of prayer among others, or is it the prayer par excellence, the sole one in relation to which all others can be defined and constituted, either by derivation or privation? Is it true that, as Feuerbach says, "audible prayer is only prayer revealing its nature."[6]

Still incomplete, a first description of prayer can situate it in an act of presence to the invisible. It is the act by which the man praying stands in the presence of a being in which he believes but does not see and manifests himself to it. If it corresponds to a

---

[6] Op. cit., p. 123.

theophany, it is first of all an anthropophany, a manifestation of man. The invisible before which man shows himself can range from the radical invisibility of the Spirit to the inward sacredness or power of a being visible by itself, like a mountain, a star, or a statue. This act of presence puts man thoroughly at stake, in all dimensions of his being. It exposes him in every sense of the word *expose* and with nothing held back. It concerns our body, our bearing, our posture, our gestures, and can include certain mandatory preliminary bodily purifications such as ablutions, vestimentary requirements such as covering or uncovering certain parts of our body, bodily gestures and movements such as raising the hands or kneeling, and even certain physical orientations. All these practices, whether they are obligatory or left to the preference of the one praying, can be gathered together in a summoned appearance that incarnates the act of presence. Even he who turns toward the incorporeal does so corporeally, with all his body. That cannot be lacking, for to say, as Saint Augustine does, that one can pray with one's body in any position whatsoever does not mean the body is bracketed in prayer and that it has no role or importance, but that in Augustine's eyes, each must adopt the most appropriate position and the one most likely to benefit his prayer.[7] With its dances and its cavorting, Hasidic movement has evidenced in this regard a lively, indeed a strange, freedom.[8] Inscribed in the body, this presence to the invisible and the summons before it include acts by which the praying man declares to God or the gods his desires, thoughts, needs, love, contrition, and so on, according to the full range of possibilities in speech—running from the act of moving ones lips without making oneself heard to the cry and passing through the mumble and the raised voice. The being before God of the one praying is an active self-manifestation to God. All the modalities of prayer are forms of this self-manifestation, be it individual or collective.

This description gives rise to a question. What do we see when we see a man praying, independently of any existential positing of the one he is addressing? We see a man who speaks alone, who

---

[7] *De diversis quaestiones ad Simplicianum*, t. 2, qu. 4 (*Quo situ corporis orandum*).

[8] L. Jacobs, *Hasidic Prayer* (London, 1972), chap. 5, "Gestures and Melody in Prayer," pp. 54ff. I would like to thank Catherine Chalier for having made this study known to me.

is alone in speaking. But speaking alone, is this the same as to speak with oneself, to speak to oneself, or to address an other absent to the senses? The two phenomena are distinguished essentially. To collapse prayer into pure soliloquy, into dialogue with oneself, is not to describe but to interpret and construct by doing violence to the phenomenon. I can indeed address myself and say "you" to myself, for example, in order to rally my flagging courage or to incite myself to some action or other. But that is in no way a prayer, and this act is opposed to the one by which I turn myself toward an other and say "you" to that other. When Kant writes that a man praying speaks "within and really *with* himself [*in und eigentlich mit sich selbst*], but ostensibly speaks the more intelligibly *with God*," when he compares the supplicant to someone who is "talking aloud to himself" and whom we suspect of "having a slight attack of madness,"[9] or when Feuerbach asserts that prayer is the "self-division of man into two beings—a dialogue of man with himself, with his heart,"[10] the essence of this speech act is mistaken and deformed, with more ill will in the first case than in the second, for the second presents itself as a constructive interpretation. It is not altogether wrong, Kant says, that we find a bit maddening the man who is caught alone and unawares "in an occupation or an attitude which can properly belong only to one who sees some one else before him." Kant distinguishes the pure *"spirit of prayer"* from the allocution or the address (*Anrede*)—the latter supposing belief in a personal presence of the other and as such being a "superstitious illusion" (*ein abergläubischer Wahn*), a "fetish-making" (*Fetischmachen*)[11]—before Schopenhauer deems all prayer that addresses a personal being "idolatry."[12] To decree a phenomenon meaningless is to too easily

---

[9] *Religion within the Limits of Reason Alone*, IV, 2, *General Remark*, pp. 185, 183 n.

[10] Op. cit., p. 123.

[11] Op. cit., p. 183. One sees how these pages could have said to Franz von Baader that Kant "speaks of prayer as a deaf man does of music" (*Sämtliche Werke*, [Leipzig, 1853], ed. Hoffmann, t. 4, p. 407,) and that he mistreated prayer more than he treated it (*behandelte oder vielmehr misshandelte*) (S.W., t. 1, p. 19).

[12] *Parerga und Paralipomena*, II, chap. 15, §178, *Ueber Theismus* [English trans., p. 378]. It remains the case that the concept of idolatry belongs properly to the religious and can be defined only with regard to faith in the true God, which renders this phrase absurd.

dismiss having to think about its meaning, and first of all having to describe it such as it appears and gives itself. The metaphysical prejudice according to which the spirit is necessarily aphonic, and all the more pure as it does not manifest itself, has, happily, never been enough to cause the human voice to fall silent.

What are the functions performed by speech in prayer? What is the importance of the address, of saying "you"? Why give voice to it? These are the questions that must, if we are to offer a better description of prayer, be broached in succession, though they are necessarily one and interlaced with each other.

That a God for whom all is transparently clear has no need for one to declare anything to him, that an omniscient God has nothing to learn from us, not even our most secret desires—this was the objection constantly addressed to the monotheistic prayer. It aims if not to suppress prayer, at least to suppress it as a speech act. But this objection is wise beyond its knowing in that it bears its own resolution within itself—namely, the function performed by speech is not to communicate any information or transmit any knowledge to our invisible interlocutor. At the beginning of his dialogue *De magistro*, Saint Augustine posits that speech performs two functions, *docere* and *discere*, to teach and to learn, to which his son Adeodatus offers the objection of the song we sing when alone. Saint Augustine then distinguishes the properly musical pleasure and the words of the song which, addressed to oneself, is *commemoratio*, where we remind ourselves of something. Adeodatus then raises a new objection: "While we are praying, we are certainly speaking, and yet it is not right to believe that God is either taught anything by us or that He is reminded." Saint Augustine's answer is complex, but essentially amounts to distinguishing in prayer an act, "the sacrifice of righteousness," which is not of itself a speech act, and a linguistic dimension, be it inward and silent or outward and sounded. The latter is then led back to the commemorative function of speech, to recollection for oneself or for others, to the collecting and gathering of our thoughts.[13]

How is this to be understood? We speak by addressing ourselves to another and by turning ourselves toward him, but it is we who

---

[13] *De magistro* I, 1 and 2 [English trans., p. 361].

are taught by this word, and it is on us that it acts. The word affects and modifies the sender, and not its addressee.★ We affect ourselves before the other and toward him. This in prayer is the first wound of the word: the yawning chasm of its addressee has broken its circle, has opened a fault that alters it. An other is silently introduced into my dialogue with myself, radically transforming and breaking it. My speech spills back over me and affects me, as would any of the words that I speak and also hear, but it affects me quite otherwise by not being destined to me, by having in it a wholly other addressee besides myself. It is precisely because I do not speak *to* myself, because I do not speak *for* myself, that my own speech, altered from the very beginning, perhaps from before the beginning, turns back upon me with such singular force.

Saint Thomas Aquinas puts it quite well: "We must pray not in order to inform God of our needs and desires but in order to remind ourselves that in these matters we need divine assistance."[14] To ask of God, that is, to carry out in words an act of demanding, is, by speaking to him, to say something about him and at the same time something about ourselves. We are made manifest to ourselves; we are in and through speech made manifest to ourselves in manifesting ourselves to him. To ask is to actually acknowledge not being the origin of every good and every gift, and it is to actually acknowledge him whom we address for what he is. All prayer confesses God as giver by dispossessing us of our egocentrism, and it does so with a word that the addressee alone renders possible in each moment of its enactment. In turning back upon me, prayer does not speak to me about myself alone.

Prayer, says Saint Bonaventure, calls for the fervor of affection,

---

★ Translator's note: As in the previous essay, what is here being translated "Word" is the French term "Parole." This French term can also be rendered "Speech," as when rendering the distinction made, in French, between *langue* and *parole*, language and speech. As such, it should be borne in mind that "Word" and "word" connote speech or a spoken word. Occasionally, context will dictate that *parole* be translated "speech"—in which case the reader should remember that this is the same term elsewhere translated as "word."

[14] *Summa theologica*, IIa IIae, q. 83, art. 2, ad 1um [English trans., vol. 39, p. 53]. Cf. art. 9, ad 5um: "Prayer is not offered to God in order to change his mind, but in order to excite confidence in us" [English trans., vol. 39, p. 75].

collectedness of thought, surety of expectation. This is why God wanted "us not only to pray mentally but also to pray verbally to arouse our affection through words and to gather our thoughts [*ad recollectionem cogitationum*] through the meaning of these words."[15] We are far from the mute spiritualism that would see in the expressed word a simple effusive movement and dispersion in exteriority, which would remain vain and superfluous before God. The movement of the word is like that of the breath drawn in and blown out. It gathers me before the other; it makes me be for him, since it paradoxically gives me what it presupposes in order to take place. It is necessary to be welcomed in order to pray, but prayer itself, as speech, is the sole thing able to embrace me and welcome me. Does this make the spoken word a simple means, some sort of an instrument in a technique designed for concentration? That can indeed be the case in certain instances. But Saint Bonaventure does not separate the gift of our voice and the signification of what we are saying. The voice is gathered and gathers us around what it says, as what it says is gathered around the one to whom it is addressed. The first function speech performs in prayer is therefore a self-manifestation before the invisible other, a manifestation that becomes a manifestation of self to self through the other, and where the presence of self to the other and of the other to self cannot be separated, as in the invisible poem of respiration evoked by Rilke. This manifestation does not merely bring to light what was there before it; it has its own light: that of an event, the event wherein what is invisible to myself illuminates me in a fashion phenomenologically different from a conversation with myself or an examination of consciousness.

The word spoken in prayer has its meaningful level, and the question about its relation to truth is raised. Aristotle, in a celebrated line from his *De interpretatione*, affirms that "prayer is a *logos* but is neither true nor false," it is not *logos apophantikos*.[16] A demand, a supplication, a lament are not, in effect, open to truth in the same manner as a predicative proposition. But prayer always has norms that determine its rectitude, and these norms put truth into play, including the truth of the *logos apophantikos*. It cannot

---

[15] *Breviloquium*, V, 10 [English trans., p. 170 (modified)].
[16] 17 A 4–5 [English trans., p. 26].

not include an explicit or implicit theology, which can be true or false, the consequence being that one could describe the thought of the divine in a determinate religion according to its prayers alone. The mere linguistic form of the demanding prayer is not enough to put out of play the question of truth. Thus Proclus makes knowledge of the gods the first step in prayer,[17] and in all religions the correctness of the divine names makes up the object of interrogation: Is God (or a god) named in a way befitting him and as he wants to be named? To be sure, this concern for rectitude can become merely pragmatic, and bear on minute corrections in the accomplishment of a rite, as with the ancient Romans for whom the fact that a priest said one word for another, or that his voice stumbled in a ritual prayer, was enough to invalidate the entire ceremony.[18] But this concerns the problem of ritual more than the problem of prayer. The latter always includes a profession of faith, which can be expressed otherwise than in its optative or imperative form.

About the first two words of the Christian prayer par excellence, the Our Father, John Cassian says that "when, therefore, we confess with our own voice that the God and Lord of the universe is our Father, we profess that we have in fact been admitted from our servile condition into an adopted sonship."[19] We do indeed affirm something about God and something about ourselves. The history of salvation, Trinitarian theology, as well as ecclesiology (for, even alone, one prays by saying "*Our* Father," and not "*My* Father"[20]) are already implied in just these two words, these vocatives.

Most certainly, the possible truth of prayer as speech act cannot be reduced solely to that of the predicative theological proposi-

---

[17] *Commentaire sur le Timée* (Paris, 1967), trans. T. Festugière, t. 2, pp. 32–33.

[18] Cf. F. Heiler, *Das Gebet*, p. 151, and D. Porte, *Les donneurs de sacré. Le prêtre à Rome* (Paris, 1989), pp. 35–36.

[19] *Conferences*, IX, 18 [English trans., p. 341]. Whence the "audemus dicere," "we dare to say," which precedes the recitation of the Our Father in the Catholic liturgy.

[20] Cf. Saint Cyprian, *De dominica oratione*, 8: "Above all the Doctor of peace and the Master of unity did not want prayer to be individual and private such that in praying each of us prays only for himself. We do not say: My father who art in Heaven. . . . For us prayer is public and communal." This passage is cited by Saint Thomas Aquinas, *Summa theologica*, IIa IIae, q. 83, art. 7, ad 1um.

tions that it utters or presupposes. It refers to the rectitude of
the prayer itself. The adverb *recte* recurs several times when Saint
Thomas Aquinas studies desire and demand in prayer. This rectitude concerns the object of the demand as well as its modality.[21]
How is this to be thought? As a preliminary to prayer, or as the
stakes of prayer itself? Isn't the truth of prayer as speech act
agonic, that of a combat and a struggle for the truth, indeed *with*
the truth?

A moral objection oftentimes raised against prayer plays on this
very question. If we are corrupt, won't our prayer bear the stamp
of this injustice in itself, and won't it thereby become a scandal?
And if we are virtuous, by our own acts and as a result of them,
what good is praying? The prayer of the just would be superfluous, and that of the unjust only one more injustice, deferring the
reform that he is obliged to make. Montaigne was struck by the
prayer of hardened sinners, which during his voyage to Rome
was good for a bit of trouble from the Holy Office.[22] Proclus,
whose thought on this matter is varied and complex, bases his
position on the Platonic thesis in the *Phaedo* which says that the
impure must not enter into contact with the pure and asserts that
"praying is appropriate only to the man who is supremely
good."[23] As for Louis-Claude de Saint-Martin, he goes so far as
to write: "Will you pray God and ask of him his gifts and favors
before being purified and having established all the virtues in
yourselves? That would be to propose that he prostitute himself."[24] Transposing this type of interrogation into contemporary
and existential terms and distinguishing an authentic and an inauthentic prayer would not fundamentally transform this moralism.
It rests on an inattentiveness to the phenomenon of prayer as
manifestation of the self before the other. This manifestation by
means of speech is groundbreaking in every instance and for all
ages, for it is the event of an encounter. Hugo von Hofmannsthal
says that each new encounter shatters us and reconfigures us, and
that is especially true of the encounter that is prayer.

---

[21] *Summa theologica*, IIa IIae, qu. 83, art. 9, respectively.

[22] *Essais*, I, 56, and for the Roman incident, *Journal de voyage en Italie*.

[23] *Commentaire sur le Timée*, t. II, pp. 33–34; cf. p. 29.

[24] *L'homme de désir* (Paris, 1973), ed. Amadou, §28, p. 59. Cf. §42, p. 77; §101,
p. 144. In a different sense, cf. §245, p. 274.

To stick with the prayer to the one God, he who addresses himself to God always does so *de profundis*, from the depths of his manifest or hidden distress, from the depths of his sin. In his prayer, he confesses the divine holiness, before which he stands and to which he addresses himself. If he truly stands before it, he is by that very standing dispossessed of all the beliefs that he could ever hold about his innermost self. In the at once discrete and inescapable light of prayer, he himself is visible from now on, and in this light he discovers that no man is worthy of prayer, if "worthy" means resting on previous merit. He consequently discovers that he lacks rectitude, and that this injustice must certainly penetrate his demands to depths he himself cannot discern. In the Bible, Moses responds to God that he does not know how to speak, and this is often the Prophets' first response to their vocation—that is to say, the very place where they hear it.

But it belongs to prayer itself that in it alone does the praying man learn that he does not know how to pray. "We do not know how to pray as we must," says Saint Paul.[25] The sorrowful and joyous adventures of the encounter take place only in the encounter itself; the shortcomings of speech open only in speaking. This is the circularity of prayer: the man praying prays in order to know how to pray, and first of all to learn that he does not know how, and he offers thanks for his prayer as a gift from God. One can be turned to God only in praying, and one can pray only by being turned toward God. Only a leap makes us enter into this circle. There are no prolegomena or preliminaries to prayer. Proclus puts it quite well: "To want to pray is to desire to turn toward the gods; this desire leads and ties the desiring soul to the divine, and that is what seems to us to be the thoroughly primary work of prayer. The act of wanting and the act of praying therefore should not constitute two steps one after the other, but one wants and one possesses prayer at the same time, according to the extent of the will."[26] With this, he resolves the aporia of an infinite regression in prayer, where it would be necessary to pray before praying and in order to do so. He says: "No matter what one prays about, he who prays will first have to offer thanks to the

---

[25] Romans 8.26.
[26] *Commentaire sur le Timée*, t. II, pp. 45–46.

gods for this, that he received from the gods the power of turning toward them."[27]

In its own eyes, prayer appears to be always surpassed and preceded by the one to whom it is addressed. It does not begin, it *responds*, and this alone is what, in the very uncertainty where its uprightness puts it, gives it confidence. The circle is not an absurd circle: it refers to the event of an encounter. This speech act does not offer its own security, but it has the security of standing in the sole place where it can in truth struggle for the truth and become upright. For the obstacles to speech dissipate only in speech, as lovers' quarrels are resolved only in love, therefore in being pursued, and not if they are set aside and expected to disappear on their own. This completes the first part of our description of prayer: the manifestation of self to the other by the word is agonic and transforming, for it is dialogue and conversation with the other in an encounter where our truth is at issue. Being before God is at stake only in and through prayer.

The Christian tradition has insisted on this agonic dimension. One of Kierkegaard's quite beautiful discourses is titled: "The true prayer is a struggle with God where one is victorious in the victory of God."[28] Several centuries earlier, one discovers Saint Macarius's powerful commentary on the passage in the Gospels where the violent seize the Kingdom of Heaven. He invites the man who is still prisoner to the hardness of his heart to "force himself to charity, when he has no charity—force himself to meekness when he has no meekness. . . ." And he goes on: "force himself to prayer when he has not spiritual prayer; and thus God, beholding him thus striving, and compelling himself by force, in spite of an unwilling heart gives him the true prayer of the Spirit."[29] What would the meekness be without the fire of this inner violence whose clarity it becomes, what would prayer be without this inward combat with the dumbness in us? This prayer that is so violent and at first uttered against our will—who can say if it is authentic or inauthentic? Doesn't the mere possibility

---

[27] Id. It is evident that the description of this circularity does not presuppose the theology of grace, which is obviously absent here.

[28] This is one of the *Four Edifying Discourses* of 1844.

[29] *Fifty Spiritual Homilies of St. Macarius the Egyptian* (Hom. 19, 3), p. 159.

that it evokes put out of play such a distinction, aiming as it does to secure the distinction between the proper and the improper?

Before offering a better description of these fortunate wounds of the Word, it behooves us to investigate what renders them possible: the address, allocution, saying "you." On this point, Feuerbach notes: "In prayer man addresses God with the word of intimate affection—*Thou*," before he interprets this saying "you" in a tendentious fashion by asserting: "he thus declares articulately that God is his *alter ego*."[30] For a philosopher who, like Karl Jaspers, makes disenchantment a virtue, this second person singular already constitutes a drift toward a mistaking of God: "If man turns to the deity in prayer, it is to him in his lonely abandonment a thou with which he would like to enter into communication. It takes for him the personal form. . . . A genuine sense of transcendence will balk at conceiving God as a personality. I quickly shrink from the impulse that would make the deity a thou for me because I feel I am profaning transcendence."[31] To be on intimate terms with the absolute, to say "you" to it, would be to make its distance unduly near, to the point that this proximity would no longer be its own, to the point of substituting for it a mythical image that I would have forged for myself.

Thus, the dialogue with God, far from being the place where I find him by finding myself, that is to say, by being first unstuck from myself, would in contrast be the place where I lose him by veiling "the abyss of transcendence" that escapes all address. To this, a historical objection can first be made: the freedom, the confidence, the heartfelt intimacy in the speech addressed to God, what the Christians call *parrèsia*, instead of decreasing and growing weaker with the recognition of his absolute transcendence, accompanies it. This is seen clearly if one compares the Greek or Roman prayer of antiquity to the Jewish prayer and the Christian prayer. Kerenyi remarks that the word 'god', *theos*, in the vocative, is introduced only by the latter pair of religions. And a formula suggesting appropriation, such as *my God*, does not signify that God has been degraded into a thing or has become the property of man; rather, it seals in speech the speaker's thorough and

---

[30] *The Essence of Christianity*, p. 122.
[31] Karl Jaspers, *Philosophy*, vol. 3, pp. 145–46.

complete belonging to the one to whom he addresses himself. For that matter, one must have a strange and narrow conception of the other, of speech, and of saying "you" to think that the address can mean only excessive familiarity. For it is only in saying "you" that objectivization runs up against an uncrossable limit; it is only in the hymn where we sing songs of celebration for the one whom we celebrate in song that "the abyss of transcendence" can be truly recognized and confessed. In fact, even silence as a mark of respect and adoration, the *favete linguis* of the Latin-speaking peoples or the euphony of the Greeks, is a destined silence, a silence before the other and for him. It is silence before You, and it makes up a possibility proper to speech, which alone can *fall into silence*, can, by the act of keeping silent, transform silence into an act of presence, and not into privation. Silence is still allocution.

A beautiful hymn from Synesius of Cyrene can bring this phenomenon to light. The first four verses begin by saying *you* (in the accusative, it is you whom I celebrate in song) and announce that the hymn is sung at all hours of the day, before the poet beckons the different beings of nature, the wind, the birds, the waters, to fall silent so that he can claim in the end: "Happily do I celebrate you with my voice, and happily too do I celebrate you with my silence, for all that the intellect says with its voice, you hear also in its silence."[32] The almost irresistible swelling of the hymn is also the embracing of silence. Nature must keep quiet so that silence might become voice, and so that in it as in a treasured locket the human voice might resound—but the latter is still voice in the silence where it is accomplished. The silence in view of divine transcendence, which is highlighted here, does not constitute the interruption or the suspension of the initial You, but its completion. The silence says *You*, beyond all names, like the opening of a gaze, but this gaze is open only through speech and remains that of speech. The silence of prayer is here a silence *heard* by God; it is still and always dialogue, and can be so only because a first silence, different and purely privative, was broken.

Prayer knows that it does not know how to pray, but it learns this only in praying. It knows this only as long as it prays, and it

---

[32] *Hymn II* (Paris, 1978), ed. and trans. Lacombrade, pp. 61–63.

is real, like all that is implied in the encounter, only in the impossible. This agonic dimension is nothing other than the ordeal of transcendence. The latter is given as such only when its distance is broached without ceasing to be distance, and it is undergone only in the ordeal of speech. Only the second person singular can open the space of such an ordeal. It is only in saying *You* that the I can be completely exposed, beyond all that it can master.

A new characteristic is added to our description of prayer: the manifestation of self to the other by the word, that is, agonic speech that struggles for its truth, is an ordeal, a suffering God, a passion for God, a theopathy. Prayer is prey to its addressee. In measuring itself by God, prayer is a speech that has always transgressed all measure, exceeded any ability to measure itself and know itself completely. In collapsing beneath him, prayer, like all lovers' speech, bears the weight of giving itself, that is to say, of losing itself. It suffers the other in coming unstuck from itself. In what way? How is the word of prayer wounded by its addressee? The man praying addresses his word to the divine ear. In distinction from a determinate human ear, this ear is always already awake, it does not need to be aroused by a call to attention. The hesitant speech of our voice resonates in and through a silent hearing that has forever preceded and awaited it. Being expected in this way renders it unexpected to itself. To be heard by God is an ordeal, speech being put to a test like no other; for our speech is exposed in all that it seeks to hide, excuse, justify, obtain. Speech appears in the attentive light of silence—the voice is truly naked.

To hear, to grant [*Ecouter, exaucer*], the word is the same: *audire, exaudire; hören, erhören*. The theological paradox stating that every real prayer is granted in one way or another has a basis in the phenomenon itself. The man praying speaks for a hearing that has always already come before his speech. The knowledge of this divine precedence to human speech makes the latter seem, in its own eyes, to be a response to this hearing, which awaits and calls. In all religions, it is asserted, however it might be interpreted, that the divine wants to be prayed to and addressed. Consequently, the speech act seems to be made possible by the silence of divine hearing; this is the silence that gives it a chance to speak. Speech is received from it; it incites speech. This is why all prayer offers thanks for itself; for even the most supplicating of demanding prayers has already received, received the power to ask of God, the power to address itself to him. Only in this way does it appear, and on that depend many of its properties as an act. The demand is always late with regard to its fulfillment. The appearing of self to self is like the moon: it gets its light from elsewhere.

In his treatise *De dono perseverentiae*, Saint Augustine, opposing the erring ways of the Pelagians, says it marvelously: "What does this mean: the Spirit itself prays, if not that it makes us pray [*interpellare facit*]." And farther along: "The cry of the spirit means making one cry [*clamare facientem*]. Thus we understand that this is also a gift of God, that we cry to God. . . . It is also a divine gift that we pray, that is, that we seek, that we ask, and that we knock, since we have received the Spirit of adoptive sons in which we cry: Abba! Father!"[33] No doubt, what is at issue concerns grace, which would call for a theological commentary; but this is also a rigorous description of prayer as speech act, made possible by its addressee, of a possibility that is already a favor granted. William of Saint-Thierry says this with as much simplicity as clarity: "When I speak to you, I turn toward you, and that too is good for me. And whatever the object of my prayer, I never pray or worship you in vain; the very act of praying brings me rich reward."[34] To speak to God is to be toward him and with him, and nothing can ever be asked of God that would not be inscribed in the space opened by this encounter and this ordeal. That is not without its consequences.

Curiously enough, Gerardus van der Leeuw in his important *Phänomenologie der Religion* dedicates only a few brief pages to prayer. He distinguishes it from adoration, which he deals with elsewhere, and which seems to him to be a higher and more pure possibility, for, he says, "prayer originates in care" and "whoever adores has therefore forgotten his prayer and now knows only God's glory."[35] In addition to ill perceiving how a prayer, at least in monotheism, could not, whatever its object, first be an act of adoration, in addition to the fact that deliverance from all worry

---

[33] *De dono perseverentiae* XXIII, 64 [English trans., p. 209 (modified), pp. 210–11 (modified)].

[34] Meditation IV,13 [English trans., p. 117].

[35] *Religion in Its Essence and Its Manifestation*, §81,1, p. 538. On prayer, cf. §62.

is not necessarily the end of religious existence (far from it!), such claims forget that prayer, even when expressing our worries, can by itself offer thanks to him who is the object of its adoration. The adoration of the Spirit who causes us to cry out takes place in the cry itself. Also, it is superficial to simply oppose a demanding prayer to a prayer without demand by considering solely the object of the prayer without paying attention to the speech act by which we make our demand and without considering the modes according to which it is turned toward its addressee. What is essential is the connection of desire and prayer, and it can serve to unify the different definitions that could be given for the latter.

In the history of the Christian tradition, two definitions were often taken up and discussed. One makes prayer an elevation of the spirit toward God, the other makes prayer a demand that God grant what is fitting.[36] The first dissociates prayer from a speech act, while the second is generally understood as vocal.[37] But both suppose desire. Saint Augustine says in a sermon: "Desire still prays even when the tongue holds silent. Desire which is never slaked is a perpetual prayer. When does prayer sleep? When desire languishes."[38] Franz von Baader, who has frequently described and meditated on the act of praying, has gone so far as to identify the will and prayer, asserting that man by his very nature, namely, as will, is a religious being, a praying. Each of the determinations of the will would be a conscious or unconscious prayer, turned toward God or toward an idol.[39]

When this desire for God appears to the man praying as a gift of God, when the very act by which he addresses a demand to God is in his eyes found in a space where God already answers for him, it is fair to describe prayer as a conversation or a dialogue with God, quite independent of extraordinary or supernatural events where we would hear voices or receive signs. The great mystical Persian poet Rûmî has described this. He evokes a man who prays fervently and to whom Satan objects: "O little chatterbox, to all these 'Allah's,' where is the 'Here I am'? No response

---

[36] Cf. Saint John Damascene, *De fide orthodoxa* III, 24, which juxtaposes the two.
[37] Cf. Saint Bonaventure, *Breviloquium* V, 10.
[38] Sermon LXXX, 7.
[39] *Sämtliche Werke*, t. II, pp. 514–15.

has come from the throne of God." This inspires doubt and discouragement, before this divine response comes to him from the mouth of a wise man: "This 'Allah' that you utter is my 'Here I am.' Your supplication, your sorrow, your fervor are My messenger to you. Your projects and your efforts to find a means to reach Me, this is in reality Me myself who would draw you toward me and free your feet. . . . In answer to each of your 'O Lord,' there are many 'Here I am' from Me."[40] The response is in the call, and reverberates in it. The vocative of the invocation is not simply the place of the praying man's presence to God, but that of God's presence to the praying man. At issue here is the same structure of preceding as in the "You would not seek me if you had not already found me" found in Saint Bernard and Pascal.

In monotheism, the description of this enveloping and intertwining of the human and divine calls can go so far as to say that it is God who prays in us. Paul Claudel says with his customary profundity that God does not accompany just our plenitude, but also our need. "It is in His company that this need in us becomes opening, utterance, and call. It is He who through our heart and our mouth invokes Himself."[41] Franz von Baader writes similarly: "The very God who prays in me will grant it in me."[42] And elsewhere, describing prayer as both a gift and a task (*Gabe, Aufgabe*), he compares it to the motions of our breath: we receive it from God, we inhale it from him (*nous l'inspirons de lui*), in order to offer it to him, in order to exhale it into him (*pour l'expirer en lui*).[43] This circulation of our breath taken in and blown out, received and offered, this "conspiracy" (*conspiration*) of the human and the divine is such that, for von Baader, prayer appears to be a function that is no less vital for the spirit than respiration is for the life of the body.[44]

The ordeal of this circulation, where the breath that we take

---

[40] Djalâl-od-Dîn Rûmî, *Mathnawî, La quête de l'Absolu* (Paris, 1990), trans. Vitray-Meyerovitch and Mortazavi, p. 542. This passage was cited by Heiler, p. 225.

[41] *La rose et le rosaire* (Paris, 1947), pp. 156–57.

[42] *S.W.*, t. VIII, p. 29. Louis-Claude de Saint-Martin already said: "You cannot pray without God himself praying with you. Who will refuse you if the one who grants is the same as the one who asks?"; see *L'homme de désir*, §271, p. 297.

[43] *S. W.*, t. II, p. 515.

[44] *S. W.*, t. II, p. 500.

for demanding is already a breath received—if it belongs to the essence of prayer—obviously happens in very different ways depending on which religion is being considered. In Christianity, the thought of the mystical body, according to which Christians make up the members of Christ, gives it a particular modality: it is accompanied by a veritable exchange of voices. If God has taken on a human voice, the relation of our voice to his is transformed. About a psalm, Saint Augustine writes, evoking Christ: "Making us with Himself, one Man, head and Body. Therefore, we pray to Him, through Him, in Him. He speaks in us in the prayer of the Psalms, which is entitled: 'A Prayer of David.' "[45]

These sorts of citations can seem to lead to strictly theological considerations, which would be something quite different from a description of prayer. All the same, they raise two decisive questions for a phenomenology. The first, already raised, is that of the breath and the voice in prayer. Why and how is prayer vocal? The second concerns the uniqueness of the speech used in prayer. One can pray freely, with the words one speaks invented to some extent, but one can also "recite" traditional prayers, such as the Psalms for Jews and Christians. What exactly does it mean to "recite" a prayer? Is the word 'recite' suitable? How can the praying man claim as his own the words composed by another in such a way that they are the highest expression of himself in this place of radical, unsubstitutable, intimate truth that is his presence to God? In what way does this appropriation of the words spoken happen?

In his voyage in Grande Garabagne, Henri Michaux evokes the god Mna, "the deafest of all and the greatest." "As soon as he is up to date, this is a god who asks only to satisfy men . . . (he can refuse them nothing)." But look! His hearing is poor, and it is only getting worse every day. So, an enormous artificial ear has been added to him. "And there are always great official wailers, priests and children of priests, with the shrillest and most penetrating voices, whose function it is to cry words of supplication, but only, as you would expect, after being preceded, for the purpose of alerting him, by men throwing firecrackers and trumpeters chosen from among the most powerfully lunged men of the

---

[45] *Enarrationes in Psalmos* 86, 1 [English trans., p. 410].

Gaurs."[46] But when one is not in Grande Garabagne, this is not, obviously, the function of the voice in prayer.

The study of the latter necessitates historical considerations; for one's apprehension of the prayer spoken aloud can vary noticeably from one age to another, and it is sometimes difficult to detach the description of the phenomenon from the critical agreement and disagreement that often surrounds it. What a divide there is, for example, between this admirable verse from Aeschylus: "When shall we show / the strength of our voices for Orestes,"[47] where prayer is literally the strength of mouths, and this distich from Angelus Silesius: "Do you then believe, poor man, that the cries of your mouth / are the song of praise which is suitable to the silent Deity?"[48] Montaigne, for his part, seems to equate the utterance of prayers with their inauthenticity, writing: "We pray out of habit and custom, or to speak more correctly, we read or pronounce our prayers,"[49] while Feuerbach sees this utterance as an essential property of prayer: "It is essential to the effectiveness of prayer that it be audibly, intelligibly, energetically expressed. Involuntarily, prayer wells forth in sound; the struggling heart bursts the barrier of the closed lips."[50]

The opposition between vocal and silent prayer is nevertheless more complex than it appears. In the ages when praying aloud was the rule, a prayer pronounced quietly, or simply murmured, could be called silent (tacitus).[51] How can we characterize Anne's prayer as it is described in the Bible? "Eli looked at her mouth. Anne spoke quite softly: her lips moved but her voice could not be heard, and Eli thought that she was drunk."[52] The Talmud will conclude from this that "one must not raise one's voice too much," but that "similarly one must not reduce prayer to a simple

---

[46] *Ailleurs* (Paris, 1962), pp. 132–33.

[47] *The Libation Bearers*, V, 719–20 [English trans., p. 120]. Claudel translates: "Ne saurons-nous par la prière / porter secours à Oreste [Can we not, with our prayers, / offer some assistance to Orestes]?"

[48] *Pèlerin chérubinique* (Paris, 1946), trans. Plard, I, 239, p. 99. Cf. the following distich speaking of the superiority of silence.

[49] *Essais* I, 56 [English trans., p. 231].

[50] *The Essence of Christianity*, p. 123.

[51] Cf. Siegfried Sudhaus, "Lautes und leises Beten," *Archiv für Religionswissenschaft* 9 (1906): 185–200. I thank François Guillaumont for having made this most useful article known to me.

[52] 1 Samuel 1.12–13. It is easily seen that he is surprised to not hear her.

meditation." "What then are we to do? Speak with your lips."[53] The Latin poet Persius will see in this a characteristic of certain Jewish prayers: *Labra moves tacitus*, you move your lips without making a sound,[54] a bit like those in our own time who do not know how to read very well. This is not a prayer that makes a sound,[55] and in this sense one can call it silent, but it is still vocal and includes the same movements as if one were pronouncing it. At the edge of silence, it is the final stage of the murmur. Where does the vocal prayer begin, and where does it end? For us, reading, even reading a religious book, is an activity that is essentially distinct from praying. But when the reading happens aloud, when, even alone, one lends one's voice to what one reads, when one reads with body and soul, the distinction is less clear-cut and can even be done away with. In the Christian Middle Ages, *lectio* drifts toward *meditatio*: in reading the Sacred Scriptures, one feeds on them, one ruminates, one tastes their flavor, and, says Jean Leclercq describing this practice, "all this activity is, necessarily, a prayer, the *lectio divina* is a prayerful reading."[56]

In antiquity, pagan as well as Jewish then Christian antiquity, the prayer that is spoken aloud and such that it can be heard is the most normal and most fashionable prayer.[57] It admits exceptions, but these are characterized precisely as exceptions, connected to particular circumstances or particular practices, and they are more like murmured prayers than entirely silent prayers. The idea even presents itself that the intensity and the force of a prayer can be marked by the clarity and liveliness with which it is said, sung, or

---

[53] *Jerusalem Talmud, Treatise Berakoth* IV. In a somewhat unexpected fashion, all this is discussed by H. A. Wolfson in his masterful work on Philo of Alexandria, *Philo* (Cambridge, Mass.: Harvard University Press, 1982), t. 2, pp. 248ff.

[54] *Satires* V, v. 184.

[55] Despite Calvin, who writes on this subject: "For even though the best prayers are sometimes unspoken, it often happens in practice that, when feelings of mind are aroused, unostentatiously the tongue breaks forth into speech, and the other members into gesture. From this obviously arose that uncertain murmur of Hannah's [1 Sam 1.13], something similar to which all the saints experience when they burst forth into broken and fragmentary speech"; *Institutes of the Christian Religion* (III, 20, 33), p. 897.

[56] *Initiation aux auteurs monastiques du Moyen Age* (Paris, 1963), pp. 72–73 [English trans., p. 73].

[57] Cf. Sudhaus, art. cited, pp. 188, 190, and W. Eichrodt, *Theology of the Old Testament*, t. I, p. 175: "The normal way of praying was to speak aloud."

cried. Not that the gods, or God, are deaf, like Mna for Michaux, and cannot hear our murmurs, but because a manifestation of self before God could not be purely spiritual and acosmic. To manifest oneself, this is to manifest oneself for God in the world, and to manifest oneself entirely.

Where does one manifest oneself entirely, if not in and through the voice, inseparably spiritual and fleshly? Distress, joy, need, gratitude want to be said and proclaimed. To pray vocally is to make one's body an essential element of the prayer. Saint Thomas Aquinas says of vocal prayer that "man ought to serve God with all that he has received from him, not only with the mind but also with the body."[58] The offering and the service of the voice, the gift of speech and the handing over of the voice, are the event in which all can be sacrificed at once, without division or restriction. For if certain religions prescribe bodily purifications prior to prayer, and if an orator can, before speaking, clear his voice, as it is said, the voice, purified and truly clear, will not be so, will not become so, except in speaking. It is not elevated and it is not transformed except in giving itself, even if it should sometimes be broken, trembling, or shaky. Instead of being the simple exterior manifestation of an interior state—an expression—it becomes an effusion that collects and an offering that concentrates. One does not receive oneself except in giving oneself; one does not exist as oneself except in projecting one's voice into the world, outside oneself. Paul Claudel says that the vocal prayer "is after all a sanctification of our breathing," which should not be confused with a technique for mastering breathing. He then goes on to say that it is "on the one hand a means for putting down vain thoughts, on the other a rhythmic purification of the disordered bubbling of our imagination, and finally a training of our sensibility and our attention."[59] The discipline introduced by the voice brings it about that speech itself listens, becomes in essence listening. The vocal prayer puts an end to the disorder of the interior babble, and thus is attention to the one to whom we address ourselves. The voice is not an instrument for itself.

A second aspect of vocal prayer, whether it be individual or

---

[58] *Summa theologica* IIa, IIae, q. 83, a. 12 [English trans., p. 83].
[59] *Emmaüs, Oeuvres complètes* (Paris, 1964), t. XXIII, p. 82.

collective, is its public nature. One prays *to* God, but ones prays *in* the world. One can set oneself apart in order to pray, but the prayer cannot in itself be secret, except as a radiant secret wanting to expose itself, since it is an act of presence and manifestation. In antiquity, the murmured or inaudible prayer is often associated with magic practices or shameful demands. The magician wants to remain the keeper of his formulae and incantations: they must not be proclaimed. And there are certain vows that we would be ashamed to utter aloud. Ancient literature provides a number of examples.[60] This is why Seneca ends one of his letters to Lucilius by citing a philosopher who asserted: "Know that thou art freed from all desires when thou hast reached such a point that thou prayest to God for nothing except what thou canst pray for openly," which itself is transposed in a lovely chiasmus: "Love among men as if God beheld you, speak with God as if men were listening."[61] Montaigne refers to the Pythagorians, who wanted prayers to God "to be public and heard by everyone, so that God should not be asked for anything indecent or unjust."[62] That can seem naïve or archaic, but makes clearly evident a property of vocal prayer: as a manifestation in the world, it has at the very least a virtual public character, and in fact it is always heard by at least one man, the one who utters it. When I am its sole witness, this speech act preserves the responsibility that is proper to it. Does this necessarily have to be a sign of naïveté rather than of taking it seriously? Is it pointless to emphasize that all human speech, even when solitary and addressed to God, always includes as its horizon the community of speech among men?

This raises the question of the respective importance of the collective and the individual prayer. Even the enemies of vocal prayer agree that it is necessary to collective prayer, which, if it can include moments of silence, still cannot be conceived without the voice. And the superiority of collective prayer is emphasized by numerous religious traditions. The Talmud goes so far as to

---

[60] Cf. the curious passage in Horace (*Letters* 1.16), cited by Montaigne, *Essais* I, 56. In the opposite sense, John Cassian (*Conferences* IX, 35) suggests as one of the motives for silent prayer, where God alone knows our demands, that the diabolical powers cannot overtake them.

[61] *Ad Lucilium Epistulae Morales* I, 10, 5 [English trans., p. 59].

[62] *Essais* I, 56 [English trans., p. 235].

claim that "only the prayers said in a synagogue are heard," and Maimonides writes that "one must associate with a community and not pray alone when one has the possibility of praying together."[63] Christianity also insists on this, as is indicated by certain passages of Scripture: "There where two or three are found to be joined in my name, I am in their midst," and if they "agree in asking for anything whatsoever, it will be granted to them by my Father who is in heaven."[64] The community of men gathered together to pray the invisible gives it a visible manifestation. It is all the more open to the invisible as it is visible, all the more spiritual as it is fleshly. In certain beliefs, this community grows beyond its visibly present members. The voice shows the invisible that calls, convokes, and assembles.

Is it thus a simple means, a simple condition sine qua non? The mutual presence of men and their common presence to God in sharing the word goes far beyond this. No one prays merely for himself, and the collectivity also prays, also speaks for those who can no longer or can not yet speak. It speaks for those who are absent or who have disappeared; it speaks for others, in their interest but also in their place. And it can be that each man, in his very solitude, is but the placeholder of the community. This is why the phenomenological difference between communal prayer and solitary prayer, where essence is at issue, is not at all identical to the empirical difference between collective prayer and individual prayer. For Plotinus, for example, who almost never invokes prayer, its truth resides in tending toward God himself with our soul, and not our words, and to pray "alone to him alone."[65] Even if many philosophers were brought together in the same place in order to pray in this way, this prayer would remain solitary in essence. As for Proclus, he clearly makes a difference between the "philosophical prayer" and the "legal prayer, that which conforms to the traditional usage of the cities," which are necessarily collective. This difference coincides with a difference between forms of speech, "the speech that one considers inwardly in scientific reflection" and "the speech whose lot is to be twice

---

[63] I am borrowing these citations from the *Cahiers d'études juives*, n.s., 1, *La prière*, pp. 10 and 16.

[64] Matthew 18.19–20.

[65] *Enneads* V, 1, 6 [English trans., p. 29]. Cf. Heiler, *Das Gebet*, p. 229.

removed from the intellect, that which is proffered outside in view of teaching and social relations."[66] Such oppositions, where the utterance of the word is a form of degradation, and where the most solitary prayer is necessarily the highest, however, are radically excluded.

In Christianity, for example, all prayer is communal by essence, since every individual prays and can pray—even when most isolated—only as a member of the mystical body of Christ, and therefore always in the Church. To be sure, the individual prayer is distinct from the collective prayer, but only as variants of the same ecclesial prayer, which the Our Father marks in its very form. Each of these two variations refers to the other as to that without which it could not be fully accomplished. The solitary prayer is always only something like a provisional detachment from the collective prayer since it is always ecclesial, and the collective prayer is nothing like an imaginary entity floating above the individuals who pronounce it, but is rooted in the act proper to each. It is indeed necessary for each to say and say again the Credo, in the first person singular, but the Christian Credo does not affirm that Christ died for me, but for us, *pro nobis*. Prayer thus founds a sui generis mode of community in and through speech.

Another characteristic manifests this: the insistence on the fact that one has to pray for oneself, the prayer for oneself being the condition of the prayer for others.[67] They are not in competition, and there is nothing egocentric in the one founding the other, for, far from divinizing me, it is that by which I stand before God and am recalled to my proper condition. This interlacing of voices and destinies gave rise to Saint Augustine's beautiful considerations on the perpetuity of prayer. This has always aroused debate, for it is asked how it is possible that an individual can pray always. The most common solution is to affirm that every action can become prayer when it is offered to God, which obviously separates prayer from a speech act. But there is at least one perpetual vocal prayer: that of the community, where, when one member falls silent, another takes up speaking where he left off. Saint Au-

---

[66] *Commentaire sur le Timée*, t. II, pp. 36 and 41.
[67] Saint Thomas Aquinas, *Summa theologica* IIa, IIae, q. 83, a. 7, ad 2 um.

gustine describes the prayer of the Church as the unceasing prayer of a single and unique man across space and time.[68] Independent of this theological perspective, the singularity of prayer, which knows itself as a voice in the chorus, as a moment in the historical community of speech, is emphasized in a clear-cut fashion.

That speech can be all the more proper to each as it does not belong to him exclusively but passes and circulates and is transmitted from one voice to another and from one life to another, consuming them and consummating them as it goes; that the highest intimacy with God is said in the speech we do not invent, but which invents us, in that it finds us and unveils us there where we were without knowing it; that the formulaic prayer, the prayer using traditional or scriptural formulae, is not a constraining prayer but the most free of all—all this forms an essential characteristic of vocal prayer. Praying is not citing, it is to be cited to appear by what one says before what one says, and in it. To be sure, in other realms of existence, I can use the words spoken by another for the purpose of communicating something quite personal and, for example, make a declaration of love by citing the verses of a poet, or express my opinion by a proverb. I appropriate these turns of speech; but it belongs to their particular stylistic effect that they be identified as a citation. In prayer, it is not the same. To say a prayer is to be appropriated by it, or to make oneself appropriate to it in a wholly other mode.

This very common phenomenon is not often meditated on or thematized. John Cassian has done so with great precision, however, when commenting on the use of the Psalms in prayer:

> Strengthened by this food on which he forever feeds, (the monk) is so run through by all the feelings expressed in the psalms that he sings them not as if they have been composed by the prophet but as if he himself were their author and they were his own personal prayer (*velut a se editos quasi orationem propriam*). . . . At the very least, he is of the opinion that they were made expressly for him (*vel certe ad suam personam aestimet eos fuisse directos*), and he knows that what they express was not realized at another moment in the person of the prophet, but rather that it is again carried out in and through him.[69]

---

[68] Cf. Emile Mersch, *Le corps mystique du Christ* (Paris-Bruxelles, 1936), t. II, pp. 106ff.

[69] *Conferences* X, 11 [English trans., pp. 383–85 (modified)].

One could not offer a better description of this actualization of the psalm in prayer. To be sure, from totally exterior considerations, some audacity can be detected in making oneself out to be something like the author of a word held to be inspired. But this is not pride, for the belief in inspiration includes precisely this dimension of perpetual novelty and actuality. To pray the psalms is not to add one theoretical interpretation to another; it is to let oneself be interpreted by them, to offer one's own life, to which they grant another speech, that of God, as the space of their resonance and their promise. Whence the temporal dimensions on which John Cassian insists in what follows: we pray the psalms by anticipating their meaning, as if we invented them, and also in remembering ourselves, in remembering our own ordeals, which are their best explanation.

This is why there is a life of prayer, "a life," says Claudel, "which brings to the domain of the spirit the surprisingly complex, varied, ingenious, and sometimes paradoxical activities of physiology," for "the Word must become flesh in us."[70] This life is sustained by the voice that gathers us and welcomes us in a place other than ourselves—before God. In the religions where God himself is Speech, it seems that prayer bursts out everywhere, as in the beautiful and surprising conclusion of Tertullian's treatise on prayer where he asserts that "every creature, even beasts of the field and wild beasts, pray" and—something that would have charmed Olivier Messiaen—that the birds, lacking hands, make an outstretched cross in the heavens with their wings, and "utter something that seems a prayer."[71] Is this just an example of someone getting carried away with himself, or is it a quite rigorous perception of the fact that the human voice, in what is unique and irreplaceable about it, is always hymnal and cannot speak without giving voice to all that has none, without bringing to speech all that remains mute or can only babble, without offering to God, with it and in it, the world as a whole wounded by the word? Philo the Jew made man into a "eucharistic" creature, a creature whose most proper act, the one integrally its own, is to offer thanks, since all that could be offered to God already belongs to

---

[70] *L'abbé Brémond et la prière*, April 1933.
[71] *De oratione* 29 [English trans., p. 45].

him, except the very act by which we thank "with whichever of
its appointed functions the voice may exercise, be it speech or
song."[72] The human voice becomes a place where the world returns to God. It gives what it does not have—which does not
mean that it gives nothing—and it can give itself only because it
is not in possession of itself, the voice being what does not belong
in all speech.

In what preceded, the exclusive insistence on vocal prayer does
not mean that we have forgotten about the varied and profound
silent prayers. But the latter can be defined and constituted only
by reference to the former. Only the voice can keep quiet, and
only speech can become silence. The withdrawal or the suspension of the voice cannot be first, and vocal prayer is always presupposed, even if there are states of the religious life where it can
become impossible or unwise. It founds all the other forms of
prayer, which suspend or interiorize the voice. And this founding
character does not mean that it is only an inchoate, rudimentary,
simple form of prayer on which more subtle, more pure, more
elevated forms of prayer would be built up little by little. It appears simple only because it is the most common, but it has all
the complexity of the voice, from cry to murmur, and that of a
speech act that can make demands, thank, interrogate, tell stories,
renounce, promise. . . . The other forms of prayer are simplifica-
tions of it; they retain only some aspect or other, already contained really or virtually in it. Saint Teresa of Avila shows that the
highest states of contemplation can be produced in vocal prayer.
This is why vocal prayer, in the full range of its forms, is something like the index of religious existence, leaving outside none
of the phenomena that constitute religion. It does not shrink back
into a world behind the scenes nor does it flee finitude since it
renders the world as a whole present to the invisible, and in manifesting us to it body and soul, it unveils to us our own condition
and our own finitude in a light without shadows, in the incandes-
cent clarity of the supplicating voice.

Why call it "wounded word"? It always has its origin in the
wound of joy or distress, it is always a tearing that brings it about
that the lips open. And it does so as it is still and otherwise

---

[72] *De plantatione*, §§130–31 [English trans., p. 279 (modified)].

wounded. Wounded by this hearing and this call that have always already preceded it, and that unveil it to itself, in a truth always in suffering, always agonic, struggling like Jacob all night in the dust to wrest God's blessing from him, and in keeping the sign of a swaying and limping by which speech is all the more confident as it is less assured of its own progress. For the man praying learns in prayer that he does not know how to pray, that he is called by a call that exceeds him in every way and seeks to introduce him into the perfect prayer—which is something whose possibility or lack thereof we cannot examine here: the prayer that would go from God to God, in a voice, and therefore in a human body, the prayer by which God would invoke himself. Wounded again is this speech on account of wanting to give voice to all the voices that keep quiet, forbidden from praying by the play of echoes where they address their individual or collective idols, or by the atrocity of the destiny they endure, whose despair does not even become a cry that would incriminate God, which can be a way of praying.

This act of a word wounded by the radical alterity of him to whom it speaks is pure address. It does not speak in order to teach something to someone, even if it always says something about ourselves and the world. It confides to the other what the other knows, and asks of him what he knows we need. Not even for a single moment is the word separate from the ordeal; it is undergone by and through itself, both by what it says and by what it does not succeed in saying and by him to whom it speaks. It itself learns from this ordeal, and this is why this wound makes it stronger, all the stronger as it will not have sought to heal it.

8

The Saturated Phenomenon

Jean-Luc Marion

> What comes into the world without troubling merits
> neither consideration nor patience.
>
> R. Char

1

THE FIELD OF RELIGION could be simply defined as whatever philosophy excludes or, in the best case, subjugates. Such a constant antagonism cannot be reduced to any given ideological opposition or any given anecdotal prejudice. In fact, it rests upon perfectly reasonable grounds: the "philosophy of religion," if there were one, would have to describe, produce, and constitute phenomena; it would then find itself confronted with a disastrous alternative: either it would be a question of addressing phenomena that are objectively definable but lose their religious specificity, or it would be a question of addressing phenomena that are specifically religious but cannot be described objectively. A phenomenon that is religious in the strict sense—that is, belonging to the domain of a "philosophy of religion" distinct from the sociology, the history, and the psychology of religion—would have to render visible what nevertheless could not be objectivized. The religious phenomenon thus amounts to an impossible phenomenon, or at least it marks the limit starting from which the phenomenon is in general no longer possible. Thus, the religious phenomenon poses the question of the general possibility of the phenomenon, more than the question of the possibility of religion.

Once this boundary is acknowledged, there nevertheless remain several ways of understanding it. Religion could not strike the possibility of the phenomenon in general with impossibility if the very possibility of the phenomenon were not defined: When does it become impossible to speak of a phenomenon, and according to what criteria of phenomenality? But the possibility of the phenomenon—and therefore the possibility of declaring a phenomenon impossible, that is, invisible—could not in its turn be determined without also establishing the terms of possibility taken in itself. By subjecting the phenomenon to the jurisdiction of possibility, philosophy in fact brings fully to light its own definition of naked possibility. The question concerning the possibility of the phenomenon implies the question of the phenomenon of possibility. Or better, when the rational scope of a philosophy is measured according to the extent of what it renders possible, that scope will be measured also according to the extent of what it renders visible—according to the possibility of phenomenality in it. Thus, according to whether it is accepted or rejected, the religious phenomenon would become a privileged index of the possibility of phenomenality.

To start out, I will rely on Kant. In Kant the metaphysical definition of possibility is stated as follows: "That which agrees with the formal conditions of experience, that is, with the conditions of intuition and of concepts, is possible [mit den formalen Bedingungen der Erfahrung . . . überkommt]." What is surprising here has to do with the intimate tie that Kant establishes between possibility and phenomenality: possibility results explicitly from the conditions of experience; among those conditions is intuition, which indicates that experience takes the form of a phenomenality—that experience has a form ("formal conditions") precisely because it experiences sensible forms of appearance. Here, therefore, possibility depends on phenomenality. Would it be necessary to conclude from this that the phenomenon imposes its possibility, instead of being subject to the conditions thereof? Not at all, because the possible does not agree with the object of experience but with its "formal conditions": possibility does not follow from the phenomenon, but from the *conditions* set for any phenomenon. Thus a formal requirement is imposed on possibility, just as Kant indicates a little bit later: "The postulate of the possibility of things requires [fordert] that the concept of things should agree

with the formal conditions of an experience in general." The access of the phenomenon to its own manifestation must submit to
the requirement of possibility; but possibility itself depends on the
"formal conditions of experience"; how, then, in the last instance,
are these "formal conditions" established that determine phenomenality and possibility together? Kant indicates an answer indirectly, but unambiguously, by underlining straightaway that
"the categories of modality . . . express only the relation of the
concept to the power of knowing."[1] The formal conditions of
knowledge are directly joined here with the power of knowing.
This means that intuition and the concept determine in advance
the possibility of appearing for any phenomenon. The possibility—and therefore also and especially the impossibility—of a phenomenon is ordered to the measure of the "power of knowing,"
that is, concretely, the measure of the play of intuition and of the
concept within a finite mind. Any phenomenon is possible that
grants itself to the finitude of the power of knowing and its requirements.

In this way Kant merely confirms a decision already made by
Leibniz. To be sure, the one thinks phenomenal possibility starting from a finite mind, while the other thinks it starting from an
infinite (or indefinite) mind; but both lead to the same conditional possibility of the phenomenon. Indeed, metaphysics obeys
the "Great Principle . . . which holds that nothing is done without sufficient reason, that is, that nothing happens without it
being possible for the one who sufficiently knows things to give
a Reason that suffices to determine why it is so and not otherwise."[2] Thus, nothing "is done," nothing "happens," in short,
nothing appears, without the attestation that it is "possible"; this
possibility, in turn, is equivalent to the possibility of knowing the
sufficient reason for such an appearance. As for Kant, for Leibniz
the right to appear—the possibility of a phenomenon—depends
on the power of knowing that implements the sufficiency of reason, which, whatever it might be, precedes what it renders possi-

---

[1] *Kritik der reinen Vernunft*, respectively A218/B265, A220/B267, and A219/
B266.

[2] *Principes de la nature et de la grâce* (Paris, 1954), ed. A. Robinet, vol. 7, p. 45.

ble. As the "power of knowing" will establish the conditions of possibility, sufficient reason already suffices to render possible that which, without it, would have remained impossible. This dependence is indicated with particular clarity in the case of the sensible. To be sure, "sensible things" appear and deserve the name of "phenomena," but they owe that name to another "reason," a reason that is different from their very appearance, and which alone suffices to qualify that appearance as a phenomenon: "The truth of sensible things consisted only in the relation of the phenomena, which had to have its reason."[3] When Leibniz opposes, among the beings that he recognizes as permanent (*Creatura permanens absoluta*), full being (*Unum per se, Ens plenum./ substantia / Modificatio*) to the diminished being that he likens to the phenomenon (*Unum per aggregationem. Semiens, phaenomenon*), one should not commit the error of imagining that the phenomenon would be ranked as half a being or a half-being only because it would suffer from an insufficiency of reason. On the contrary, it is precisely because it enjoys a perfectly sufficient reason that the phenomenon regresses to the rank of half a being; it is precisely as "phaenomena bene fundata"[4] that the phenomena admit their being grounded, and therefore conditioned by a reason that alone is sufficient and which they themselves do not suffice to ensure. If reason can ground the phenomena, this is so first because it must save them; but reason would not have to do this if one did not first admit that, left to themselves, these phenomena would be lost. For appearance actually to appear does not suffice to justify its possibility; it must still resort to reason, which—while itself not having to appear—alone renders possible the brute actuality of the appearance, because it renders the possibility of that appearance intelligible. The phenomenon attests its lack of reason when and because it receives that reason; for it appears only under condition, as a conditional phenomenon—under the condition of what does not appear. In a metaphysical system, the possibility of appearing never belongs to what appears, nor phenomenality to the phenomenon.

---

[3] *Nouveaux Essais*, IV, II, 84, in *Die philosophischen Schriften*, ed. C. Gerhardt, vol. 5, p. 355.

[4] Ep. CXXXIII to Des Bosses, ed. cit., vol. 2, p. 506.

2

It is this aporia that phenomenology escapes all at once in opposing to the principle of sufficient reason the "principle of all principles," and thus in surpassing conditional phenomenality through
a phenomenality without condition. The "principle of all principles" posits that "every originarily *donating* intuition [*Anschauung*]
is a source of right [*Rechtsquelle*] for cognition, that everything
that offers itself to us originarily in 'intuition' ['*Intuition*'] is to be
taken quite simply as it gives itself out to be, but also only within
the limits in which it is given there."[5] There could be no question
here of determining the decisive importance of this principle, nor
its function within the whole of the other principles of phenomenology.[6] It will suffice here to underscore some of its essential
traits.

According to the first essential trait, intuition no longer intervenes simply as a de facto source of the phenomenon, a source
that ensures its brute actuality without yet grounding it in reason,
but as a source of right, justificatory of itself. Intuition is itself
attested through itself, without the background of a reason that is
yet to be given. In this way, according to Husserl, the phenomenon corresponds in advance to the phenomenon according to
Heidegger: that which shows itself on the basis of itself. To put it
plainly: on the basis of itself as a pure and perfect appearance of
itself, and not on the basis of another than itself that would not
appear (a reason). Intuition is sufficient for the phenomenon to
justify its right to appear, without any other reason: far from having to give a sufficient reason, it suffices for the phenomenon to
give itself through intuition according to a principle of sufficient
intuition. But intuition becomes sufficient only inasmuch as it
operates without any background, originarily, as Husserl says;
now, it operates originarily, without any presupposition, only inasmuch as it furnishes the originary data, inasmuch, therefore, as
it gives itself originarily. Intuition is justified by right on the basis
of itself only by making a claim to the unconditioned origin. It

---

[5] *Ideen* I, §24, Hua. III, p. 52; English trans. by F. Kersten (The Hague: Martinus Nijhoff, 1982), p. 44 (modified).

[6] On this point, see M. Henry, "Quatre principes de la phénoménologie," in
Revue de Métaphysique et de Morale, 1991, n. 1.

cannot justify this claim without going so far as to mime the sufficient reason to be rendered (*reddendae rationis*), that is, by rendering itself, by giving itself in person. Indeed, *donation* alone
indicates that the phenomenon ensures, in a single gesture, both
its visibility and the full right of that visibility, both its appearance
and the reason for that appearance. Nevertheless, it still remains
to be verified whether the "principle of all principles" in point of
fact ensures a right to appear for all phenomena, whether it indeed
opens for them an absolutely unconditioned possibility, or
whether it renders them possible still only under some condition.
Now, it happens that the principle of the *donating* intuition does
not authorize the absolutely unconditioned appearance, and thus
the freedom of the phenomenon that gives itself on the basis of
itself. To be sure, this is not because the intuition as such limits
phenomenality, but because it remains framed, as intuition, by
two conditions of possibility, conditions that themselves are not
intuitive but that are nevertheless assigned to every phenomenon.
The second and third traits of the "principle of all principles"
contradict the first, as conditions and limits—a condition and a
limit—contradict the claim to absolute possibility opened by the
donating intuition.

Let us first consider a second trait of the "principle": it justifies
every phenomenon, "but also only [*aber auch nur*] within the limits in which" that phenomenon is given. This restriction attests to
a twofold finitude of the *donating* instance of intuition. First, there
is a factual restriction: intuition admits "limits [*Schranken*]": these
limits, in whatever way one understands them (since Husserl
hardly makes them clear here), indicate that not everything is
capable of being given perfectly; right away, intuition is characterized by scarcity, obeys a logic of shortage, and is stigmatized by
an indelible insufficiency—we will have to ponder over the moti-
vation, the status, and the presuppositions of this factual short-
coming. But—secondly—this restriction can already be
authorized by a limitation de jure: any intuition, in order to give
within certain factual "limits," must first be inscribed by right
within the limits (*Grenze*) of a horizon; likewise no intentional
aim of an object, signification, or essence can operate outside of
a horizon. Husserl indicates this point by means of an argument
that is all the stronger insofar as it is paradoxical: considering what

he nevertheless names "the limitlessness [*Grenzenlosigkeit*] that is presented by the immanent intuitions when going from an already fixed lived-experience to new lived-experiences that form its horizon, from the fixing of these lived-experiences to the fixing of their horizon; and so on," he admits that any lived-experience is continually referred to new, as yet unknown lived-experiences, and therefore to a horizon of novelties that are irreducible because continually renewed. But precisely, this irrepressible novelty of the flux of consciousness remains, by right, always comprehended within a horizon, even if these new lived-experiences are not yet given: "a lived-experience that has become an object of an ego's look and that therefore has the mode of being looked at, has for its horizon lived-experiences that are not looked at" (*Danach hat ein Erlebnis, das zum Objekt eines Ichblickes geworden ist, also den Modus des Erblickes hat, seinen Horizont nichterblickter Erlebnisse*)[7] The horizon, or, according to its etymology, the delimitation, exerts itself over experience even there where there are only lived-experiences that are not looked at, that is, where experience has not taken place. The outside of experience is not equivalent to the experience of the outside, because the horizon in advance seizes the outside, the nonexperienced, the not looked at. One cannot escape here the feeling of a fundamental ambiguity. With this horizon, is it a question of what is not looked at as not looked at, a question of the simple recognition that all lived-experience is grasped in the flux of consciousness, and is therefore oriented in advance toward other lived-experiences that are yet to arise? Or is it not rather a question of the treatment, in advance, of the non-lived-experiences that are not looked at as the subjects of a horizon, and therefore a question of the inclusion within a limit—be it that of the flux of consciousness—of anything that is not looked at, a question of the a priori inscription of the possible within a horizon? Thus we must ask whether the "principle of all principles" does not presuppose at least one condition for *donation*: the very

---

[7] *Ideen* I, §83, Hua. III, p. 201; English trans., p. 197 (modified). The connection made here by Husserl between the horizon of lived-experiences and the Kantian idea will assume all of its importance below. Will it be objected that the horizon is defined solely by the lack of intuition? Undoubtedly not, since signification, even without intuition, is given as such.

horizon of any *donation*. Does not the second trait of the "principle of all principles"—that of any horizon at all—contradict the absoluteness of intuitive *donation*?

The third trait of the "principle of all principles" has to do with the fact that intuition gives what appears only by giving it "to us." There is nothing trivial or redundant about this expression; it betrays a classic ambiguity of the *Ideen*: the *donation* of the phenomenon on the basis of itself to an *I* can at every instant veer toward a constitution of the phenomenon through and on the basis of the *I*. Even if one does not overestimate this constant threat, one must at least admit that *donation*, precisely because it keeps its originary and justifying function, can give and justify nothing except before the tribunal of the *I*; transcendental or not, the phenomenological *I* remains the beneficiary, and therefore the witness and even the judge, of the given appearance; it falls to the *I* to measure what does and does not give itself intuitively, within what limits, according to what horizon, following what intention, essence, and signification. Even if it shows itself on the basis of itself, the phenomenon can do so only by allowing itself to be led back, and therefore reduced, to the *I*. Moreover, the originary primacy of the *I* maintains an essential relation with the placement of any phenomenon within the limits of a horizon. Indeed, "every *now* of a lived-experience has a horizon of lived-experiences—which also have precisely the originary form of the 'now,' and which as such produce *an originary horizon* [*Originaritätshorizont*] *of the pure I*, its total originary *now* of consciousness."[8] In this way the "principle of all principles" still presupposes that all *donation* must accept the *I* as its "now." The requirement of a horizon is but one with that of the reduction: in each case it is a matter of leading phenomenological *donation* back to the *I*. But, that being the case, if every phenomenon is defined by its very reducibility to the *I*, must we not exclude straightaway the general possibility of an absolute, autonomous—in short, irreducible—phenomenon? By the same token, is not all irreducible possibility decidedly jeopardized?

"The principle of all principles," through originarily *donating*

---

[8] *Ideen* I, §82, Hua. III, p. 200; English trans., p. 196 (modified). See also *Formal and Transcendental Logic*, §99, Hua. XVII, p. 257.

intuition, undoubtedly frees the phenomena from the duty of rendering a sufficient reason for their appearance. But it thinks that *donation* itself only on the basis of two determinations that threaten its originary character: the horizon and the reduction. Phenomenology would thus condemn itself to missing almost immediately what the *donating* intuition nevertheless indicates to it as its own goal: to free the possibility of appearing [*l'apparaître*] as such. We should stress that it is obviously not a question here of envisaging a phenomenology without any *I* or horizon, for, clearly, it would then be phenomenology itself that would become impossible. On the contrary, it is a question of taking seriously the claim that, since the "principle of all principles," "higher than actuality stands *possibility*,"[9] and of envisaging this possibility radically. Let us define it provisionally: What would occur, as concerns phenomenality, if an intuitive *donation* were accomplished that was absolutely unconditioned (without the limits of a horizon) and absolutely irreducible (to a constituting *I*)? Can we not envisage a type of phenomenon that would reverse the condition of a horizon (by surpassing it, instead of being inscribed within it) and that would reverse the reduction (by leading the *I* back to itself, instead of being reduced to the *I*)? To declare this hypothesis impossible straightaway, without resorting to intuition, would immediately betray a phenomenological contradiction. Consequently, we will here assume the hypothesis of such a phenomenon, at least in the capacity of an imaginary variation allowing us to test a movement to the limit in the determination of any phenomenality and allowing us to experience anew what possibility means—or gives. Some limits remain, in principle, irrefutable and undoubtedly indispensable. But this does not mean that what contradicts them cannot for all that, paradoxically, be constituted as a phenomenon. Quite on the contrary, certain phenomena could—by playing on the limits of phenomenality— not only appear at those limits, but appear there all the more. Within this hypothesis, the question of a phenomenology of religion would no doubt be posed in new terms, as much for religion as for phenomenology.

---

[9] *Sein und Zeit*, 10th ed. (Tübingen, 1963), §7, p. 38.

3

We are justified in evoking the possibility of an unconditioned and irreducible phenomenon, that is, a phenomenon par excellence, only inasmuch as such a possibility truly opens itself. We therefore have to establish that this possibility cannot be reduced to an illusion of possibility, through a movement to the limit that would exceed nothing other than the conditions of possibility of phenomenality in general. In short, we have to establish that an unconditioned and irreducible phenomenon, with neither delimiting horizon nor constituting *I*, offers a true possibility and does not amount to "telling tales." To arrive at this guarantee, we will proceed indirectly at first by examining the common definition of the phenomenon, since there is a definition as much in metaphysics according to Kant as in phenomenology according to Husserl; we will then attempt to specify whether that definition—which, moreover, subjects every phenomenon to a horizon of appearance and a constituting *I*—is justified by an opening of phenomenality, or whether it does not rather confirm its essential closure. In other words, it will be a matter of specifying the ground of the limitation that is brought upon the phenomenon by its common definition, in order to indicate exactly what possibility would, by contrast, remain open to an unconditional and irreducible acceptation of phenomenality.

All along the path of his thinking, Husserl maintains a definition of the phenomenon that is determined by its fundamental duality: "The word 'phenomenon' is ambiguous [*doppelsinnig*] in virtue of the essential correlation between appearance and that which appears [*Erscheinen und Erscheinenden*]."[10] This correlation

---

[10] *Idee der Phänomenologie*, Hua. II, p. 14; English trans. by W. P. Alston and G. Nakhnikian (The Hague: Martinus Nijhoff, 1970), p. 11. See *Logische Untersuchungen*, III, §3: "Appearances [*Erscheinungen*] in the sense of objects appearing [*erscheinenden*] as such, but also in respect of phenomena as the experiences in which the phenomenal things appear"; and V, §2: "We cannot too sharply stress the equivocation that allows us to characterize as a phenomenon [*Erscheinung*] not only the lived-experience in which the appearing [*des Erscheinen*] of the object consists . . . , but also the object appearing [*erscheinende*] as such." (ed. Niemeyer [Tübingen, 1901], vol. 2, pp. 231 and 349; English trans. by J. N. Findlay [London: Routledge & Kegan Paul, 1970], vol. 2, pp. 439 and 538 [modified]).

is organized according to several different but interlinked pairs—intention/intuition, signification/fulfillment, noesis/noema, and the like—and thus only better establishes the phenomenon as what appears as a correlate of appearance (*apparition*). This is indeed why the highest manifestation of any phenomenon whatever, that is, the highest phenomenality possible, is achieved with the perfect adequation between these two terms: the subjective appearing (*l'apparaître subjectif*) is equivalent to that which objectively appears (*l'apparaissant objectif*). "And so also, *eo ipso*, the ideal of every fulfillment, and therefore of a *significative* fulfillment, is sketched for us; the *intellectus* is in this case the thought-intention, the intention of meaning. And the *adaequatio* is realized when the object meant is in the strict sense *given* in our intuition, and given precisely as it is thought and named. No thought-intention could fail of its fulfillment, of its last fulfillment, in fact, insofar as the fulfilling medium of intuition has itself lost all implication of unsatisfied intention."[11] It is certainly important to stress the persistence here, in a territory that is nevertheless phenomenological, of the most metaphysical definition of truth as *adaequatio rei et intellectus*. But it is even more important to stress the fact that adequation defines not only the truth, but above all "the ideal of ultimate fulfillment."[12] This limit case of perception is equivalent to what Husserl, in a Cartesian fashion, names *evidence*. More precisely, the objective truth is achieved subjectively through evidence, considered as the experience of the adequation made by consciousness. Now, this ideal of evidence, which is supposed to designate the maximum and the extreme of any ambition to truth, nevertheless claims, with a very strange modesty, only an "adequation," a simple equality. The paradigm of ideal equality weighs so heavily that Husserl does not hesitate to repeat it in no less than four figures: (a) "the full agreement between the meant and the given as such [*Übereinstimmung zwischen Gemeintem und Gegebenem*]"; (b) "the idea of the absolute adequation [*Adäquation*]" between the ideal essence and the empirically contingent act of evidence; (c) the "ideal fulfillment for an intention"; (d) and, fi-

---

[11] *Logische Untersuchungen*, VI, §37, loc. cit., vol. 3, p. 118; Eng. trans., p. 762 (modified).

[12] *Logische Untersuchungen*, VI, §37, loc. cit., vol. 3, p. 116; Eng. trans., p. 761. See p. 118; Eng. trans., p. 762.

nally, "the truth as rightness [Rechtigkeit] of our intention."[13] What is surprising, however, resides not so much in this insistent repetition as in the fact that the adequation it so explicitly seeks remains nonetheless a pure and simple ideal: "The ideal of an ultimate fulfillment," "that ideally fulfilled perception," an "idea of absolute adequation as such."[14] Now, how can we not understand these two terms in a Kantian manner where the ideal is the object of the idea? Consequently, since the idea remains a concept of reason such that its object can never be given through the senses, the ideal as such (as object of the idea) will never be given.[15] Thus, if adequation, which produces evidence subjectively, still constitutes an "ideal" for Husserl, we would have to conclude that it is never, or at least rarely, realized. And with it, truth itself is rarefied or made inaccessible. Why, therefore, does adequate evidence most often remain a limit case, or even an excluded case? Why does the equality between noesis and noema, essence and fulfillment, intention and intuition, seem inaccessible—or almost so—at the very moment when it is invested with the dignity of truth? Why does Husserl compromise the return to the things themselves by qualifying evidence and truth with ideality?

---

[13] Logische Untersuchungen, VI, §39, loc. cit., vol. 3, respectively, pp. 122 and 123; Eng. trans., pp. 765, 766 (modified).

[14] "ideale Fülle für eine Intention," §39, p. 123; Eng. trans., p. 766; "Ideal der leizten Erfüllung," title of §37, p. 118; Eng. trans., p. 761; "Das Ideal der Adäquation," title of chap. V, p. 115; Eng. trans., p. 760.

[15] "It is obvious that reason, in achieving its purpose, that, namely, of representing the necessary complete determination of things, does not presuppose the existence of an essence [nicht die Existenz eines solchen Wesen . . . voraussetze] that corresponds to this ideal, but only the idea of such an essence, and this only for the purpose of deriving from an unconditioned totality of complete determination the conditioned totality, that is, the totality of the limited" (Kritik der reinen Vernunft, A577/B606; Eng. trans., Norman Kemp Smith, modified). This definition of the ideal by Kant—the unconditioned but nonexistent totality that allows reason to determine the conditioned but existent limitation—covers fairly exactly the Husserlian ideal of fulfillment: unconditioned and complete, but not actualized, equality, in relation and comparison to which is measured the meaning [visée] that is actualized but intuitively poor. The difference has to do with the fact that for Kant the ideal of reason coincides strictly with God, whereas Husserl will have to wait for the final developments of his teleology of spirit in order to identify the ideal of fulfillment with God. See the classic work of A. Ales Belo, Husserl. Sul problema di Dio (Rome, 1985), and the texts that are gathered and commented on by J. Benoist, "Husserl: Au-delà de l'onto-théologie," Les Etudes philosophiques 4 (1991).

Answer: because the equality that Husserl maintains de jure between intuition and intention remains for him in fact untenable. Intention (almost) always (partially) lacks intuition, just as meaning (*signification*) almost always lacks fulfillment. In other words, intention and meaning surpass intuition and fulfillment. "A surplus in meaning [*ein Überschuss in der Bedeutung*] remains, a form that finds nothing in the phenomenon itself to confirm it," because in principle "the realm of meaning is much wider than that of intuition."[16] Intuition remains essentially lacking, poor, needy, indigent. The adequation between intention and intuition thus becomes a simple limit case, an ideal that is usually evoked by default. One could not argue against this by putting forward the fact that evidence is regularly achieved in mathematics and formal logic; for this fact, far from denying the failure of evidence, confirms it. Indeed, the ideal of adequation is realized precisely only in those domains where the intention of meaning, in order to be fulfilled in a phenomenon, requires only a pure or formal intuition (for example, space in mathematics), or even no intuition at all (for example, empty tautology in logic); mathematics and formal logic offer, precisely, only an ideal object—that is, strictly speaking, an object that does not have to give itself in order to appear, in short, a minute or zero degree of phenomenality; evidence is adequately achieved because it requires only a poor or empty intuition. Adequation is realized so easily here only because it is a matter of phenomena without any (or with weak) intuitive requirements.[17] There would be good reason, moreover,

---

[16] *Logische Untersuchungen*, VI, §§40 and 63, loc. cit., vol. 3, pp. 131 and 192; Eng. trans., pp. 775 and 825 (modified). Heidegger too speaks of "ein Überschuss an Intentionen," in *Prolegomena zur Geschichte des Zeitbegriffs*, §6, G.A. 20, p. 77.119.

[17] Descartes had clearly indicated that the privilege of the mathematical type of object (and therefore phenomenon) is due to its "purum et simplex" character, which presupposes nothing that experience renders uncertain (*Regulae ad directionem ingenii* II, AT X, 365, 16ff.); this privilege of certitude is paid for with an equal poverty of intuitive given, of "matter," such that it procures at one and the same time a real content and an irreducible uncertainty. This is also why the *intuitus* ensures certitude only for objects that are without matter (and poor in intuition, if not purely formal) like mathematical idealities, or for objects that are quasitautological (and therefore poor in intuition), like "uniusquisque intueri se existere, se cogitare" (see ibid., III, 368, 21ff., and Commentary in my *Sur l'ontologie grise de Descartes* [Paris, 1975; 2nd ed., 1981], §6, pp. 41–43 and §7, pp. 49–53). One of the reasons for the progressive abandonment of *intuitus* by

to wonder about the privilege that is so often granted by theories of knowledge (from Plato to Descartes, from Kant to Husserl) to logical and mathematical phenomena: they are erected as models of all the others, while they are distinguished therefrom by their shortage of intuition, the poverty of their *donation*, even the unreality of their objects. It is not self-evident that this marginal poverty could serve as a paradigm for phenomenality as a whole, nor that the certitude it ensures would be worth the phenomenological price one pays for it. Whatever the case may be, if the ideal of evidence is realized only for intuitively poor phenomena, when it is, on the contrary, a matter of plenary phenomena, that is, of the appearance of the "things themselves" to be given intuitively, adequation becomes an ideal in the strict sense, that is, an event not (entirely) given, due to a (minimally, partial) failure of intuition. The equality required by right between intuition and intention is lacking—for lack of intuition. The senses deceive, not at all through a provisional or an accidental deception, but through an inescapable weakness: even an indefinite sum of intuited outlines will never fill intention with the least real object. When it is a question of a thing, the intentional object always exceeds its intuitive donation. Its presence remains to be completed by appresentation.[18] What keeps phenomenology from allowing phenomena to appear without reserve, therefore, is, to begin with, the fundamental deficit of intuition that it ascribes to them—with neither recourse nor appeal. But the phenomenological "breakthrough" postulates this shortage of intuition only as a result of metaphysical decisions—in short, Husserl here suffers the consequences of decisions made by Kant.

For it was Kant who first, always defining the truth by *adaequatio*,[19] inferred therefrom the parallel between intuition and the

---

Descartes after 1627–1628 is undoubtedly found here: an object is known all the more certainly insofar as it requires a *lesser* intuitive fulfillment and content.

[18] See the *Cartesianische Meditationen*, §§50–54. We should stress that appresentation— "the surplus [*Überschuss*] in perception of what is not authentically perceived in it"—intervenes not only in order to know another, but already with the knowledge of the worldly object (§55, Hua. I, p. 151). Descartes also admits that adequate knowledge remains impossible not only for the idea of infinity (AT VII, 368, 1–3), but also for that of any object whatsoever, however limited it may be: "conceptu rerum adaequato, qualem nemo habet, non modo de infinito, sed nec forte etiam de ulla alia re quantumvis parva" (AT VII, 365, 3–5).

[19] *Kritik der reinen Vernunft*, A58/B82.

concept, which are supposed to play a tangentially equal role in the production of objectivity. "Without sensibility no object would be given to us, without understanding no object would be thought. Thoughts without content are empty, intuitions without concepts are blind. It is, therefore, just as necessary to make our concepts sensible (that is, to add the object to them in intuition), as to make our intuitions intelligible (that is, to bring them under concepts). These two powers or capacities cannot exchange their functions. The understanding can intuit nothing, the senses can think nothing."[20] In principle, the phenomenon, and therefore the real object, appears in the strict measure that the intuition and the concept not only are synthesized, but also are balanced in that synthesis. *Adaequatio*—and therefore the truth—would thus rest on the equality of the concept with the intuition. However, Kant himself does not hesitate to disqualify this parallelism; for, if the concept corresponds to the intuition, it nevertheless radically depends on it. Indeed, if the concept thinks, it limits itself in this way to rendering intelligible, after the fact and by derivation, what intuition for its part, principally and originarily, alone can give: "Our knowledge springs from two fundamental sources of the mind. . . . Through the first [receptivity] an object is given [*gegeben*] to us, through the second the object is thought"; "There are two conditions under which alone the knowledge of an object is possible, first, intuition, through which it is given, though only as phenomenon [*nur als Erscheinung gegeben word*]; second, the concept, through which an object is thought corresponding to this intuition."[21] To be sure, the intuition remains empty, but blindness is worth more here than vacuity: for even blinded the intuition remains one that gives, whereas the concept, even if it alone can allow to be seen what would first be given to it, remains as such perfectly empty, and therefore just as well incapable of seeing anything at all. Intuition without the concept, even though still blind, nevertheless already gives matter to an object; whereas the concept without intuition, although not blind, nevertheless no longer sees anything, since nothing has yet been given to it to be seen. In the realm of the phenomenon, the intuition, rather than

---

[20] *Kritik der reinen Vernunft*, A51/B76.
[21] *Kritik der reinen Vernunft*, A50/B74, A92/B125.

the concept, is king: before an object is seen and in order for it to be seen, its appearance must be given; even if it does not see what it gives, intuition alone enjoys the privilege of giving: "the object cannot be given to a concept otherwise than in intuition [*nicht anders gegeben werden, als in der Anschauung*]"; for "the category is a simple function of thought, through which no object is given to me, and by which alone what can be given in intuition is thought [*nur was in der Anschauung gegeben werden mag*]"; or again, "intuitions in general, through which objects can be given to us [*uns Gegenstände gegeben werden können*], constitute the field, the whole object, of possible experience." Thus, intuition does not offer a simple parallel or complement to the concept; it ensures the concept's condition of possibility—its possibility itself: "intuitions in general, through which objects can be given to us [*gegeben werden können*], constitute the field or whole object of possible experience [*möglicher Erfahrung*]."[22] The phenomenon is thought through the concept; but in order to be thought it must first be given; and it is given only through intuition. The intuitive *mise en scène* conditions conceptual objectivation. Inasmuch as it is alone and anteriorly *donating*, intuition breaks in its own favor its parallelism with the concept. Henceforth, the scope of intuition establishes that of phenomenal *donation*. Phenomenality is indexed according to intuition.

Now, through a stunning tactical reversal, Kant stresses this privilege of intuition only in order better to stigmatize its weakness. For if intuition alone gives objects, there falls to human finitude only an intuition that is itself equally finite, and in this case sensible. Consequently, all the eventual objects that would necessitate an intellectual intuition are excluded from the possibility of appearing. Phenomenality remains limited by the defect of what renders it partially possible: intuition. What gives (intuition inasmuch as sensible) is but of a piece with what is lacking (intuition inasmuch as intellectual). Intuition determines phenomenality as much by what it refuses to it as by what it gives to it. "Thought is the act which relates given intuition [*gegebene Anschauung*] to an object. If the mode of this intuition is not in any way given [*auf keinerlei Weise gegeben*], then the object is merely transcendental

---

[22] *Kritik der reinen Vernunft*, A239/B298, then A95 and A253.

and the concept of understanding has only transcendental employment."[23] To think is more than to know the objects given by (sensible) intuition; it is to think all those objects that no (intellectual) intuition will ever give, to measure the immense cenotaph of phenomena that never appeared and never will appear, in short, to presume intuition's absence from possible phenomena. For intuition, which alone gives, essentially lacks. What gives is lacking. A paradox follows: henceforth, the more phenomena give themselves in sensibility, the more also grows the silent number of all the phenomena that cannot and need not claim to give themselves in sensibility. The more intuition gives according to the sensible, the more evident becomes its failure to let what is possibly phenomenal appear—a phenomenality that is henceforth held as impossible. The limitation of intuition to the sensible indirectly shows, as much as the directly given phenomena, the shadow of all those that it cannot let appear. The finitude of intuition is attested to with the permanence—which Kant admits is "necessary"—of the idea. The idea, even though, or rather because, it is a "rational concept to which no corresponding object can be given in the senses [*in den Sinnen*]," remains nevertheless *visable*[24] if not *visible* in all the sensible appearances from which it is excluded. "Absent from every bouquet," the flower of thought, according to the "glory of long desire,"[25] calls for sensible flowers and survives them; likewise the idea, in letting itself be aimed at *outside* of the conditions established for phenomenality, marks that much more the limits thereof. In the quasi phantomlike mode of a nonobject, the idea attests to the limits of an intuition that was not able to give the idea. It is therefore by not being sensible that the idea proves the failure of sensible intuition—in it and in general.

The phenomenon is characterized by its lack of intuition, which gives it only by limiting it. Kant confirms that intuition is

---

[23] *Kritik der reinen Vernunft*, A247/B304.

[24] *Translator's* note: That which can be aimed at, meant, or intended; from *viser,* to aim at.

[25] Kant, *Kritik der reinen Vernunft*, A327/B383 (*notwendig*), and A339/B397 (*unvermeidlich Schein*). Mallarmé, respectively, *Variations sur un sujet* and *Prose pour des Esseintes*, in *Oeuvres complètes*, "Pléiade," ed. H. Mondor (Paris, 1965), pp. 361 and 56.

operative only under the rule of limitation, of lack and of necessity, in short, of nothingness [*néant*], by undertaking to define
reciprocally the four senses of nothingness starting from intuition.
Everything happens as if it were with intuition first, and with
intuition considered as essentially lacking, failing, and limited, that
nothingness in all its dimensions could be defined. The list of the
four senses of nothingness amounts in effect to a review of four
modes of intuition's failure. (a) Nothingness can be taken as *ens
rationis*. This is defined as "the object of a concept to which there
corresponds no intuition that might be given [*keine anzugebende
Anschauung*]." Intuition first produces nothingness in being unable to give any intuition corresponding to a being of reason; its
limitation to the sensible finally induces a first nothingness. (b)
Nothingness can be taken as *nihil privativum*. This is defined as
"the concept of the lack of an object," that is, as a double lack of
intuition; first as a concept, and therefore as what by definition
lacks intuition; and then as the concept representing the very lack
of intuition, which alone gives an object; a double lack of intuition produces a second nothingness. (c) Nothingness can be
taken as *nihil imaginativum*. This acceptation is paradoxically significant: in principle, imagined nothingness would have to distance itself from nothingness, since here a minimum of intuition
(precisely, the imagined) would have to give a minimum of being.
But Kant does not grant even this positivity to intuition, admitting only a "simple form of intuition" and reducing it to an
"empty intuition." It should be noted that "empty" elsewhere
returns to the concept, and that intuition does not even have any
more right here to its "blind" solitude—since it is true that here
the form of intuition is likened to the empty form of the concept.
The form of intuition is reduced to a third nothingness. (d) Finally
nothingness can be taken as *nihil negativum*. As an "empty object
without concept," it would seem to be defined by the failure in
it of the concept and not of intuition; likewise, as "the object of
a concept that contradicts itself," it would seem to admit of a
purely logical explanation, and not an intuitive one. But,
strangely, such is not the case, since Kant puts forward an example—a two-sided rectilinear figure—that can be conceived only
in space, and therefore in intuition. Moreover, as he specified
earlier, "there is no contradiction in the concept of a figure that

is enclosed between two straight lines, since the concepts of two figures and of their meeting contain no negation of a figure; the impossibility does not arise from the concept in itself, but in connection with its construction in space."[26] The concept lacks because the object contradicts itself; but this contradiction is not logical; it results from the contradiction of the conditions of experience—here from the requirements of construction in space; it is therefore a matter of a contradiction according to intuition, and thus according to the finitude of that intuition. Nothingness is expressed in many ways, as is Being elsewhere, but that polysemy is organized entirely on the basis of different absences of finite and sensible intuition. Intuition's failure characterizes it fairly essentially, so that nothingness might itself be inflected in its voids.

We were asking: How is the phenomenon defined when phenomenology and metaphysics delimit it within a horizon and according to an *I*? Its definition as conditioned and reducible is well accomplished through a de-*finition*: the phenomena are given by an intuition, but that intuition remains finite, either as sensible (Kant), or as most often lacking or ideal (Husserl). Phenomena suffer from a deficit of intuition, and thus from a shortage of *donation*. This radical lack has nothing accidental about it, but results from a phenomenological necessity. In order that any phenomenon might be inscribed within a horizon (and there find its condition of possibility), it is necessary that that horizon be delimited (it is its definition), and therefore that the phenomenon remain finite. In order for a phenomenon to be reduced to an obviously finite *I* who constitutes it, the phenomenon must be reduced to the status of finite objectivity. In both cases, the finitude of the horizon and of the *I* is indicated by the finitude of the intuition itself. The phenomena are characterized by the finitude of *donation* in them, so as to be able to enter into a constituting horizon and to be led back to an *I*. But, conversely, one could also conclude from this equivalence of the determinations that unconditioned and irreducible phenomena would become possible only if a nonfinite intuition ensured their *donation*. But can a nonfinite intuition even be envisaged?

---

[26] *Kritik der reinen Vernunft*, A290–2/B347–9; see A220/B268 and A163/B204. See G. Granel, "Le *nihil privatum* en son sens kantien," *Philosophie* 14 (1987), reprinted in *Ecrits logiques et politiques* (Paris: Galilée, 1990).

4

The impossibility of an unconditioned and irreducible phenomenon thus results directly from the determination of the phenomenon in general by the (at least potential) failure of intuition in it. Every phenomenon would appear as lacking intuition and as marked by this lack to the point of having to rely on the condition of a horizon and on the reduction toward an *I*. There would be no phenomenon except that which is essentially poor in intuition, a phenomenon with a reduced *donation*.

Having arrived at this point, we can pose the question of a strictly inverse hypothesis: In certain cases still to be defined, must we not oppose to the restricted possibility of phenomenality a phenomenality that is in the end absolutely possible? To the phenomenon that is supposed to be poor in intuition can we not oppose a phenomenon that is saturated with intuition? To the phenomenon that is most often characterized by a defect of intuition, and therefore by a deception of the intentional aim and, in particular instances, by the equality between intuition and intention, why would there not correspond the possibility of a phenomenon in which intuition would give *more, indeed unmeasurably more*, than intention ever would have intended or foreseen?

This is not a matter of a gratuitous or arbitrary hypothesis. First, because in a certain way it falls to Kant—nevertheless the thinker of the intuitive shortage of the common phenomenon—to have envisaged and defined what we are calling a *saturated phenomenon*. There is nothing surprising in that. Indeed, if the "rational idea can never become a cognition because it contains a concept (of the supersensible) for which no adequate intuition can ever be given"—a phenomenon that is not only poor in, but deprived of, intuition—it nevertheless offers only one of the two faces of the idea, which is defined in general as the representation of an object according to a principle, such that it nonetheless can never become the cognition thereof. Thus to the rational idea—a representation according to the understanding—there corresponds the "aesthetic idea"—a representation according to intuition—which itself can never become a cognition, but for an opposite reason: "because it is an intuition (of the imagination) for which no ade-

quate [*adäquat*] concept can ever be found."²⁷ Inadequacy always
threatens phenomenality (or, better, suspends it); but it is no
longer a matter of the nonadequation of the (lacking) intuition
that leaves a (given) concept empty; it is a matter, conversely, of
a failure of the (lacking) concept that leaves the (overabundantly
given) intuition blind. Henceforth, it is the concept that is lacking, no longer intuition. Kant stresses this unambiguously: in the
case of the aesthetic idea, the "representation of the imagination
furnishes much to think [*viel zu denken veranlasst*], but to which
no determinate thought, or concept, can be adequate [*adäquat sein
kann*]." The excess of intuition over any concept also prohibits
"that any language ever reach it completely and render it intelligible,"²⁸ in short, allow an object to be seen in it. It is important to
insist here particularly on this: this failure to produce the object
does not result from a shortage of *donation* (as for the ideas of
reason), but indeed from an excess of intuition, and thus from an
excess of *donation*—which "furnishes much to think." There is an
excess of *donation*, and not simply of intuition, since, according to
Kant (and, for the main part, Husserl), it is intuition that gives.
Kant formulates this excess with a rare term: the aesthetic idea
remains an "inexposable [*inexponible*] representation of the imagination." We can understand this in the following way: because it
gives "much," the aesthetic idea gives more than any concept can
expose; to "expose" here amounts to arranging (ordering) the
intuitive given according to rules; the impossibility of this conceptual arrangement issues from the fact that the intuitive over-

---

²⁷ *Kritik der Urteilskraft*, §57, note 1, Ak. A., vol. 5, p. 342. [English trans. by
Werner S. Pluher (Indianapolis: Hackett, 1987); modified].

²⁸ *Kritik der Urteilskraft*, §49, op. cit., p. 314; [Eng. trans., p. 182, modified].
One should not object that the aesthetic idea is here called a "representation of
the imagination" and is not related to intuition since, a few lines lower, intuition
is purely and simply assimilated to the "representation of the imagination" ("Be-
griff, dem keine Anschauung [*Vorstellung der Einbildungskraft*] adäquat sein kann")
(ibid.). There are other confirmations of this elsewhere: "die Einbildungskraft,
als Vermögen der Anschauung" (§39, p. 292); "eine Anschauung (der Einbildungskraft)" (§57, note 1, p. 342). Moreover, there is nothing surprising in this,
since already in 1787, the second edition of the first *Critique* explicitly specified
this tie: "Imagination is the power of representing in intuition an object that is
not itself present. Now, since all our intuition is sensible, the imagination, by
virtue of the subjective condition under which alone it can give to the concepts
of understanding a corresponding intuition, belongs to *sensibility*" (§24, B151).

abundance is no longer exposed within rules, whatever they may be, but overwhelms them; intuition is no longer exposed within the concept, but saturates it and renders it overexposed— invisible, not by lack of light, but by excess of light. The fact that this very excess should prohibit the aesthetic idea from organizing its intuition within the limits of a concept, and therefore from giving a defined object to be seen, nevertheless does not disqualify it phenomenologically, since when recognized in this way for what it is, this "inexposable representation" operates according to its "free play."[29] The difficulty consists simply in attempting to comprehend (and not only to repeat) what phenomenological possibility is put into operation when the excess of *donating* intuition thus begins to play freely.

The path to follow from here on now opens more clearly before us. We must develop as far as possible the uncommon phenomenological possibility glimpsed by Kant himself. In other words, we must attempt to describe the characteristics of a phenomenon that, contrary to most phenomena, which are poor in intuition and defined by the ideal adequation of intuition to intention, would be characterized by an excess of intuition, and thus of *donation*, over the intention, the concept, and the aim. Such a phenomenon will doubtless no longer allow the constitution of an object, at least in the Kantian sense. But it is not self-evident that objectivity should have all the authority in fixing phenomenology's norm. The hypothesis of a phenomenon saturated with intuition can certainly be warranted by its outline in Kant, but above all it must command our attention because it designates a possibility of the phenomenon in general. And in phenomenology, the least possibility is binding.

5

We will outline the description of the saturated phenomenon according to the guiding thread of the categories of the understand-

---

[29] *Kritik der Urteilskraft*, §57, note 1, twice "inexponible Vorstellung," ibid., p. 342ff. For the positive use of this rare term, see the "exponible Urteile," in *Logik*, §31, A.A. vol. 9, p. 109.

ing established by Kant. But, in order to do justice to the excess of intuition over the concept, we will use them in a negative mode. The saturated phenomenon in fact exceeds the categories and the principles of the understanding—it will therefore be *invisable* according to quantity, unbearable according to quality, absolute according to relation, and incapable of being looked at [*irregardable*] according to modality.

First, the saturated phenomenon cannot be aimed at. This impossibility stems from its essentially unforeseeable character. To be sure, its *donating* intuition ensures it a quantity, but such that it cannot be foreseen. This determination is better clarified by inverting the function of the axioms of intuition. According to Kant, quantity (the magnitudes of extension) is declined through a composition of the whole on the basis of its parts; this "successive synthesis" allows one to compose the representation of the whole according to the representation of the sum of the parts; indeed, the magnitude of a *quantum* has the property of implying nothing more than the summation of the *quanta* that make it up through addition. From this homogeneity follows another property: a quantified phenomenon is "foreseen in advance [*schon . . . angeschaut*] as an aggregate (a sum of parts given in advance) [*vorher gegebener*]."[30] Such a phenomenon is literally foreseen on the basis of the finite number of its parts and of the magnitude of each one among them. Now, these are precisely the properties that become impossible when a saturated phenomenon is at issue. Indeed, since the intuition that gives it is not limited, its excess can be neither divided nor put together again by virtue of a homogenous magnitude and finite parts. It could not be measured on the basis of its parts, since the saturating intuition surpasses the sum of these parts by continually adding to it. Such a phenomenon, which is always exceeded by the intuition that saturates it, would instead have to be called incommensurable, not measurable (immense), unmeasured [*démesuré*]. This lack of measure [*démesure*], furthermore, does not always or initially operate through the enormity of an unlimited quantity. It is marked more often by the impossibility of applying a successive synthesis to it, a synthesis allowing one to foresee an aggregate on the basis of the sum of its parts. Since the

---

[30] *Kritik der reinen Vernunft*, A163/B204.

saturated phenomenon exceeds any summation of its parts—which, moreover, often cannot be counted—we must forsake the successive synthesis in favor of what we will call an *instantaneous synthesis*, the representation of which precedes and goes beyond that of possible components, rather than resulting from them according to foresight.

We find a privileged example of this with amazement. According to Descartes, this passion strikes us even before we know the thing, or rather precisely because we know it only partially: "One can perceive of the object only the first side that has presented itself, and consequently one cannot acquire a more particular knowledge of it."[31] The "object" delivers to us only a single "side" (we could also say *Abschatung*) and immediately imposes itself on us with such a force that we are overwhelmed by what shows itself, eventually to the point of fascination. And yet the "successive synthesis" was suspended as early as its first term. This, then, is because another synthesis has been achieved, a synthesis that is instantaneous and irreducible to the sum of possible parts. Any phenomenon that produces amazement imposes itself upon the gaze in the very measure (or, more precisely, in the very lack of measure) that it does not result from any foreseeable summation of partial quantities. Indeed, it amazes because it arises without any common measure with the phenomena that precede it, without announcing it or explaining it—for, according to Spinoza, "nullam cum reliquis habet connexionem."[32] Thus, for at least two phenomenological reasons, the saturated phenomenon could not be foreseen on the basis of the parts that would compose it through summation. First, because intuition, which continually saturates the phenomenon, prohibits distinguishing and summing up a finite number of finite parts, thus annulling any possibility of foreseeing the phenomenon. Next, because the saturated phenomenon most often imposes itself thanks to amazement, where it is precisely the nonenumeration and the nonsummation of the parts, and thus the unforeseeability, that accomplish all intuitive *donation*.

---

[31] *Passions de l'Ame*, §73, AT XI, 383, 7–10. See §78: "one stops one's attention on the first image of the objects that have presented themselves, without calling for any other knowledge of them" (ibid., 383, 14–17).

[32] *Ethica* III, appendix, definition IV.

Second, the saturated phenomenon cannot be borne. According to Kant, quality (intensive magnitude) allows intuition to give a degree of reality to the object by limiting it, eventually as far as negation: every phenomenon will have to admit a degree of intuition and that is what perception can anticipate. The foresight at work in extensive magnitude is found again in intensive magnitude. Nevertheless, an essential difference separates them: foresight no longer operates in a successive synthesis of the homogenous, but in a perception of the heterogeneous—each degree is marked by a break with the preceding, and therefore by an absolutely singular novelty. Since he privileges the case of the poor phenomenon, Kant analyzes this heterogeneity only on the basis of the simplest cases: the first degrees starting from zero, imperceptible perceptions, and so on. But in the case of a saturated phenomenon, intuition gives reality without any limitation (or, to be sure, negation). It reaches an intensive magnitude without (common) measure, such that, starting from a certain degree, the intensity of the real intuition exceeds all the anticipations of perception. In face of that excess, perception not only can no longer anticipate what it is going to receive from intuition, but above all it can no longer bear the degree of intuition. For intuition, which is supposed to be "blind" in the realm of poor phenomena, in a truly radical phenomenology proves instead to be blinding. The intensive magnitude of the intuition that gives the saturated phenomenon is unbearable for the gaze, just as this gaze could not foresee that intuition's extensive magnitude.

Bedazzlement characterizes what the gaze cannot bear. Not bearing does not amount to not seeing; for one must first perceive, if not see, in order to experience this incapacity to bear. It is in fact a question of something visible that our gaze cannot bear; this visible something is experienced as unbearable to the gaze because it weighs too much upon that gaze; the glory of the visible weighs, and it weighs too much. What weighs here is not unhappiness, nor pain, nor lack, but indeed glory, joy, excess: "O/ Triumph!/ What Glory! What human heart would be strong enough to bear/ That?"[33] Intuition gives too intensely for the

---

[33] Claudel, *Tête d'or*, Théâtre 1, "Pléiade" (Paris, 1956), p. 210. Glory weighs: the Hebrew says this with one word. Obviously, we are here extremely close to the works of J.-L. Chrétien on *L'inoubliable et l'inespéré* (Paris, 1991).

gaze to be truly able to see what already it can no longer receive, nor even confront. Indeed, this blinding concerns the intensity of the intuition and it alone, as is indicated by cases of blinding in face of spectacles where the intuition remains quantitatively ordinary, even weak, but of an intensity that is out of the ordinary: Oedipus blinds himself for having seen his transgression, and therefore a quasi-moral intensity of intuition; and He whom no one can see without dying blinds first by his holiness, even if his coming is announced by a simple breath of wind. Because the saturated phenomenon, due to the excess of intuition in it, cannot be borne by any gaze that would measure up to it ("objectively"), it is perceived ("subjectively") by the gaze only in the negative mode of an impossible perception, the mode of bedazzlement. Plato described this perfectly in connection with the prisoner in the Cave: "let one untie him and force him suddenly to turn around [ἀνίστασθαι] . . . and to lift his gaze toward the light [πρὸς τὸ φῶς ἀναβλέπειν], he would suffer in doing all that, and, because of the bedazzlements, he would not have the strength to see face on [διὰ τὰς μαρμαρυγὰς ἀδυνατοῖ καθορᾶν] that of which previously he saw the shadows." It is indeed a question of "suffering" in seeing the full light, and of fleeing it by turning away toward "the things that one can look at [ἃ δύναται καθορᾶν]." What keeps one from seeing are precisely the "eyes filled with splendor."[34] Moreover, this bedazzlement is just as valid for intelligible intuition as it is for sensible intuition. First, because the Myth of the Cave, in the final analysis, concerns the epistemological obstacles to intelligibility, of which the sensible montage explicitly offers one figure; next, because the idea of the Good also and above all offers itself as "difficult to see" (μόγις ὁράσθαι), certainly not by defect, since it presents "the most visible of beings," but indeed by excess—because "the soul is incapable of seeing anything . . . saturated by an extremely brilliant bedazzlement [ὑπὸ λαμπροτέρου μαρμαρυγῆς ἐμπέπλησται]."[35] What in all these cases prohibits one from seeing is the sensible or intelligible light's excess of intensity.

---

[34] Plato, *Republic*, 515c and 517a. The term μαρμαρυγή originally designates vibration (for example, that of the feet of dancers, in *Odyssey*, 8.265), and then the vibration of overheated air, and thus mirage and bedazzlement.

[35] Plato, *Republic*, 517bc and 518a.

Bedazzlement thus becomes a characteristic—universalizable to any form of intuition—of an intuitive intensity that goes beyond the degree that a gaze can sustain. This is not a question of some exceptional case, which we would merely mention as a matter of interest along with the poor phenomenon, itself thought to be more frequent and thus more or less normative. On the contrary, it is a question of an essential determination of the phenomenon, which is rendered almost inevitable for two reasons. (a) The Kantian description of intensive magnitudes, in other respects so original and true, nevertheless maintains a resounding silence concerning the most characteristic notion of intensive magnitude: the maximum. For even if it can undoubtedly not be defined objectively, there is always a subjective maximum, the threshold of tolerance. Bedazzlement begins when perception passes beyond its subjective maximum. The description of intensive magnitudes would necessarily and with priority have to take into consideration their highest degrees, and therefore the subjective maximum (or maximums) that the bedazzlements signal. (b) As previously with unforeseeability, so bedazzlement designates a type of intuitive *donation* that is not only less rare than it would seem to a hasty examination, but above all decisive for a real recognition of finitude. Finitude is experienced (and proved)[36] not so much through the shortage of the given before our gaze, as above all because this gaze sometimes no longer measures the amplitude of the *donation*. Or rather, measuring itself against that *donation*, the gaze experiences it, sometimes in the suffering of an essential passivity, as having no measure with itself. Finitude is experienced as much through excess as through lack—indeed, more through excess than through lack.

6

Neither *visable* according to quantity, nor bearable according to quality, a saturated phenomenon would be absolute according to relation as well: that is, it would shy away from any analogy of experience.

---

[36] *Translator's* note: s'éprouve (et se prouve).

Kant defines the principle of such analogies as follows: "Experience is possible only through the representation of a necessary connection of perceptions." Now, simple apprehension by empirical intuition cannot ensure this necessary connection; on the contrary, the connection will have to produce itself at once through concepts and in time: "Since time cannot itself be perceived, the determination of the existence of objects in time can be made only through their connection in time in general, and therefore only through concepts that connect them in general." This connection connects according to three operations: inherence of accident in substance, causality between cause and effect, and community between several substances. But Kant establishes them only by bringing three presuppositions into play. It is thus the possible questioning of these that will again define the saturated phenomenon. First presupposition: in all occurrences, a phenomenon can manifest itself only by respecting the unity of experience, that is, by taking place in the tightest possible network of ties of inherence, causality, and community, which assign to the phenomenon, in a hollow so to speak, a site and a function. This is a matter of a strict obligation: "This entire manifold must be unified [*vereinigt werden soll*]." "An analogy of experience is, therefore, only a rule according to which the unity of experience must arise from perceptions [*entspringen soll*]."[37] For Kant, a phenomenon appears, therefore, only in a site that is predefined by a system of coordinates, a system that is itself governed by the principle of the unity of experience. Now it is here that another question creeps in: Must every phenomenon, without exception, respect the unity of experience? Can one legitimately rule out the possibility that a phenomenon might impose itself on perception without one for all that being able to assign to it either a substance in which to dwell as an accident, or a cause from which it results as an effect, or even less an interactive *commercium* in which to be relativized? Further, it is not self-evident that the phenomena that really arise—as opposed to the phenomena that are poor in intuition, or even deprived entirely of intuition—can right from the first and most often be perceived according to such analogies of perception; it could be, quite the reverse, that they occur without

---

[37] *Kritik der reinen Vernunft*, A177/B220 and A180/B222.

being inscribed, at least at first, in the relational network that ensures experience its unity, and that they matter precisely because
one could not assign them any substratum, any cause, or any communion. To be sure, after a bit of analysis, most can be led back,
at least approximately, to the analogies of perception. But those,
and they are not all that rare, that do not lend themselves to this
leading-back henceforth assume the character and the dignity of
an event—that is, an event or a phenomenon that is unforeseeable
(on the basis of the past), not exhaustively comprehensible (on
the basis of the present), nor reproducible (on the basis of the
future), in short, absolute, unique, occurring. We will therefore
call it a *pure event*. We are here taking that which has the character
of event [*l'événementiel*] in its individual dimension as much as in
its collective dimension. Henceforth, the analogies of experience
could concern only a fringe of phenomenality, the phenomenality
typical of the objects constituted by the sciences, a phenomenality
that is poor in intuition, foreseeable, exhaustively knowable, reproducible, while other layers—and historical phenomena first of
all—would be excepted.

The second presupposition concerns the very elaboration of the
procedure that allows one to ensure the (at once temporal and
conceptual) necessity and thus the unity of experience. Kant presupposes that this unity must always be achieved through recourse
to an analogy. For "all the empirical determinations of time must
[*müssen*] stand under the rules of the general determination of
time, and the analogies of experience . . . must [*müssen*] be rules
of this kind." In short, it is up to the analogies of experience and
to them alone actually to exercise the regulation of experience by
necessity, and thus to ensure its unity. Now, at the precise moment of defining these analogies, Kant himself recognizes the fragility of their phenomenological power: indeed, in mathematics,
analogy remains quantitative such that through calculation it gives
itself the fourth term and truly constructs it; in this way the equality of the two relations of magnitude is "always constitutive" of
the object and actually maintains it in a unified experience. But,
Kant specifies, "in philosophy, on the contrary, analogy is not the
equality of two *quantitative* relations but of two *qualitative* relations; and from three given members we can obtain a priori
knowledge only of the relation to a fourth, not of the fourth

member itself. . . . An analogy of experience therefore will be a rule according to which the unity of experience . . . must arise from [*entspringen soll*] perceptions, and it will be valid as the principle of objects (phenomena) in a manner that is not *constitutive* but only *regulative*."[38] To put it plainly, when it is a question of what we have called poor phenomena (here, mathematical), intuition (here, the pure intuition of space) is not such that it could saturate the phenomenon and contradict in it the unity and the preestablished necessity of experience; in this case, the analogy remains quantitative and constitutive. In short, there is analogy of experience provided that the phenomenon remains poor. But, as soon as the simple movement to physics (not even to speak of a saturated phenomenon) occurs, analogy can no longer regulate anything, except qualitatively: if A is the cause of effect B, then D will be in the position (quality) of effect with respect to C, without it being possible to identify what D is or will be, and without it being possible to construct it (by lack of pure intuition) or to constitute it. Kant's predicament culminates with the strange employment, within the analytic of principles, of principles whose usage remains purely "regulative," which can be understood in only one sense: the analogies of experience do not really constitute their objects, but instead express subjective needs of the understanding. Let's suppose, for the moment, that the analogies of perception, thus reduced to a simple regulative usage, must treat a saturated phenomenon: the latter already exceeds the categories of quantity (unforeseeable) and quality (unbearable); it gives itself already as a pure event. Henceforth, how could an analogy—especially one that is simply regulative—assign to the phenomenon—especially necessarily and a priori—a point whose coordinates would be established by the relations of inherence, causality, and community? This phenomenon would escape all relations because it would not maintain any common measure with these terms; it would be freed from them, as from any a priori determination of experience that would eventually claim to impose itself on the phenomenon. In this sense, we will speak of an *absolute phenomenon*: one untied from any analogy with any object of experience whatsoever.

---

[38] *Kritik der reinen Vernunft*, A177/B220 and A179/B222. See also A665/B693.

This being the case, the third Kantian presupposition becomes questionable. The unity of experience is developed on the basis of time, since it is a matter of "the synthetic unity of all phenomena according to their relation in time."[39] Thus, Kant posits, and is the first no doubt to do so, not only time as the ultimate horizon of phenomena, but above all that no appearance can dawn without a horizon that receives it and that it rejects at the same time. This signifies that before any phenomenal breakthrough toward visibility, the horizon first waited in advance. And it signifies that every phenomenon, in appearing, is in fact limited to actualizing a portion of the horizon, which otherwise remains transparent. A current question concerns the identity of the horizon (time, Being, the Good, and so on). This should not, however, mask another question that is simpler albeit rougher: Could certain phenomena exceed every horizon? We should specify that it is not a matter of dispensing with a horizon in general—which would undoubtedly prohibit all manifestation—but of freeing oneself from the delimiting anteriority proper to every horizon, an anteriority that is such as to be unable not to enter into conflict with a phenomenon's claim to absoluteness. Let us assume a saturated phenomenon that has just gained its absolute character by freeing itself from the analogies with experience. What horizon can it recognize? On the one hand, the excess of intuition saturates this phenomenon so as to make it exceed the frame of ordinary experience. On the other hand, a horizon, by its very definition, defines and is defined; through its movement to the limit, the saturated phenomenon can manage to saturate its horizon. There is nothing strange about this hypothesis—even in strict philosophy where, with Spinoza, for example, the unique substance, absorbing all the determinations and all the individuals corresponding thereto, manages to overwhelm with its infinitely saturated presence ("infinitis attributis infinitis modis") the horizon of Cartesian metaphysics, by leaving therein no more free space for the finite (absolute and universal necessity). Such saturation of a horizon by a single saturated phenomenon presents a danger that could not be overestimated, since it is born from the experience—and from absolutely real, in no way illusory, experi-

---

[39] *Kritik der reinen Vernunft*, A177/B220 and A182/B224.

ence—of totality, with neither door nor window, with neither other [autre] nor Other [autrui]. But, strangely, this danger results less from the saturated phenomenon itself than from the misapprehension of it. Indeed, when it arises, it is most often treated as if it were only a common law phenomenon or a poor phenomenon. In fact, the saturated phenomenon maintains its absoluteness and, at the same time, dissolves its danger, when one recognizes it without confusing it with other phenomena, and therefore when one allows it to operate on several horizons at once. Since there are spaces with $n + 1$ dimensions (whose properties saturate the imagination), there are phenomena with $n + 1$ horizons. One of the best examples of such an arrangement is furnished by the doctrine of the transcendentals: the irreducible plurality of *ens, verum, bonum,* and *pulchrum* allows one to decline the saturated phenomenon from the first Principle in perfectly autonomous registers, where it gives itself to be seen, each time, only according to one perspective, which is total as well as partial; their convertibility indicates that the saturation persists, but that it is distributed within several concurrent horizons. Or rather the saturation increases because each perspective, already saturated in itself, is blurred a second time by the interferences in it of other saturated perspectives.[40] The plurality of horizons therefore allows as much that one might respect the absoluteness of the saturated phenomenon (which no horizon could delimit or precede), as that one might render it tolerable through a multiplication of the dimensions of its reception.

There remains nevertheless one last thinkable, although extreme, relation between saturated phenomenon and horizon: that no horizon nor any combination of horizons tolerate the abso-

---

[40] It would be necessary to develop here some privileged examples: the plurality of accounts, of literary genres, of testimonies, and of hermeneutics of the same event (the multiple accounts of the crossing of the Red Sea, the irreducible plurality of the Gospels) clearly indicates that a saturated phenomenon is at issue. But the doctrine of the four senses of Scripture, assigning a plurality of different and compossible senses, proves that even a text can sometimes (in the case of the Jewish and Christian Scriptures, although in essentially divergent senses) appear as a saturated phenomenon. This goes as well for texts that are not (directly) religious: thus, it is clear that the irreconcilable plurality of literary treatments of single themes (thus dramatic models, the very notion of literary imitation, and so on), even of constantly renewed interpretations and stagings of standard works, points to saturated phenomena.

luteness of the phenomenon precisely because it gives itself as absolute, that is, as free from any analogy with common law phenomena and from any predetermination by a network of relations, with neither precedent nor antecedent within the already seen (the foreseen)—in short, a phenomenon saturated to the point that the world could not accept it. Having come among its own, they did not recognize it; having come into phenomenality, the absolutely saturated phenomenon could find no room there for its display. But this opening denial, and thus this disfiguration, still remains a manifestation.

Thus, in giving itself absolutely, the saturated phenomenon gives itself also as absolute: free from any analogy with the experience that is already seen, objectivized, and comprehended. It frees itself therefrom because it depends on no horizon. On the contrary, the saturated phenomenon either simply saturates the horizon, or it multiplies the horizon in order to saturate it that much more, or it exceeds the horizon and finds itself cast out from it. But this very disfiguration remains a manifestation. In every case, it does not depend on that condition of possibility par excellence—a horizon, whatever it may be. We will therefore call this phenomenon *unconditioned*.

7

Neither *visable* according to quantity, nor bearable according to quality, nor absolute according to relation, that is, unconditioned by the horizon, the saturated phenomenon finally gives itself as incapable of being looked at according to modality.

The categories of modality are distinguished from all the others, Kant insists, in that they determine neither the objects themselves, nor their mutual relations, but simply "their relation to thought in general," in that they "express only the relation to the power of knowing," "nothing other than the action of the power of knowing."[41] In fact, between the objects of experience and the power of knowing, it is not only a question of a simple relation, but of the fact that they "agree." This agreement determines the

---

[41] *Kritik der reinen Vernunft*, A74/B100, A219/B266, and A234/B287.

possibility of phenomena to be (and therefore also their actuality and necessity) in the measure of their suitability to the *I* for and through whom the experience takes place. "The postulate of the possibility of things requires [*fordert*] therefore that their concept agree [*zusammenstimme*] with the formal conditions of an experience in general."[42] The phenomenon is possible in the strict measure that it agrees with the formal conditions of experience, thus with the power of knowing that fixes its attention on them, and therefore finally with the transcendental *I* itself. The possibility of the phenomenon depends on its reduction to the *I*.

This being the case, we can envisage a reversal of Kant's pronouncement and ask: What would occur phenomenologically if a phenomenon did not "agree" with or "correspond" to the *I*'s power of knowing? The Kantian answer leaves hardly any doubt: this phenomenon quite simply would not appear; or better, there would not be any phenomenon at all, but an object-less perceptive aberration. If this answer remains meaningful for a poor or common law phenomenon, does it still hold for a saturated phenomenon? In fact, the situation in this case becomes much different. In the face of saturation, the *I* most certainly experiences the disagreement between the at least potential phenomenon and the subjective conditions of its experience; consequently, the *I* cannot constitute an object therein. But this failure to objectivize in no way implies that absolutely nothing appears here: intuitive saturation, precisely inasmuch as it is invisible, intolerable, and absolute (unconditioned), imposes itself in the capacity of a phenomenon that is exceptional by excess, not by defect. The saturated phenomenon refuses to let itself be looked at as an object, precisely because it appears with a multiple and indescribable excess that suspends any effort at constitution. To define the saturated phenomenon as a nonobjective or, more exactly, nonobjectivizable, object in no way indicates a refuge in the irrational or the arbitrary; this definition refers to one of its distinctive properties: although exemplarily visible, it nevertheless cannot be looked at. We here take "to look at"—*regarder*—literally: *re-garder* exactly reproduces *in-tueri* and must therefore be understood on the basis of *tueri*, *garder*—but in the sense of "to keep an eye on . . . ," "to

---

[42] *Kritik der reinen Vernunft*, A225/B273 and A220/B267.

keep half an eye on . . . ," "to have (to keep) in sight. . . ."
Regarder therefore implies being able to keep the visible that is
seen under the control of the one who is seeing and who is,
consequently, a voyeur. And it is certainly not by chance that
Descartes entrusts the *intuitus* with maintaining in evidence what
the *ego* reduces to the status of *objectum*. To define the saturated
phenomenon as incapable of being looked at [*irregardable*]
amounts to envisaging the possibility in which a phenomenon
would impose itself with such a surfeit of intuition that it could
neither be reduced to the conditions of experience, and thus to
the *I* who sets them, nor, all the same, forego appearing.

Under what figure, then, would it appear? It appears in spite of
and in disagreement with the conditions of possibility of experience—by imposing an impossible experience (if not already an
experience of the impossible). Of the saturated phenomenon
there would be only a counterexperience. Confronted with the
saturated phenomenon, the *I* cannot not see it, but neither can it
look at it as its object. It has the eye to see it, but not to look after
it [*pour le garder*]. What, then, does this eye without a look [*cet oeil
sans regard*] actually see? It sees the overabundance of intuitive
donation, not, however, as such, but as it is blurred by the overly
short lens, the overly restricted aperture, the overly narrow frame
that receives it—or rather, that no longer accommodates it. The
eye apperceives not so much the appearance of the saturated phenomenon as the blur, the fog, and the overexposure that it imposes on its normal conditions of experience. The eye sees not so
much another spectacle as its own naked impotence to constitute
anything at all. It sees nothing distinctly, but clearly experiences
its impotence before the unmeasuredness of the visible, and thus
above all experiences a perturbation of the visible, the noise of a
poorly received message, the obfuscation of finitude. Through
sight it receives a pure *donation*, precisely because it no longer
discerns any objectivizable given therein. Let us call this phenomenological extremity a *paradox*. The paradox not only suspends
the phenomenon's relation of subjection to the *I*, it actually inverts that relation. Far from being able to constitute this phenomenon, the *I* experiences itself as constituted by it. It is constituted
and no longer constituting because it no longer has at its disposal
any dominant point of view over the intuition that overwhelms

it; in space, the saturated phenomenon engulfs it with its intuitive flood; in time, it precedes it through an interpellation that is always already there. The *I* loses its anteriority and finds itself, so to speak, deprived [*destitué*] of the duties of constitution, and is thus itself constituted: it becomes a *me* rather than an *I*. It is clear that on the basis of the saturated phenomenon we meet here with what we thematized elsewhere under the name of the subject on its last appeal: the *interloqué*.[43] When the *I* finds itself, from the constituting *I* that it remained in face of common law phenomena, constituted by a saturated phenomenon, it can identify itself as such only by admitting the precedence of such a phenomenon over itself. This reversal leaves it *interloqué*, essentially surprised by the more original event that detaches it from itself.

Thus, the phenomenon is no longer reduced to the *I* that would look at it. Incapable of being looked at, it proves irreducible. There is no drift or turn here, not even a "theological" one, but, on the contrary, an accounting for the fact that in certain cases of *donation* the excess of intuition could no longer satisfy the conditions of ordinary experience; and that the pure event that occurs cannot be constituted as an object and leaves the durable trace of its opening only in the *I/me* that finds itself, almost in spite of itself, constituted by what it receives. The constituting subject is succeeded by the constituted witness. As a constituted witness, the subject remains the worker of truth, but no longer its producer.

8

In order to introduce the concept of the saturated phenomenon in phenomenology, we have just described it as *invisable* (unforeseeable) according to quantity, *unbearable* according to quality, but also *unconditioned* (absolved from any horizon) according to relation, and *irreducible* to the *I* (incapable of being looked at) according to modality. These four characteristics imply the term-for-term reversal of all the rubrics under which Kant classifies the

---

[43] See "Le sujet en dernier appel," *Revue de Métaphysique et de Morale*, 1991, no. 1.

principles and thus the phenomena that these determine. However, in relation to Husserl, these new characteristics are organized in a more complex way; the first two—the *invisable* and the *unbearable*—offer no difficulty de jure for the "principle of all principles," for what intuition gives can quantitatively and qualitatively exceed the scope of the gaze; it is sufficient that intuition actually give it. The case is not the same for the last two characteristics: the "principle of all principles" presupposes the horizon and the constituting *I* as two unquestioned presuppositions of anything that would be constituted in general as a phenomenon; but the saturated phenomenon, inasmuch as it is unconditioned by a horizon and irreducible to an *I*, pretends to a possibility that is freed from these two conditions; it therefore contradicts and exceeds the "principle of all principles." Husserl, who nonetheless surpassed the Kantian metaphysics of the phenomenon, must himself be surpassed in order to reach the possibility of the saturated phenomenon. Even and especially with the "principle of all principles" Husserl maintains a twofold reserve toward possibility. Nevertheless, that reserve of Husserl *toward* possibility can prove to be a reserve of phenomenology itself—which still maintains a reserve *of* possibility, in order itself to be surpassed toward a possibility without reserve. Because it gives itself without condition or restraint, the saturated phenomenon offers the paradigm of the phenomenon without reserve. Thus, in the guiding thread of the saturated phenomenon, phenomenology finds its ultimate possibility: not only the possibility that surpasses actuality, but the possibility that surpasses the very conditions of possibility, the possibility of unconditioned possibility—in other words, the possibility of the impossible, the saturated phenomenon.

The saturated phenomenon must not be understood as a limit case, an exceptional, vaguely irrational, in short, a "mystical," case of phenomenality. On the contrary, it indicates the coherent and conceptual completion of the most operative definition of the phenomenon: it alone truly appears as itself, of itself, and starting from itself,[44] since it alone appears without the limits of a

---

[44] "das Sich-an-ihm-selbst-zeigende," Heidegger, *Sein und Zeit*, § 7, p. 31, 12. See "das an ihm selbst Offenbare von ihm selbst her sehen lassen," *Prolegomena zur Geschichte des Zeitbegriffs*, §2, G. A. 20 (Frankfurt am Main, 1979), p. 117. The "von ihm selbst her" indeed indicates an appearance "of itself" in the strict sense of "starting from itself."

horizon and without the reduction to an *I*. We will therefore call this appearance that is purely of itself and starting from itself, this phenomenon that does not subject its possibility to any preliminary determination, a *revelation*. And—we insist on this—here it is purely and simply a matter of the phenomenon taken in its fullest meaning.

Moreover, the history of philosophy has a long-standing knowledge of such saturated phenomena. One could go so far as to maintain that none of the most important metaphysicians has avoided the description of one or more saturated phenomena, even at the price of a head-on contradiction of his own presuppositions. Among many fairly obvious examples, let us simply call to mind Descartes and Kant. (a) Descartes, who everywhere else reduces the phenomenon to the idea and the idea to the object, nevertheless thinks the idea of infinity as a saturated phenomenon. According to quantity, the idea of infinity is not obtained by summation or successive synthesis, but "tota simul"; thus, the gaze [*intueri*] becomes the surprise of admiration [*admirari*].[45] According to quality, it admits no finite degree, but a *maximum*: "maxime clara et distincta," "maxime vera."[46] According to relation, it maintains no analogy with any idea at all: "nihil univoce"; indeed, it exceeds every horizon since it remains incomprehensible, capable only of being touched by thought: "attingam quomodolibet cogitatione"[47] According to modality, far from letting itself be led back to a constituting *I*, it comprehends the *I* without letting itself be comprehended by it: "non tam capere quam a ipsa capi,"[48] such that perhaps even the *ego* could also be interpreted at times as one who is called [*un interpellé*]. But furthermore, would it not suffice to translate "idea of infinity" word for word by "saturated phenomenon" in order to establish our conclusion? (b) Kant furnishes an example of the saturated phenomenon that is all the more significant insofar as it does not concern, as does

---

[45] AT VII, respectively 371, 25 and 52, 15. Infinity is never potential but always *actu*, 47, 19.

[46] AT VII, 46, 8, 12.

[47] Respectively, "nihil . . . univoce illi et nobis convenire," AT VII, 137, 22 (see 433, 5–6 or *Principia Philosophiae* I, § 51); *attingere*, AT VII, 139, 12 (see 52, 5 and 46, 21).

[48] AT VII, 114, 6–7. This is why here, and here alone, *intueri* is equivalent to *adorare*.

Descartes's, rational theology: in fact, it is a question of the sublime. We relied above on the "aesthetic idea" to challenge the principle of the shortage of intuition and to introduce the possibility of a saturation. In fact, already with the doctrine of the sublime we are dealing with a saturated phenomenon. Indeed, according to quantity, the sublime has neither form nor order, since it is great "beyond all comparison," absolutely and not comparatively (absolute, schlechthin, bloss).[49] According to quality, it contradicts taste as a "negative pleasure" and it provokes a "feeling of inadequacy," a feeling of "monstrosity."[50] According to relation, it very clearly escapes any analogy and any horizon since it literally represents "unlimitedness [Unbegrenztheit]."[51] According to modality, finally, far from agreeing with our power of knowing, "it can seem [erscheinen mag] in its form to contradict the purpose [zweckwidrig] of our faculty of judgment"; the relation of our faculty of judgment to the phenomenon is therefore reversed, to the point that it is the phenomenon that hereafter "looks at" the I in "respect."[52] The Kantian example of the sublime would thus permit us to widen the field of application for the concept of the saturated phenomenon.

From now on we can recapitulate. Phenomena can be classified, according to their increasing intuitive content, in three fundamental domains. (a) The phenomena that are deprived of intuition or that are poor in intuitions: for example, formal languages (endowed with categorial intuition by Husserl) or mathematical idealities (whose pure intuition is established by Kant). (b) The common law phenomena, whose signification (aimed at by intention) can ideally receive an adequate intuitive fulfillment, but that, right at the start and most of the time, do not reach such

---

[49] Kritik der Urteilskraft, respectively §25, op. cit., vol. 5, p. 248; Formlosigkeit, §24, p. 247; Unordnung, §23, p. 246; "über alle Vergleichung," and schlechthin §25, p. 248 (and §26, p. 251).

[50] Kritik der Urteilskraft, respectively §23, op. cit., p. 245; Gefühl der Unangemessenheit, §26, p. 252; Ungeheuer, §26, p. 253.

[51] Kritik der Urteilskraft, respectively Unbegränzheit, §23, p. 244. See "keine angemessene Darstellung," p. 245.

[52] Kritik der Urteilskraft, §23, p. 245. See subjektive Unzweckmässigkeit, §26, p. 252; Widerstreit of the subjective end, §27, p. 258. Respect (Achtung) comes in at §27, p. 257. Here we follow P. Lacoue-Labarthe, "La vérité sublime," in Du sublime (Paris, 1988).

fulfillment. In these first two domains, the constitution of objects is rendered possible precisely because the shortage of intuition authorizes comprehension, foresight, and reproduction. (c) There remain, finally, the saturated phenomena, which the excess of intuition shields from objective constitution. Conveniently, we can distinguish two types. (i) First, pure historical events: by definition nonrepeatable, they occur most often without having been foreseen; since through a surfeit of intuitive given they escape objectivation, their intelligibility excludes comprehension and demands that one move on to hermeneutics;[53] intuitive saturation surpasses a single horizon and imposes multiple hermeneutics within several horizons; finally, the pure historical event not only occurs to its witness (the nonconstituting *I*) without the latter comprehending it, but itself, in return, comprehends the *I* (the constituted *I*): the *I* is comprehended on the basis of the event that occurs to it in the very measure that the *I* itself does not comprehend the event. Pure events offer a type of saturated phenomenon that is historical and thus communal and in principle communicable. (ii) Such is not always the case for the second type: the phenomena of revelation. Let us repeat that by *revelation* we here intend a strictly phenomenological concept: an appearance that is purely of itself and starting from itself, that does not subject its possibility to any preliminary determination. Such revealed phenomena occur principally in three domains. First, the picture as a spectacle that, due to excess of intuition, cannot be constituted but still can be looked at (the idol). Next, a particular face that I love, which has become invisible not only because it dazzles me, but above all because in it I want to look and can look only at its invisible gaze weighing on mine (the icon). Finally, the theophany, where the surfeit of intuition leads to the paradox that an invisible gaze visibly envisages me and loves me. And it is here that the question of the possibility of a phenomenology of religion would be posed in terms that are not new (for it is only a matter of pushing the phenomenological intention to its end), but simple.

In every case, recognizing the saturated phenomena comes

---

[53] Such is the objective of P. Ricœur, particularly with *Temps et récit*, 3: *Le temps raconté* (Paris, 1985). Our analyses quite obviously owe much to his decisive works.

down to thinking seriously "aliquid quo majus cogitari nequit"—
seriously, which means as a final possibility of phenomenology.[54]

This text has profited from several helpful readings. We wish to
thank in particular B. Besnier, N. Depraz, and D. Franck for their
remarks.

Translated by Thomas A. Carlson.

---

[54] See our study on an exemplary case of the saturated phenomenon, the argument of Saint Anselm, wrongly called "ontological," "L'argument relève-t-il de l'ontologie," *Questions cartésiennes* (Paris, 1991) (or *Archivio di Filosofia* 1–2 [Rome, 1990]).

9

Speech and Religion:
The Word of God

Michel Henry

By "Word of God," we mean first of all the Scriptures.* Thus
it concerns a text, like all the others, written in a language that
can be comprehended according to principles that are relevant to
language in general. This language can be called a "word" because it can take the form of a sonorous utterance and also because, according to what is evident in the significations that it
conveys, it is addressed to someone.

All the same, the word of the Scriptures bears a distinctive characteristic: it is not merely addressed to someone, to us men, but
it is addressed to us by God. Understanding the word of the Scriptures is possible only if the divine provenance of this word is
perceived at the same time as it is.

This is why the text of the Gospels (to which, lacking time, we
will limit ourselves) displays a constant attempt at legitimization,
making reference to other sacred texts, to the Prophets whose
confirmation, or something like it, they give themselves out to
be.

The most categorical affirmation of the divine provenance of
the evangelic word resides in the quotation marks that punctuate
the story. In these instances, it is Christ himself who speaks; it is

---

* *Translator's note*: As in the previous essays, what is here being translated as
"Word" is the French term "Parole." This French term can also be rendered as
"Speech," as when rendering the distinction made, in French, between *langue*
and *parole*, language and speech. As such, it should be borne in mind that
"Word" and "word" connote speech or a spoken word. Occasionally, context
will dictate that *parole* be translated as "speech"—in which case the reader should
remember that this is the same term elsewhere translated as "word." In the title
of this essay, both "Speech" and "Word" translate *parole*.

the very word of God that we hear—and that is so because Christ is defined as the Word of God. Organized around this divine Word, the evangelical text as a whole is transformed, dismissed from its linguistic station, banished from its properly textual place toward its divine referent: not only the words spoken by Christ, but his acts—washing feet, remitting sins, resurrecting the dead.

It is still the case that these acts are said, like the words of Christ. Both are significations borne by linguistic terms, moments, and parts of a language, of a speech, incapable of doing anything but adding meaning to meaning, without crossing the abyss that separates all signifying truth from reality itself, not to mention this Archi-reality to which one gives the name "God." The words of Christ stand out from between the quotation marks with an impressive force, but these words are words, a language whose referential reality is never posited by it. After all, this collection of texts is perhaps only making up a clever tale whose central character is invented or, if Christ really existed, perhaps, as Rilke suggests, "he was played the fool by his love as was Mohammed by his pride." And in such a case, the words of the Gospel, in spite of their loftiness and their profundity, are still human words, not bearing in them the mark of their divinity. For, as Sartre said, "It is always I who decide that this voice is the voice of an angel."

The question is therefore this: composed of linguistic terms and of significations, language, a word homogeneous with every other—can the evangelic word attest in some way to its divine provenance, thereby establishing its truth, the divinity of Christ, that is, the truth of what he says and what he does? In other words, how is one to know that the Scriptures are the word of God? Who, what word will tell us this?

And here is our answer: there exists another Word besides that which, composed of linguistic terms, forms the substance of the Scriptures. This other Word differs by nature from all human words; it includes neither linguistic terms nor significations, neither signifier nor signified; it does not have a referent; it does not come from a speaker properly speaking; and it is not addressed to some interlocutor, to anyone, whoever he might be, who would exist before it—before it has spoken. It is this other word that tells us that the word delivered in the Scriptures is of divine provenance. And it is this other Word, telling us that the evangelic word is of divine origin, that alone is the Word of God.

Let us therefore examine the nature of these two words, each in turn—the one set forth in the Scriptures, like unto the word that men use among themselves; and this other word, more ancient, which is the sole one to let us understand that the word delivered by the Scriptures is of divine provenance—this other word that is the Word of God.

The human word is based on language, which is composed of signs relating to objects. In this regard, the linguistic term is an instrument, a means, which by conferring a name on something that is already there allows one to have power over it, to manipulate it symbolically. But however one might conceptualize it, this instrumental function refers to a phenomenological essence that is the essence of the Word. For the linguistic term can say the thing only if it gives it to be seen, if "it delivers the thing as thing into the bursting forth of the appearing [*das Ding als Ding zum Scheinen bringt*]."[1] To speak truly, in the term that names the thing, the Word does not just render visible the being about which it is spoken or what is said about it; it does this only because previously it let appear, because, according to Heidegger, it grants the arrival in presence itself—because it gives Being.

The term to designate the phenomenological essence of the word inasmuch as it lets appear and thus gives Being, is Logos. There is therefore a co-belonging of Logos to Being and Being to Logos, but this does not indicate any reciprocity between these two terms. It is only because the Word grants the appearing that, at the same time, it grants Being. In other words, Being does not have any word that would be proper to it; it does not have a name. It does not have a name not because it would be beyond all names, but in contrast because there is always a name before it. A Word has always already spoken before it, one that delivers the appearing to which Being owes Being and beings with it.

Only if the Word that frees the appearing comes before Being is it necessary to say not what it "is," but what sort of appearing it frees, what sort of appearing appears as the very essence of the Word as Logos. It no longer suffices to assert that the Word is

---

[1] Heidegger, *Unterwegs zur Sprache* (Neske Pfüllingen, 1959), p. 256.

phenomenological through and through, that its essence is phe-nomenality as such; it is incumbent upon us to recognize how it is phenomenalized, that is to say, what is the pure phenomenolog-ical material of which it is made. The final question relative to the word, no longer the question of the essence of the word (*das Wesen der Sprache*) but of the word of the essence (*die Sprache des Wesens*), is the question of knowing how the Word speaks, in what tongue, and, in this fashion, what it says.

Now explicitly in Heidegger, and implicitly in most theories of language, the phenomenality that serves as support for the saying of the word is interpreted as that of the world. According to Hei-degger, "To say means to show, to make appear, *to present a world in a clearing.*" Or: "*The Said gives the 'is' in the clearing.*"[2] Already in *Sein und Zeit,* the word, as an existential of *Dasein* (discourse), found its explicit phenomenological possibility in the opening of Being-in-the-world. In other forms of thought, across different systems of conceptualization, the phenomenality that supports the word, which, for example, grounds the relation of the sign and the thing, is always the light of an "Outside." It is accordingly the coming outside of this Outside—a sort of original exterioriza-tion of exteriority, finding its origin there and consisting in its very deployment—that constitutes the clearing power of this light, its Lighting. Thus, to say, to express, is to exteriorize and to make seen in this way, while the expressed is what is outside [*Das Ausgesprochene ist gerade des Draussensein*].[3] Let us call this Word that finds its phenomenological possibility in the coming outside of an Outside the Word of the World.

What is said in the Word of the World displays several charac-teristics.

1. It is given by showing itself outside, like an "Image."

2. It is automatically given as a nonreality. Consider, for exam-ple, the snow, the bell, the evening about which Trakl speaks in the poem "Winter Evening."[4] The poet having called them by their names, these things come into presence and yet they do not

---

[2] Ibid., respectively, pp. 214, 215; English trans., p. 107 (modified), p. 108 (modified): "*Sagen Heisst: Zeigen, Erscheinen lassen, lichtend-verbergend-freigebend Darreichen von Welt*"; "*Die Sage gibt das 'ist' in das gelichtete Freie.*"

[3] Heidegger, *Sein und Zeit* (Niemeyer, 1941), p. 162; English trans., p. 205.

[4] *Unterwegs zur Sprache,* pp. 17–22.

take a place among the objects that surround us in the room where we are standing. They are present, but in a sort of absence: present in that they appear, absent in that, though appearing, they are not there. What sort of appearing gives, lets beings appear such that, thus giving them Being, it withdraws Being by the same move, gives it as not being? What Logos is carried out like a murder? It is the Logos that reigns in the Word that the poet speaks, in the Word of the World, Logos whose appearing is the World as such.

3. It is therefore not only the things said by the poet that come to presence in a sort of absence, that show themselves as not being. This is the case for all beings. For "all can be said." The Saying of the World on which the poet himself relies, as well as every man who speaks in this Saying, is such that, showing what it is made of, it withdraws Being from all that it shows. And this is because *giving in Exteriority and thus placing each thing in its own exteriority, it empties them of their own reality.* If a difference must be made between the things about which the poet speaks and those that surround me in the room where I am, it is precisely not the word of the poet, *it is not the appearing of the World that can make it.* But what will I say about myself, seated in this room, making an effort to read and to understand? What does the Word of the World say about the *ego*?

This word wants to make the *ego* visible by positing it before, by installing it in the light of a clearing, that is, in the language of modern metaphysics, by representing it. But if the *ego* in its ipseity expels all conceivable exteriority from itself and therefore its light, the *ego*'s appearing before itself can signify only its own disappearance. Thus Lacan reduces the subject to the fact of saying itself to the intention of an other and the *cogito* to its utterance. Holding, in the wake of Kojève and Hegel, that by virtue of its constitutive negativity, the subject can be posited only by denying itself, Lacan finds the saying of the Word of the World to be an exemplary illustration of his theses, or perhaps even their ground. The subject who is said in language by abolishing all real referent is itself abolished therein. Saying "I" is to say "I am not"; "it is in sum always to say 'I am dead,' or 'I am nothing.' " The self-utterance of the subject is the utterance of this nothing. Or "the subject of the utterance disappears by appearing in the subject of what is uttered."[5] It appears only in this disappearing, snatched up by it, such that its act of birth is also its obituary.

Descartes did not share the romantic theories of language to which we just alluded, but every analysis of the *cogito* that means to stick to its utterance, to the texts in which it is formulated, runs up against the same aporia—namely, in itself *cogito* is the contrary of what the word of men says about it. Thus this word that makes visible and that wants to see says that *cogito* is what is seen clearly, evidently—while in itself, having issued from hyperbolic doubt, *cogito* happens when all evidence has been annihilated—when the Word of the World has fallen silent.

We arrive now at our question: What do the Gospels say about the *ego*, what do they say about us? They say that we are the Sons. Now Sons and filiation are found only in Life. In the world, by contrast, no such thing as birth is possible. Things are not born, and, for this reason, they do not die, except metaphorically. In the world, things appear and disappear without anything living ever being able to arrive in their appearance or being able to disappear in their disappearance.

Only Sons have a birth; they are born in Life, begotten by it, being one of the living only as such, as Sons. Life is the Word of God. To understand Life as the very Word of God is possible, however, only if by this term "word" we refrain from understanding something that might resemble the words that men speak. The Word of God no doubt has one characteristic in common with the Word of the World: it is phenomenological through and through. This is why the saying of the divine word is a revelation. But how does the divine word reveal, what sort of appearing does it deliver, and what does it say to us? This is the crucial question; it is that of phenomenology—of a phenomenology that grasps itself—and perhaps also that of theology, a theology that grasps itself—not as discourse on God but as the Word of God himself. The Word of God reveals, speaks, as Life. Life, that is to say, the original word, is the Archi-Revelation as self-revelation, as autoaffection. This is to say that life reveals in such

---

[5] Mikkel Borch-Jacobsen, *Le lien affectif* (Aubier, 1991), p. 132. One finds, in this remarkable work, a radical requestioning of much of what contemporary thought has taken for granted.

a way that what it reveals is itself and nothing other. It affects in such a way that the content of its affection is itself and nothing other. In distinction from the Word of the World, which points away from itself and always speaks of something else, of something else that in this Word is carried outside itself, thrown out of line, deprived of its own reality, reduced to an image, to a content without content, at once opaque and nonetheless empty—the Word of Life gives life. It is called the Word of Life because its Logos is Life, namely, self-givenness, self-enjoyment.

Giving in this way, speaking this Logos, Life begets its Sons in it. The transcendental birth of Sons, of those who, in the Word of the World, will be called *ego*, self, men, individuals, persons, and so on, is a birth intelligible in life and in it alone. And this is because there is no other way to come into life except through life itself. In the process of its incessant coming into itself, which is that of its eternal autoaffection, life undergoes itself in such a way that a Self results each time from this ordeal as identical to its pure "undergoing itself." Such an ordeal is singular on principle, undergoing what it undergoes, phenomenologically defined by the content of this ordeal. Life is the essence of ipseity; it is carried out by giving birth to the latter, by giving birth to it in it and without ever departing from itself. But all ipseity, as living, is a singular Self.

Thus life is begotten, carried out, undergone as a singular Self, as this Self that I myself am. Life autoaffects itself as myself. If with Eckhart, one calls life "God," then one will say with him: "God is begotten as myself." But this Self begotten in Life, holding the singularity of its Self only from ipseity and holding its ipseity only from the eternal autoaffection of life, bears the latter in it, inasmuch as it is borne by it and arrives in each instant in life only through it. Thus life communicates itself to each of the Sons by penetrating him as a whole, such that there is nothing in him that would not be living, and moreover nothing—inasmuch as its Self arrives only in the autoaffection of life itself—that would not contain in itself this eternal essence of life. "God gives birth to me as himself."[6]

The mystery of the transcendental birth of Sons in Life stems

---

[6] Meister Eckhart, *Sermon 6*; English trans., p. 187.

from the fact that in this birth two passivities collapse into each other: the radical passivity of life vis-à-vis the Self in its eternal autoaffection (in theological language, the eternal *jouissance* of God) and, on the other hand, the passivity of the singular Self begotten in this autobegetting of absolute life. For, this Self is passive with regard to itself only within the autoaffection of Life that begets it and the passivity proper to this life. Life throws the Self into itself inasmuch as it is thrown into itself, in its eternal autoaffection and thus through it. The phenomenality of these two passivities—that of Life, that of the Self—is the same. It is a nonecstatic pathos, which is why neither of them can be said to be even the least bit passive in relation to something exterior in the phenomenological sense and thus visible.

The fact that the Self can subsist only in the eternal autoaffection of Life in it invites us to make a more precise distinction between two concepts of this autoaffection. The autoaffection that expresses the essence of absolute life signifies that the latter affects itself in the twofold sense that it is carried out as productive of its own affection and at the same time as the content of this affection. Life is what affects and what is affected. This life can be called absolute because it needs nothing other than itself to exist. Phenomenologically, there is after all nothing else to it. This is why this life can still be called infinite, because the finitude of the ecstatic horizon of a world is totally foreign to it. It can be called eternal because the temporality that deploys this ecstatic horizon has no place in it either. The phenomenological passivity that characterizes all life inasmuch as it is pure self-enjoyment—even in sorrow—can just as well be thought as a pure Act since in the case of this absolute life, it is it itself that produces the affection constitutive of its essence, which is self-begotten.

In the case of the autoaffection of the singular Self that I am, autoaffection has changed its meaning. The Self autoaffects itself; it is the identity of the affector and the affected, but in such a way that it has not itself posited this identity. The Self autoaffects itself only insofar as absolute life autoaffects itself in it. Passive, it is so not just in regard to itself and each of the determinations of its life, in the way that each suffering is passive vis-à-vis itself and is possible only as such, getting its affective tenor only from this passivity whose pure phenomenological tenor is affectivity as such. The Self is passive first in regard to the eternal process of the autoaffection of the life that begets it and is forever begetting it. This passivity of the Self in life is not a metaphysical determination posited by thought; it is a phenomenological determination constitutive of the Self's life and which, as such, is forever being lived by it. This determination is so essential, the ordeal that is undergone so unrelenting, that our life is nothing other than this feeling of being lived. If one sticks to the experience proper to it, the Self therefore should not be called what autoaffects itself, but what is found unrelentingly autoaffected. How is it that the specific mode of the singular Self's passivity as autoaffected in the eternal autoaffection of Life does not define simply a general characteristic of its own life? How is it that this particular mode of passivity begets in this life all its essential modalities, which are as such pathetic—for example, the anxiety or the drive that originates directly in the phenomenological structure of the Self and is identical to it? Here is not the place to show this. For us, the problem is rather to understand the relation between these two passivities collapsed each into the other in the transcendental birth of the Self as the birth of a Son in Life. In sum, the issue is this: by pushing phenomenology to its limit, as radical phenomenology, as material phenomenology, to understand man's relation to God, to at least circumscribe what, as phenomenology, it can say about this relation.

What this phenomenology has established, at the point we have arrived at in our analysis, is the quasi-identity of the essence of man and that of God, namely, Life. Such an essence is not merely phenomenological; it is that of an Archi-phenomenality. It is this Archi-phenomenality of life which makes it a Word, an Archi-word that speaks of nothing else but itself, at once the how and the content of what it says, of what it says *to us*, inasmuch as in its saying a singular self is built up. If we are in the word and speak only in its wake, if this word is addressed to us[7] and enjoins us in such a way that no one can evade it, this is simply because, as Word of Life finding its essence in Life, it is first in itself, in an absolute immanence that nothing can break. Next, it is because

---

[7] Above, cf. *Unterwegs zur Sprache*, particularly pp. 241, 179, 257, 180; English trans., p. 111–12, 75, 126, 76.

in the immanence of its autoaffection, a singular Self is begotten each time, to which it is addressed henceforth and to which it can address itself and address itself inevitably—in this autoaffection that has become no longer the autoaffection of Life but that of the Self.

This phenomenological essence common to man and God grounds their phenomenological relation, begets man as a man who knows God—"*ein Gott wissender Mensch*"[8]; "we worship what we know"[9]—while, begetting man in the autoaffection of his own autobegetting, God knows man, reads the depths of his heart in the very act by which he begets him. This commonality of a phenomenological essence could be expressed metaphorically by saying: the Eye with which I see God and the Eye with which God sees me is but one and the same Eye—it being understood that phenomenologically speaking, here there is neither Eye nor vision nor world, nor anything like that.

That man knows God is an outrageous proposition, one barely heard today. What is it other than the inevitable response to the most simple question: Is it conceivable that the living know nothing of life? Where and how, why, what formidable hatred for life has gathered in the world where we live that the innermost certainty that life has of living has been hidden, not simply hidden, but to speak truly, denied, thus committing in this long series of murders that is the history whose horror Voltaire saw, a quite particular murder, a theoretical murder in some ways, general, putting to death no one in particular, but stripping each living thing of its living quality and doing so by stripping life of what makes it life. But let us leave aside these questions that pertain to modernity and return to our own question, which belongs to no time and now stands out in its simplicity: What do the living know about life?

In a certain sense, nothing, if it is a matter of that knowing that guides the modern world and modern thought. And this is because such a knowing is excluded from the internal structure of life. In another sense, inasmuch as the essence of the living stems from the Archi-revelation of life, doesn't it know all there is to

---

[8] Eckhart, *Sermon 10.*
[9] John 4.23.

know about it? Let us try to glimpse this extraordinary knowing, without anything held back or left over, where in the absolute immanence of a pathetic autoaffection, the living has already laid hold of all that which, in this taking possession, is henceforth under its power, one of its powers. For it is but the most humble drive, the most elementary act that presupposes—in order to be carried out without thought, without representation, without imagination, without perception, without conception, without being preceded in any way, and without wanting, without showing itself in any world—nothing but the autoaffection of the living contemporaneous with its transcendental birth and identical to it.

Isn't it significant that Heidegger, when he wanted to think life, taking his inspiration from the biologists of his time, was compelled to turn to the immanence of an original being-in-possession-of-itself belonging to the drive and its specific phenomenality, thought negatively as fascination (*Benommenheit*), or else in categories totally foreign to the analytic of *Dasein*, as Didier Franck has shown.[10] And if in other texts Heidegger believed he could radically separate philosophy and theology and affirm that "faith does not arise from *Dasein*,"[11] isn't this simply because the analytic of *Dasein*, like the later thought of Being, was entirely ignorant of life? For Faith is not some sort of lesser knowledge deprived of its own position and thus of all possible justification. It is simply a name for the unshakeable certainty that life has of living and for its hyperknowing. Faith does not come from the fact that we believe, it comes from the fact that we are the living in life. It is our condition as Sons that makes us believe what we believe, namely, that we are Sons; and it is for this reason alone that Faith can befall us.

Does the living know everything about life? Haven't we said that the autoaffection of the living differs from the autoaffection of life insofar as only the second produces itself in the sense of an absolute autoaffection. If the singular Self is autoaffected in its

---

[10] Cf. "L'Etre et le Vivant," *Rev. Philosophie*, no. 7, p. 73–92; English trans., "Being and the Living," in *Who Comes after the Subject?* (New York: Routledge, 1991), ed. Eduardo Cadava, Peter Connor, and Jean-Luc Nancy.

[11] *Phänomenologie und Theologie*, in *Wegmarken*, GA, 9, p. 52; English trans., p. 9 (modified).

transcendental birth—that is to say, begotten as a Self—only in the autoaffection of life, doesn't the latter precede it as an already to which it will never be able to return, as a past that it will never be able to rejoin and that will remain forever closed to it—an absolute past? In his magnificent work *L'inoubliable et l'inespéré*,[12] Jean-Louis Chrétien reintroduced the concept of the Immemorial. I will take it up here to designate the antecedence of life to all the living.

That there is no memory of the Immemorial means first that we cannot represent it, form a memory of it, relate to it by any thought whatsoever. The Archi-ancient never turns toward thought. In this sense the Immemorial is struck by an insurmountable Oblivion. This Oblivion is not something like the correlate or flip side of a possible memory; it is not the forgetting into which memory changes when we no longer think of it. In their mutual correlation, forgetting and memory each proceed from a single place, from that place that is freed by the Word of the World, from "that clearing that every appearance must seek out and every disappearance must leave behind."[13] In the Immemorial of the antecedence of Life no clearing of this sort is ever given out, and this is so simply because there is no possible memory or forgetting of it, no conversion of the one into the other. Now the absolute Oblivion that banishes all memory and all forgetting, that never goes out to meet thought—does this forgetting bar all access to the Immemorial or does it constitute this access as such?

That thought does not have to remember, that the clearing where all appears appears and all that disappears disappears, does not open the path to the Immemorial but forbids access to it—this is what renders untenable the claim to submit God to the priority of Being, and this is what justifies the problematic of Jean-Luc Marion.[14] For one can well say "God is," but as Being itself is subordinated to the priority of the givenness of appearing, the meaning of Being is decided only in the latter. From now on, submitting God to the priority of Being implies at least two ab-

---

[12] Desclée de Brouwer (Paris, 1991).

[13] *Unterwegs zur Sprache*, p. 257; English trans., p. 126.

[14] *Dieu sans l'Être* (Fayard, 1982; rev. ed., P.U.F., 1991); English trans., *God without Being* (Chicago: University of Chicago Press, 1991).

surdities. The first is the presupposition that God is in himself foreign to Revelation and consequently obliged to ask an exterior revelation for the right to show himself in it, in the place that it assigns to him and in the way that it prescribes. But the second presupposition is even more mistaken because it has already identified the light to which God would owe his shining for us with that which is deployed in the Difference of the world and things—thus reserving, it is true, a small corner for God in the Fourfold. One must therefore reverse Heidegger's propositions, according to which "the experience of God and of his manifestedness, to the extent that the latter can indeed meet man, flashes in the dimension of Being"[15]; "the sacred . . . comes into the light of appearing only when Being has been clarified beforehand."[16] For it is only when this light of appearing is extinguished, outside the clearing of Being, that access to the Immemorial is possible—in Oblivion.

The Oblivion that passes beyond all memory belonging to thought, and thus all conceivable Memory, gives us access to the Immemorial. We can mitigate the paradoxical character of this thesis by validating it in the case of our Self itself. For it must be observed that in the *ego*'s relation to itself, that is to say, in the ipseity of its Self, there is no memory. The project that seeks the essence of my self in its unity and sameness and wants to ground the latter on memory as the sole faculty capable of unifying its fragmented states is one of the most superficial in philosophical thought. For if it is a matter of the *living ego* and thus of its life, any intrusion of a memory separating from the Self what it would present to it as itself would have already destroyed the very possibility of the Self, namely, the autoaffection of life and the ipseity in it. Far from gathering life into a possible unity and thus into unity with itself, memory deploys a place where no life is possible, only what no longer is and as such, as remembered object, never was. Husserl saw clearly that a life given in retention would be a life in the past. But a life in the past is a phenomenological nonsense, something that excludes the very fact of living.

---

[15] Seminar at Zurich. Cited and commented on by J.-L. Marion in *Dieu sans L'Être*, p. 92 and p. 93, n. 15; English trans., p. 61 and p. 211, n. 16. See also Jean Greisch, *Heidegger et la question de Dieu* (Paris, 1980), p. 334.

[16] *Questions III* (Gallimard, 1966), p. 114.

This is why the idea of a subjectivity self-constituting itself in retention and protention would mean only self-suppression for the living defined transcendentally by such a subjectivity. There is life as there is affect: only in the present. Not in this present that itself comes into time and in it slips into the past, which is only a temporal form, but in what stands outside time and thus outside all memory—in the Oblivion of the Immemorial. This is why if it is said of the Immemorial of the antecedence of life to the living that it is an absolute past, it must be seen that in this absolute past there is nothing of the past. For this antecedence is that of life, while in the past there is only death. What is more, it is only on condition of excluding all past, and thus all memory, from the self that the Immemorial designates the antecedence of life and thus its absolute essence.

To better understand the Self's relation to the life that precedes it in Oblivion, it is necessary to grasp more clearly what this Oblivion signifies in the Self's relation to itself. Far from separating my self from itself, from dispossessing it of a quality or a power, Oblivion integrates this power into my self as what is so inward that, being able neither to represent it nor to think it, it can no longer lose it and bears it in itself as an innate capacity belonging to it and which has been put in it since forever. Of this belonging to my self in Oblivion, of all its powers, the Body offers the most striking example. It is only in the Oblivion of its Body that the self is found in possession of all its powers, one with them, in such a way that in this Oblivion they precede and inhabit it as the very forces that life confided to it in the act by which it begets it eternally. In contrast, all movement of the living body is interrupted at once if it is placed or forced outside itself in the Exteriority of a "world." All thought of the Body destroys it, renders action impossible, as the modern dualism imputed to Descartes demonstrates. This is because, standing in Oblivion, the Body could be glimpsed by thought only if the latter does not attain it and leaves its power to act intact.

It is not just particular experiences that establish this. It is a universal law of the Self that wherever it seeks to show itself—either as apprehended object or if it casts itself ahead of itself in a project—a limitless nostalgia penetrates it along with an irrepressible feeling of impotence. This nostalgia is only too evident in the case of memory which never proposes to life anything but its own absence. It can also be spotted in the indefinite progress of knowing, in the speech of men that itself never stops, in every form of being-in-the-world insofar as the ipseity of the Self is identified with it or with a mode in which it is enacted, with the resoluteness or abiding character of a decision. Finally, this same nostalgia or despair can be found in all action that intends an objective referent or believes itself able to be defined thus.

The Oblivion constitutive of the ipseity of the Self is its absolute immanence. An immanent Self is a nonconstituted Self, nonconstituted as Self—Self without Self, without image of itself, without anything being able to take the aspect or the form of a Self for it, without anything being proposed to it in this form, as Self or even as this Self that it is. Self without face and that will never admit being seen. Self in the absence of all Self. In such a way this absence of Self in the Self is constitutive of its ipseity as well as of all that will be possible on the basis of it. For it is only because no image of itself is interposed like a screen between it and itself that the Self is thrown into itself without protection and with such violence that nothing will ever defend it from this, no more than from itself. It is only because this violence is perpetrated against it on account of its being one of the living in life and thus in self-Oblivion that the Self is possible as this Self to which no memory will ever refer its image, that nothing will ever separate or deliver it from itself so that it is this Self that is forever.

Doesn't the Oblivion that constitutes the ipseity of the Self bear within it something like the shadow of a more ancient forgetting—a more obscure zone in the obscurity of the Night of absolute subjectivity? Actually, the Immemorial does not merely circumscribe the domain of a specific phenomenology: this nonecstatic pathos where, in the immanence of its ipseity, without memory and without Self, the Self accomplishes itself as a "living [vivre]." Immemorial means that when the Self arrives in and through this ipseity, the autoaffection of absolute life is already accomplished. Immemorial thus does not first designate the Self's memoryless relation to itself but, more essentially, its relation to life. As this relation no longer to self but to life is itself forgotten, this phenomenological homogeneity does not yet exhaust a dif-

ference that must be explained in full, does not say if this difference is itself phenomenological.

There are therefore two autoaffections: that of life which autoaffects itself absolutely and thus autobegets itself and that of the
Self autoaffected and thus begotten as Self in Life. Nevertheless,
there is but one life, the living live nowhere else but in this single
and unique life that begets itself absolutely. Thus the autoaffection
in which the autoaffected Self arrives at its condition as Self is not
other than the autoaffection of absolute life. That the power of
self-begetting itself would never be the Self's own deed but only
that of the autoaffection of life, and that thus the Self would live
only begotten in it, means precisely that the autoaffection that
throws it in itself is that of life, that there is none other besides the
former, and that there is thus nothing else in it but this absolute
autoaffection. This, then, is why God begets me "as himself,"
why the Self is passive vis-à-vis itself only inasmuch as it is passive
vis-à-vis absolute life, why, finally, to the forgetting of self in
which the Self is given to itself as a Self without Self, the Oblivion
of Life is added—which is the greatest forgetting of all, the Immemorial in which alone we are the living, where our transcendental
birth is carried out.

The transcendental birth of the *ego* thus has nothing to do with
our birth as a man—not only because the latter appears as an
arrival in the world and is understood as such, while our transcendental birth as the Self's coming into its Self stands entirely outside the world. In addition to this radical phenomenological
difference and as its consequence, our transcendental birth is opposed to our birth as a man because in distinction from the latter—which designates only a moment in the time and history of
this man, a moment at the end of which, having cut the umbilical
cord, he will set out as an almost autonomous being following,
nay creating, his own destiny—our transcendental birth never
ends if it is true that the arrival of the Self in its Self as autoaffected
in the autoaffection of absolute life happens only inasmuch as this
autoaffection happens. Being a Son does not designate the result
of some event that happened at another moment and is now past.
Being a Son designates a condition, the Condition from which
no one can cut himself off and for which he can make no other
arrangements, "gift that must be received each day without being

able to make any other arrangements for it."[17] Our transcendental birth is never past because there is no past in the Self, because there is no past in the absolute past of the Immemorial of the antecedence of Life. This is why if we say that we are born in this transcendental birth, we have to say also, more profoundly, that we are "unborn,"[18] never separated from the autobegetting of life, being begotten only in it. There is thus all the more reason for us to say that we are uncreated, since by creation one means that of the world.

We have described the Self's self-forgetting before describing its forgetting of Life. The second forgetting nonetheless precedes the first since the Self is related to itself only on the Basis of Life, of its absolute autoaffection. If the Self is related to itself only in life, it can be said that there is no self anywhere but in God. More precisely: "In him we have life."[19] It is necessary to pass through God, through life, in order to come fully into life, just as the Self must pass through this life in order to come fully to itself and each of its "states." That God—or, if one prefers, Life—is more intimately within me than myself is not a mystical pronouncement, but a phenomenological one. It is included in the affirmation that we are Sons. The affirmation that we are Sons—the living in life—is not a simple tautology, it overturns just about everything that has ever been said about man since man has been spoken about, since the Word of the World has spoken of man.

That the Oblivion of Life gives access to Life and the forgetting of the self to the Self, are notions that might seem strange. Forgetting Life, that is what we do every day and all day; but for all that we do not cease to be the living. That the Oblivion of Life, far from separating us from Life or from our Self, gives us access to both makes sense only in a phenomenology—a phenomenology of life that does not demand the unveiling of its object from a process of intentional elucidation nor from the clearing of Being, but from this object itself, precisely from Life and the original world of its Archi-revelation. It is because Life is revealed in the radical immanence of its pathetic autoaffection that it does not

---

[17] *Dieu sans l'Être*, p. 247; English trans., p. 175 (modified).
[18] "I am unborn," Eckhart, *Sermon 52*; English trans., p. 202.
[19] Paul, Acts 17.28.

care for itself nor desire to be seen, that it does not think and especially does not think about itself or remember itself, that it lives in Oblivion. In this Oblivion, life never stops embracing itself and never quits itself. If there is something "that one can forget without losing," as Jean-Louis Chrétien says of the Plotinian Good,[20] this is only because this "something," this "Good," is only a name for Life. It is only to the extent that the Nonecstatic to which no thought ever fully arrives is not a phenomenological Nothing but precisely the phenomenological essence of the pathos in which Life arrives and arrives incessantly in itself in its eternal Archi-revelation—only to this extent is the Oblivion of this Nonecstatic, the Oblivion of the Immemorial, changed into what cannot be lost. What can never be remembered is precisely what can never be forgotten. The phenomenology of the Immemorial is the same thing as a phenomenology of the Unforgettable: it leads irresistibly from the first to the second. This phenomenology must be named at least once: " 'Unforgettable' is a suffering of what we lack the power to detach ourselves." The unforgettable is "the misfortunes themselves to the extent that they cannot be put behind us."[21]

Because Life in its Oblivion archi-reveals itself, it is a Word, we have said. Every Word must be heard and understood. In what does this Understanding consist? Of the Word, Heidegger says, "We hear it only because we belong within it [*Wir hören Sie nur weil in sie gehören*]."[22] How do we belong to the Word? This is what must be made clear if the mode of this belonging is the only thing that tells the nature of the Understanding. And it is here that the phenomenological presupposition that commands the worldly interpretation of the Word, at the same time that it hides its original essence, denatures the relation that it must maintain with those to whom "understanding" falls. As soon as the Understanding is taken as being-open-to-the-world and when this existential de-

---

[20] *L'inoubliable et l'inespéré*, p. 41.

[21] Ibid., p. 106.

[22] *Unterwegs zur Sprache*, p. 255; English trans., p. 124 (modified). *Translator's note:* The English "Understanding" here translates the French *entendre* as these are the respective English and French language renderings of Heidegger's *Verstehen* to which Henry refers in this passage. It should be borne in mind that the French *entendre* also carries the meaning *to hear* in the sense of hearing something spoken to one.

termination counts as much for the speaking as for the hearing that are grounded on the Understanding structured like it,[23] it follows that there is hearing only with regard to what is outside itself; it also follows that in this Gap constitutive of the Understanding as well as the hearing that rests on it, a fundamental uncertainty slips in: differing in principle from what is said and understood, I am reduced to its subject, to conjectures and interpretations.

This is what stands out clearly and distinctly in the privileged case where it is supposed that it is the same one who speaks and hears, who consequently listens to his own word. Isn't it remarkable that in this situation—namely, that of the moral conscience and its call, a call explicitly defined as that which *Dasein* addresses to itself—this call, issued from *Dasein* but coming to it in the opening of the world, comes to it "from afar" even if it is cast "unto afar."[24] The object of many mistaken interpretations, this distant and mysterious call demands, if it is to be comprehended, that one take on a bold problematic whose ultimate result repeats the initial phenomenological presupposition, claiming that *Entschlossenheit* is nothing other than *Erschlossenheit* itself grasped in its truth. What remains simply presupposed in this presupposition is the thesis claiming *Dasein* is "mine," so that the exterior identity of the caller and the called in the moral conscience can pass for an ontological theory of the essence of ipseity, which exists nowhere else but in life.

At the same time, it is, in the lectures of the 1950s, the affirmation of a "we" belonging to the Word, taking a place in it, steeped in it, that seems groundless. And nonetheless, for every word it must be known who hears it and how. This connection of the Word and the Understanding which is appropriate to it in its essential ipseity and singularity inasmuch as it is that of a "we," that is to say, of an "I" or of a "me," escapes from the contingency of a factual correlation only if it is phenomenologically grounded. Being phenomenologically grounded does not mean simply:

---

[23] "*Reden und Hören grunden im Verstehen . . . Nur wer schon versteht, kann zuhören*"— "Both talking and hearing are based upon understanding . . . Only he who already understands can listen"; p. 164; English trans., p. 208.

[24] "*Gerufen wird aus der Ferne in der Ferne*"—"The call is from afar unto afar"; *Sein und Zeit*, p. 271; English trans., p. 316.

showing itself, appearing. No more than to a speculative affirmation, the belonging of a "we" to the word could not belong to a simple observation, in the sense of what can be seen. Being grounded phenomenologically means—for this "we," for this "self," for this "*ego*," for the "listeners" whoever they might be, as well as for the link that has already inscribed and buried them in the word—that the latter precedes them radically, but in such a way that, exhausting its essence in life and confiding to them this essence which is its own, it at the same time confides to them their ipseity, an ipseity that belongs to them and by whose effect they find themselves determined in themselves as Selves and *egos*. What the Word of Life confides to those who hear it is their own "existence." Between it and each of them there is an absolute relation. If this existence is each time that of a self, that of an "each individual," this is so only to the extent that the Word that gives it bears the ipseity in itself and, giving its own essence, giving this ipseity, it gives each to itself as this self that it is insurmountably and forever.

But because the Word of Life consists in life and the latter never goes outside itself, something remains to this Word of Life confided to each of the living: standing only in itself, it stands in itself only insofar as it holds it in itself, in its own life, in this unique life that is literally that of all the living, that which gives them life as a life that is each time their own and that is theirs only inasmuch as it remains in itself, as it is its own—it in them, and them in it.

How do we belong to the Word of Life, how do we understand it, if this Understanding is other than the mode of this belonging? We belong to the Word of Life in the autoaffection where we are begotten: our understanding is our birth—our Son-ly condition. I am forever hearing the sound of my birth. Because understanding the Word of Life (the hearing in which I hear this Word) is equivalent to my own life begotten in the autobegetting of absolute life, this Understanding affords no freedom to him who understands. It is not the Understanding of a call to which the living would have license to respond or not. To respond to the call, to understand it appropriately, but also to be able to avoid it, it is always too late. Always already, life throwing itself into itself has thrown us into ourselves, into this Self that is like unto no other and that marks our irreplaceable place in life. Here, as the advertisement for the Great Circus of Oklahoma says, "Here there is a place for everyone."[25]

This place is given in life by Life, a place that intrudes upon that of no one else, never taken from another nor occupied by him, because in the autoaffection of life which gives the Self to itself, life is given in its entirety, without division or any part kept in reserve. Who has ever been free of birth, and who, receiving life, has never received it in its entirety, crushed beneath its profuseness and bearing it inside as what, making it a Self, grants to it in each instant, in its autoaffection which is that of life, the capacity to grow by itself and thus to "live"? For to live is nothing other than that: to grow by oneself, to be exceeded by oneself, inasmuch as the Self itself is exceeded by life, exceeded by what makes it a Self.

In this way, the Understanding in which we understand the Word of Life can be grasped by a model different from that of life itself. Because this Understanding is our birth, our primal belonging to life, its phenomenological substance is exhausted in the passivity of the living autoaffected in the autoaffection of absolute life and in the pathos proper to this passivity and constituting it: it is Suffering and Joy. Suffering and Joy are the fruits of life, its unique Word—in the final analysis, the sole thing that anguished men amid the troubles of the world desire to understand. But what does this Word say to them? Nothing other than itself, namely, their own "existence"—the ineffable happiness of the ordeal and of living.

It is thus that an abyss separates the Word of Life from that of the world. The Word of the World is not merely different from all that it says, the appearing in which it is deployed stemming only from the Difference as such. Such Difference manifests an absolute indifference, the indifference of this word to all that it says, since it can say anything and everything, as the light cares not for what it illuminates, letting it slip out of the clearing that it opens, like an object that is lost without ever taking precautions against it. The most obvious, most simple, most terrible characteristic of this indifference found in all Difference and implied by it

---

[25] Kafka, *Amerika*.

is surely the following: *never does the classification of what is said in the Word of the World result from the classification of this word, namely, from the mode of appearing that it conveys.* Whether it be a stone, a tree, a broken tool, an equation, a goat, or a hydroplane, it matters little as long as the nature of what is disclosed owes nothing to its disclosure, as long as the latter, its saying—not penetrating the inner essence of what it says and, in that way, grasping nothing—is limited to a simple observation, to saying and to repeating: "that is," "there is."

Life is so little a stranger to what it reveals that it resides in it as its very own essence—it contains and retains it in itself with an unbreakable grip and as was described above: as this eternal autoaffection in the autoaffection of which it became one of the living. This is the reason why, in distinction from the Word of the World, *The Word of Life confers its classification on what it reveals,* never disclosing it outside itself as what would have no relation with it, as anything whatsoever, but in it as that whose flesh it is. And this is why, in distinction from the beings about which the Word of the World speaks—entering or exiting from the clearing at the whim of this Word or owing to the gratuitousness of the discourse that speaks, remembers, or forgets them and that can hearken back to what it speaks about just as well as to what it says about this—he who is born of the Word of Life does not have the leisure to remove himself from the Parousia of its Revelation. Whether it be remembered or forgotten depends only on thought, not on its condition as living. Life has only one word, this word never hearkens back to what it said and no one can evade it. This Parousia without memory and without project, this Parousia of the Word of Life, it is our birth.

At the end of this short journey a question arises: Since immemorial Life has begotten us as its Sons and showered us with good, and since this birth is incessantly being accomplished in us, what need is there for a Memorial? We speak nonetheless of the Scriptures, and these Scriptures in their entirety—what are they if not a Memorial? What is more, what they say to us in the farthest reaches of what they want to convey, isn't this done to preserve in memory, to celebrate this Memorial together? In the Gospels in any case, isn't this extreme point the institution of the Eucharist: "Do this in memory of me"?[26]

One could contemplate establishing the necessity of this Memorial on the very nature of the Immemorial. Because the latter consists in an unfathomable Oblivion, we could gain some knowledge of it only through what is said to us about it in the Scripture, and thus by a sort of favor granted to he who is gifted with reading them. This, it seems, is Chrétien's thesis: "The necessity for Scripture comes precisely from the fact that it is the sole memorial of what is inaccessible to our memory."[27] But what would happen if the knowledge of the Scriptures, that is to say, the assurance of their divine provenance, could be established only in the place held by the Immemorial itself and thus by means of it? Truthfully, it is not the memorial that grounds our access to the Immemorial, but the latter alone that, giving us to understand who it is, at the same time gives us the possibility of understanding, by recognizing it, every conceivable authentic memorial as the memorial of the Immemorial.

How can we not notice that, in the words that report the institution of the Eucharist, a strange displacement occurs. That which must be preserved in memory is not exactly words, not even those that relate the institution of the Eucharist: "Do this." From the beginning, with unexpected force, the text designated another place besides its own, the one where something like "Doing" happens. But doing, we have tried to show, is possible only in the Oblivion of the body, which is possible only in the most abysmal Oblivion, there where I am Son, in the place of my birth.

The Scriptures say that we are the Sons. Relative to their worldly word, this referent—the condition Son—is external to them. But this referent that is external is what we are as one of the living; this is the essence of the divine Word that begets us in each instant. By saying: "You are the Sons," the Word of the Scriptures points away from itself and indicates the place where another word speaks. To speak truly, everything affirmed by this word of the Scriptures carries out the displacement that leads out

---

[26] Luke 22.20.
[27] Op. cit., p. 116.

of it to this other place where the Word of Life speaks. For example, all Christian "morality" has this radical phenomenological signification of referring *from the word that makes visible by absenting to the one that begets in Life.* "It is not those who say to me: Master! Master! who will enter into the Kingdom of Heaven, but he who does the will of my Father."[28] Here alone reigns the word whose saying is a doing, the Word of Life that makes us the living. And it is not the word of the Scriptures that gives us to understand the Word of Life. It is the latter, by begetting us at each instant, by making Sons of us, which reveals in its own truth, the truth that the word of the Scriptures acknowledges and witnesses. He who hears this word of the Scriptures knows that it speaks truly, for the Word that institutes it in life hears itself in it.

What need have we of the Scriptures? Are they there only to be acknowledged after the fact, on the basis of a truth that we already bear in us and which in its prior accomplishment, in the already accomplished accomplishment of life in us, could easily do away with them? By virtue of the Oblivion that defines its ownmost phenomenological essence, life is ambiguous. Life is what knows itself without knowing itself. That it knows all at once is neither extra nor added on. The knowing by which one day life knows what it knew ever since forever without knowing it is not of another order than that of life itself. It is life itself that knows at one fell swoop what it knew ever since forever. The knowing by which life knows what it knew ever since forever without knowing it is an upheaval in life itself. In such an upheaval, life undergoes its autoaffection as the autoaffection of absolute Life; it suffers the depths of its own Basis and is suffered as identical to it. To the extent that life is susceptible of this upheaval, it is Becoming.

When we ask if life already knows all that it knows and if in this case something more can still befall it, we are speaking of it in the manner that one speaks of things which, in their releasement, already are all that they are. Life "is" not. Still less could it be "all that it 'is.'" That life is Becoming means: possibility remains open in it so that in it the autoaffection that strikes each of the living with the seal of its indelible ipseity—this autoaffection is under-

---

[28] Matthew 7.21.

gone as that of absolute life. That this limitless emotion in which the autoaffection of each of the living is undergone as that of the absolute life in it and thus as its own essence—as this essence of life which is also its own—that such an emotion as the Revelation of its own essence befalls him who reads the Scriptures and inasmuch as these say to him nothing other than his condition as Son—there is nothing surprising here as soon as it is noted that this Son-ly condition is precisely his own and that thus *the condition of Faith is always posited*. Only the god can make us believe in him, but he inhabits our own flesh.

For this reason, the emotion that delivers the living to eternal life rises up in it each time that the truth of life is revealed to it, and all the more surely as it is revealed in its ownmost proper way—namely, as a revelation that is not first addressed to the Intellect but that consists in the very affectivity of life, as happens in the case of art that has no other end but to awaken in us the powers of life according to the impulsive, dynamic, and pathetic modalities that are its own.

But the upheaval of life that opens it emotionally onto its own essence does away with all condition in the sense of an encounter, of a circumstance or an occasion, of every cultural form of whatever order. It is and can be born from life itself as this rebirth that gives it to suddenly undergo its eternal birth. The Spirit blows whither it will.★

★ The first part of this text was the object of a presentation made at the Colloque Castelli (Rome, January 1992). It was published in the acts of this colloquium, *Archivio di Filosofia* 1–3 (1992).

ENGLISH-LANGUAGE
EDITIONS CITED

Aeschylus. *The Libation Bearers*. In *The Oresteia*. Translated by David Grene and Wendy Doniger O'Flaherty. Chicago: University of Chicago Press, 1989.

Aristotle. *De Interpretatione*. In *The Complete Works of Aristotle*. Edited by Jonathan Barnes. Princeton, N.J.: Bollingen Series, Princeton University Press, 1984.

Augustine. *De dono perseverentiae*. *The De dono perseverentiae of St. Augustine*. Translated by Sister Mary Alphonse Lesousky, OSU. Washington, D.C.: The Catholic University of America Press, 1956.

————. *De Magistro*. *Concerning the Teacher*. In *Basic Writings of St. Augustine*, vol. 1. Edited by Whitney J. Oates. New York: Random House, 1948.

————. *Enarrationes in Psalmos*. *Expositions on the Book of Psalms*. In *A Select Library of Nicene and Post-Nicene Fathers of the Christian Church*, vol. 10. Edited by A. Cleveland Coxe. Grand Rapids, Mich.: Eerdmans, 1983.

Bonaventure. *Breviloquium*. *Breviloquium*. Translated by Erwin Esser Nemmers. London: Herder Book Co., 1946.

Calvin, John. *Institutes of the Christian Religion*. Translated by Ford Lewis Battles. Philadelphia: Westminster Press, 1960.

Eckhart, Meister. *Sermon 6*. In *Meister Eckhart: The Essential Sermons, Commentaries, Treatises, and Defense*. Translated by Bernard McGinn and Edmund Colledge. New York: Paulist Press, 1981.

————. *Sermon 10*. In *Meister Eckhart: Teacher and Preacher*. Edited by Bernard McGinn. New York: Paulist Press, 1986.

————. *Sermon 52*. In *Meister Eckhart: The Essential Sermons, Commentaries, Treatises, and Defense*. Translated by Bernard McGinn and Edmund Colledge. New York: Paulist Press, 1981.

Feuerbach, Ludwig. *Das Wesen des Christentums. The Essence of Christianity.* Translated by George Eliot. Buffalo, N.Y.: Prometheus Books, 1989.

Heidegger, Martin. *Phänomenologie und Theologie.* "Phenomenology and Theology." In *The Piety of Thinking.* Translated by James G. Hart and John C. Maraldo. Bloomington: Indiana University Press, 1976.

————. *Sein und Zeit. Being and Time.* Translated by John Macquarrie and Edward Robinson. San Francisco: Harper & Row, 1962.

————. *Unterwegs zur Sprache. On the Way to Language.* Translated by Peter D. Hertz. New York: Harper & Row, 1971.

Husserl, Edmund. *Cartesianische Meditationen. Cartesian Meditations.* Translated by Dorion Cairns. The Hague: Martinus Nijhoff, 1960.

————. *Idee der Phänomenologie. The Idea of Phenomenology.* Translated by W. P. Alston and George Nakhnikian. The Hague: Martinus Nijhoff, 1970.

————. *Ideen. Ideas.* Translated by F. Kersten. The Hague: Martinus Nijhoff, 1982.

————. *Krisis. The Crisis of European Sciences and Transcendental Phenomenology.* Translated by David Carr. Evanston, Ill.: Northwestern University Press, 1970.

————. *Logische Untersuchungen. Logical Investigations.* Translated by J. N. Findlay. London: Routledge & Kegan Paul, 1970.

————. Preface to *Logische Untersuchungen. Introduction to the Logical Investigations: A Draft of a Preface to the Logical Investigations 1913.* Translated by Philip J. Bossert and Curtis Peters. The Hague: Martinus Nijhoff, 1975.

Jaspers, Karl. *Philosophie. Philosophy.* Translated by E. B. Ashton. Chicago: University of Chicago Press, 1971.

John Cassian. *Conferences.* Translated by Boniface Ramsey. New York: Paulist Press, 1997.

Kant, Immanuel. *Kritik der reinen Vernunft. Critique of Pure Reason.* Translated by Norman Kemp Smith. New York: St. Martin's Press, 1965.

————. *Kritik der Urteilskraft. Critique of Judgment.* Translated by Werner S. Pluher. Indianapolis, Ind.: Hackett, 1987.

————. *Religion innerhalb der Grenzen der blossen Vernunft. Religion within the Limits of Reason Alone.* Translated by Theodore M. Greene and Hoyt Hudson. New York: Harper & Row, 1960.

Leclercq, Jean. *Initiation aux auteurs monsatiques du Moyen Âge. The Love of Learning and the Desire for God.* Translated by Catherine Misrahi. New York: Fordham University Press, 1982.

Macarius. *Fifty Spiritual Homilies of St. Macarius the Egyptian.* Edited by A. J. Mason. New York: Macmillan, 1921.

Marion, Jean-Luc. *Dieu sans l'être. God without Being.* Translated by Thomas A. Carlson. Chicago: University of Chicago Press, 1991.

Montaigne, Michel de. *Essais. The Complete Essays of Montaigne.* Translated by Donald Frame. Stanford, Calif.: Stanford University Press, 1958.

Philo. *De plantatione.* In *Philo III.* Translated by F. H. Colson. New York: G. P. Putnam's Sons, 1930.

Plotinus. *Enneads.* Translated by A. H. Armstrong. Cambridge, Mass.: Harvard University Press, 1984.

Schopenhauer, Arthur. *Parerga und Paralipomena. Parerga and Paralipomena: Short Philosophical Essays.* Translated by E. F. J. Payne. Oxford: Clarendon Press, 1974.

Seneca. *Ad Lucilium Epistulae Morales*, vol. 1. Translated by Richard M. Gummere. New York: G. P. Putnam's Sons, 1925.

Tertullian. *De oratione.* In *Tertullian's Treatises.* Translated by Alexander Souter. New York: Macmillan, 1919.

Thomas Aquinas. *Summa theologica. Summa theologiae.* New York: Blackfriars, 1964.

van der Leeuw, Gerardus. *Phänomenologie der Religion. Religion in Essence and Manifestation.* Translated by J. E. Turner. Gloucester, Mass.: Peter Smith, 1967.

William of St. Thierry. *The Works of William of St. Thierry*, vol. 1. Translated by Sister Penelope, CSMV. Spencer, Mass.: Cistercian Publications, 1971.